Justice: Deconstruction and Hermeneutics

Social and Critical Theory

A CRITICAL HORIZONS BOOK SERIES

VOLUME 32

The titles published in this series are listed at *brill.com/sct*

Justice: Deconstruction and Hermeneutics

Interviews with Contemporary Thinkers

By

Sema Cevirici Atilla

BRILL

LEIDEN | BOSTON

Library of Congress Cataloging-in-Publication Data

Names: Atilla, Sema Cevirici, editor.
Title: Justice : deconstruction and hermeneutics / edited by Sema Cevirici Atilla.
Description: Boston, Massachusetts : Brill, 2025. | Series: Social and critical theory a critical horizons book series, 1572-459X ; 32 | Includes bibliographical references and index.
Identifiers: LCCN 2025011409 (print) | LCCN 2025011410 (ebook) | ISBN 9789004727779 (hardback) | ISBN 9789004732902 (ebook)
Subjects: LCSH: Justice. | Justice, Administration of–Philosophy. | Hermeneutics. | Justice (Philosophy)
Classification: LCC K240 .J87 2025 (print) | LCC K240 (ebook) | DDC 340/.114–dc23/eng/20250314
LC record available at https://lccn.loc.gov/2025011409
LC ebook record available at https://lccn.loc.gov/2025011410

Typeface for the Latin, Greek, and Cyrillic scripts: “Brill”. See and download: brill.com/brill-typeface.

ISSN 1572-459X
ISBN 978-90-04-72777-9 (hardback)
ISBN 978-90-04-73290-2 (e-book)
DOI 10.1163/9789004732902

This book is printed on acid-free paper and produced in a sustainable manner.

Contents

Foreword: Does Justice Exist? VII
Notes on Contributors XI

Introduction 1

1 God and Justice: John D. Caputo 7

2 Ethics and Justice: Simon Critchley 25

3 Hermeneutics and Justice: Richard Kearney 36

4 Law and Justice: Michel Rosenfeld 58

5 Deconstruction and Justice: Christopher Norris 73

6 Democracy and Justice: Samir Haddad 94

7 Human Rights and Justice: Seyla Benhabib 113

8 Pragmatism and Justice: Richard J. Bernstein 127

9 Post-Anarchism and Justice – I: Todd May 136

10 Post-Anarchism and Justice – II: Saul Newman 146

11 Post-Anarchism and Justice III: Lewis Call 155

12 Human Nature and Justice: Noam Chomsky 164

Afterword: Is Justice a Spectral Effect? 171

Index 177

FOREWORD

Does Justice Exist?

One way to think about the book that follows is that its subject matter does not exist, and that is what is so important about it, why it is so much loved and desired and deserving of our respect. I have long been fascinated with the saying, "*Fiat justitia, ruat coelum.*" Let justice be done, even if the sky were to fall. Let justice be done if the whole earth, if the entire cosmos, were to perish. Let justice be done, no matter what. Let justice be done if it goes unnoticed, unacknowledged, unacclaimed. Let it be done even if I even if I am made to suffer for being just by the powers of injustice. Let justice be done no matter the cost. Let justice flow like water across the land. Let justice soar far above power, fame, and wealth, in all its transcendent glory, "beyond being," as Plato would say, which is said in praise of justice, not in denial, as exceeding being, not falling short. Throw caution to the winds! Put ourselves in harm's way. Risk having the heavens fall down on our heads. All for justice.

Still, the downside of soaring above and beyond being is that the power belongs to the powers that be, so that the eminent hyper-being of justice must make its way without the power of being. Derrida had something like this in mind when he said that justice is "unconditional without sovereignty," that is, justice calls upon us unconditionally but without an army or the police, without the strong arm of the law to enforce what it is calling for. In a nonviolent demonstration against injustice, the protesters have girded their loins with justice, but the police are girded with gun belts. Justice demands but it cannot command. Justice solicits, entices, pleads, inspires, but justice, left to its own resources, cannot be realized. The prophets had this in mind when they lamented, "Why, O Lord, do the wicked prosper while the righteous suffer?" Because they can; they always have and they always will. They have the power to mock justice, to flaunt it, and the only thing that could stop the powerful is the weak force of honor and shame, but they are shameless and without honor, so nothing stops them. They have the power.

Justice without force is impotent, Pascal said, and power without justice is tyrannical, which is why he added, "And so, since it was not possible to make the just strong, the strong have been made just." We can try to make the powers that be just, things like the state and the institutions, the courts and the police, but why can we not make justice strong? Because justice is not a real being, a material object or even an immaterial entity. Then is it nothing at all? Surely, there is justice. To be sure, but this thing is not a thing, not something that is;

it is beyond being. Its very eminence is also its embarrassment. In Derrida's deadly serious quip, the status of justice is not ontological but hauntological; it is a ghost, a specter. The spectral operation is neither to be nor not to be but to spook, to haunt, to call upon us. The specter stirs up the dangerous memory of the dead, *les revenants,* whose death must not be in vain, and the hope of something coming, *les arrivants,* promising the children a world in which justice will reign. By hauntological Derrida meant, in part, that every promise is also a threat, so be careful what you pray for, but hauntological also meant, to speak more straightforwardly, axiological, as in *axios*, what is intrinsically worthy of love and admiration, what commands our respect (even if it cannot command our action), what is prized in and for itself, honored for itself. Justice is loved, desired, dreamt of, prayed for, pursued, fought and died for, but justice of itself does not exist.

But even if justice, in itself, does not exist, *there is* (*es gibt, il y a*) justice. But where *is there*? Justice, in itself, is not a real thing but justice is not unreal. Then, where is justice to be found? And how?

Are there not just laws? To be sure, and the more the better, but we must be cautious. Laws are universals which can turn into monsters when it comes to singulars, which tend to be exceptions. It happens all too often that following the letter of the law results in the worst injustice. Even when laws are made with the best of intentions, they can have unforeseen consequences which end up producing injustice. It is because the convergence of law and justice is always imperfect, never finished, that laws must be repealable, amendable, deconstructible, while justice in itself, if there is such a thing, is undeconstructible.

Are there no just institutions? To be sure, and the more the better, but here we are even more wary because, when push comes to shove, institutions tend to protect themselves, not the cause of justice; they compromise their mission in favor of their survival. Institutions, like laws, can become monsters, inspired by self-interest, not justice.

But are there not just persons? To be sure, and the more the better, but such people would be the last ones to say such a thing. They are always conscious of their faults, "I more than others," and conscious too that nothing says they will not betray justice in the future, when they are forced to make a difficult and terrible choice.

Then at least there are particular acts of justice, here and now? To be sure, and this is perhaps as close as we can get to meeting justice in the flesh, to encounter it in its lived reality, transiently, in the particularity of the concrete situation. But even here we must exercise caution because very often the choices we make in the concrete, good choices, urgent and undeferrable choices, come down to compromises, choosing the lesser evil, where every alternative is bad, where the choice we make is bad, but, as we often hear it said, the only thing worse is all the alternatives.

That is why I think we do better to say, with an irony born of a deep respect for justice, not from skepticism but from love, not from despair but from hope, that justice does not exist. Justice does not subsist, justice insists. Justice does not exist; justice calls for existence. The actual existence of justice is *up to us*, here and now, in the concrete, factical situation. Justice will not come riding on a white horse to save us. If we want to talk about a Messiah, Walter Benjamin said, then we must realize that *we* are the messianic generation, the ones the dead have been waiting for to make right the wrongs that were done to them. This is Levinas's point about the *me voici*, that justice puts us in the accusative, in a double sense; it accuses us, makes us guilty, and it puts us on the receiving end of an address, a call coming from the ones who demands justice, making us responsible.

That is also why I think, once again not from cynicism but from reverence, that there is something to be said for turning our attention to injustice, to an inventory of injustices, over which the idea of justice hovers likes a white light or a hallowed spirit, bringing out every fault, exposing every blemish. Treat the idea of justice as something in the making, in process, always behind us, reminding us of those who died unjustly, and always ahead of us, calling us, luring us forward, letting our implicit sense of justice gradually become explicit in examining the injustice of this and that. We will know justice by the victims of injustice, when justice is missing, miscarried, misunderstood and especially when it is used as a disguise for vengeance, when some of the worst crimes are committed in the name of justice. The best theory of justice just may be the theory of the lesser evil, where the choice is urgent but there are no good choices, and so we make the least bad choice. The book of justice is not a book of essences but an encyclopedia of injustices, the way the Oxford English Dictionary defines a word by way of an inventory of its actual uses over the years. Our idea of justice is sharpened by our eye for injustice.

Sema Cevirici Atilla has undertaken a work of love, made a contribution to the cause of justice, by exploring a variety of approaches taken to justice on the part of a number of creative and provocative thinkers, each of whom has something different to say. Together, they hold up to us the prism of justice, of what justice demands, what justice deserves, because justice in itself, if there is such a thing, is not *one* thing. It means something different, makes different demands, in different contexts. Justice does not have an essence; it has a history. Justice is not an infinite ideal we can see and approach asymptotically but an infinitival expectation, meaning that, even as justice cannot be deferred, justice is also always to-come and that it must feel its way in the face of an unforeseeable future. Justice does not come in the declarative, but in the imperative. Justice is not an essence, but an insistence, a call which in each case makes a unique and singular demand upon us. Justice is the totality of such instances just where we will never reach totalization. These cases have at most what Wittgenstein called a family resemblance, but it is a growing family, composed of generations now long dead and of generations belonging to an unforeseeable future.

So, we can all be grateful to Sema Cevirici Atilla for the work that follows, which explores a variety of views of justice, coming from diverse figures, speaking from different circumstances, offering their counsel about how to make the dream of justice come true.

John D. Caputo
Thomas J. Watson Professor Emeritus of Religion
Syracuse University

David R. Cook Professor Emeritus of Philosophy
Villanova University

Notes on Contributors

John D. Caputo

John David Caputo was born in 1940 in the US. He completed his B.A. at LaSalle University in 1962. He finished his master's degree at Villanova University in 1964 and his Ph.D. at Bryn Mawr College in 1968. Caputo is the Thomas J. Watson Professor of Religion and Humanities at Syracuse University and the David R. Cook Professor Emeritus of Philosophy at Villanova University. He is a philosopher and a theologian who specializes in radical theology, post-modern Christianity, and continental philosophy of religion. Professor Caputo has created the theological movement called weak theology. In his work, he mainly deals with hermeneutics, phenomenology, deconstruction, and theology. Some of his influential books are *Radical Hermeneutics* (1987), *The Prayers and Tears of Jacques Derrida* (1997), *Philosophy and Theology* (2006) and *The Weakness of God: A Theology of the Event* (2006).

Simon Critchley

Simon Critchley was born in Hertfordshire, England. He is the Hans Jonas Professor of Philosophy at the New School for Social Research in New York and a professor of philosophy at The European Graduate School. He obtained his M.Phil. from University of Nice and his Ph.D. from University of Essex in 1988, which would be the foundation of his later work *The Ethics of Deconstruction.* He worked as a visiting professor at the University of Oslo, Cardozo Law School, the University of Sydney and the University of Notre Dame. His work mainly focuses on continental philosophy, history of philosophy, phenomenology, literature, ethics, and politics. He published numerous books such as *Deconstruction and Pragmatism* (1996), *Ethics-Politics-Subjectivity: Essays on Derrida, Levinas, and Contemporary French Thought* (1999) and *Infinitely Demanding: Ethics of Commitment, Politics of Resistance* (2007). Critchley won the Kanani Prize in Philosophy in 1985.

Richard Kearney

Richard Kearney is the Charles B. Seelig Chair of Philosophy at Boston College. He was born in 1954 in Ireland and completed his B.A. at University of Dublin in 1975. After doing his masters at McGill University with his advisor Charles Taylor, Kearney completed his Ph.D. with Paul Ricoeur at Universite Paris Ouest Nanterre La Defense. He worked as a visiting professor at University College Dublin, the University of Paris (Sorbonne) and the University of Nice. His research interests are hermeneutics, contemporary continental philosophy, philosophy of religion, and aesthetics. His work mostly focuses on narrative imagination, hermeneutics, radical hospitality, and phenomenology. Professor Kearney currently teaches the following courses at Boston College: Narrative Imagination, Carnal Hermeneutics, Phenomenology of Eros, Hermeneutics of Religion. Among his books are *Strangers, Gods and Monsters* (2003), *Anatheism: The Returning to God After God* (2011) and *Radical Hospitality: From Thought to Action* (co-authored with Melissa Fitzpatrick, 2021).

Michel Rosenfeld

Michel Rosenfeld is the University Professor of Law and Comparative Democracy, Justice Sydney L. Robins Professor of Human Rights and Director of the Program on Global and Comparative Constitutional Theory at the Benjamin N. Cardozo School of Law where he teaches courses such as Comparative Constitutionalism, Constitutional Law, and Liberalism and its Critics and Concepts of Justice. He finished his B.A. in 1969, M.A. in 1971, M.Phil. in 1978 and Ph.D. in 1991 at Columbia University and his J.D. at Northwestern University in 1974. Rosenfeld's research elaborates on the concepts of constitutional law, justice, constitutional secularism, democracy, and liberalism. His well-known books include *The Identity of the Constitutional Subject: Selfhood, Citizenship, Culture, and Community* (2010), *Law, Justice, Democracy and the Clash of Cultures: A Pluralist Account* (2011) and *A Pluralist Theory of Constitutional Justice; Assessing Liberal Democracy in Times of Rising Populism and Illiberalism* (2022).

Christopher Norris

Christopher Norris (b. 1947) is a Distinguished Research Professor in Philosophy at the University of Cardiff, Wales. In 1975, he received his Ph.D. in English at University College London. After teaching English Literature, he moved to the Philosophy Department via Literary Theory in 1991. He was a visiting professor at Berkeley, City University of New York, Dartmouth College and the University of Santiago de Compostela. His research interests include philosophy of language, epistemology, philosophy of science, modern continental philosophy, aesthetics, and literary theory. He expands on deconstruction and the work of Jacques Derrida in his books and articles. He has authored more than thirty books on literary theory, continental philosophy, deconstruction, politics, and music. Some of his well-known books are *The Deconstructive Turn* (1984), *The Truth About Postmodernism* (1993) and *Philosophy of Language and the Challenge to Scientific Realism* (2003). Recently, he has published poetry and philosophical verse.

Samir Haddad

Samir Haddad completed his B.Sc. in Mathematics at Australian National University. He obtained his B.A. in Philosophy and Women's Studies in 1998. In 2006, he received his Ph.D. in Philosophy from Northwestern University with his dissertation *Derrida, Arendt, and the Inheritance of Democracy*. Haddad is currently teaching philosophy at both undergraduate and graduate levels at Fordham University. Some of the courses that he teaches are French Philosophies of Education, Latin American Philosophy, Education and Democracy, Philosophical Ethics, Politics and Biopower, and Rethinking Citizenship. His research interests include 20th century continental philosophy, contemporary French philosophy, deconstruction, democratic theory, and philosophy of education. He published his first book *Derrida and the Inheritance of Democracy* in 2013.

Richard J. Bernstein

Richard J. Bernstein was born in 1932. He completed his Ph.D. at Yale University in 1958. He taught at Haverford from 1966 to 1989. He was the Vera List Professor Emeritus of Philosophy in the Philosophy Department at The New School for Social Research in New York. Dr. Bernstein was one of the leading figures of American pragmatism. His research interests included hermeneutics, American pragmatism, social and political philosophy, critical theory, and Anglo-American philosophy. He was the author of *Beyond Objectivism and Relativism: Science, Hermeneutics, and Praxis* (1983), *The Abuse of Evil: The Corruption of Politics and Religion since 9/11* (2006), *Pragmatic Encounters* (2015) and *Ironic Life* (2016). The philosopher passed away on July 4th, 2022.

Seyla Benhabib

Seyla Benhabib is a Turkish-American philosopher born in 1950. She is the Eugene Meyer Professor of Political Science and Philosophy at Yale University and a senior research scholar and adjunct professor of law at Columbia Law School. She completed her B.A. in Humanities at American College for Girls in Istanbul and another B.A. in Philosophy at Brandeis University. She received her Ph.D. in Philosophy from Yale University in 1977. Benhabib taught philosophy courses at Boston University, SUNY at Stony Brook and New School for Social Research before working at Yale University. She also taught at the University of Cambridge and Harvard University. Her areas of specialty include 19th and 20th century European social and political philosophy, citizenship and migration studies, feminist theory, democratic theory, migration and refugee studies, and German legal and political thought. Among her influential books are *Situating the Self: Gender, Community and Postmodernism in Contemporary Ethics* (1992), *The Claims of Culture: Equality and Diversity in the Global Era* (2002) and *The Rights of Others: Aliens, Citizens and Residents* (2004).

Noam Chomsky

Noam Chomsky (b. 1928) is an American theoretical linguist, educator, philosopher, social critic and political activist. He is a Laureate Professor of Linguistics at the University of Arizona and an Institute Professor Emeritus at the Massachusetts Institute of Technology. Though he is widely recognized as the founder of modern linguistics, he is a leading figure in analytic philosophy, cognitive psychology and the philosophies of mind and language. In 1955, Chomsky received his Ph.D. in linguistics from the University of Pennsylvania. He has published more than 150 books on linguistics, philosophy, intellectual history, international affairs, and U.S. foreign policy. Among his numerous books are *Language and Mind* (1968), *Chomsky on Anarchism* (2005), *Aspects of the Theory of Syntax* (1965), *The Minimalist Program* (1992), *On Power and Ideology* (1987) and *The Culture of Terrorism* (1988). The philosopher passed away in 2024.

Todd May

Born in 1955, Todd May received his Ph.D. from The Pennsylvania State University in 1989 with his dissertation *Psychology, Knowledge, Politics: The Epistemic Grounds of Michel Foucault's Genealogy of Psychology*. He is currently Class of 1941 Memorial Professor of Philosophy at Clemson University. His areas of specialization are twentieth century continental philosophy, phenomenology, existentialism, structuralism, poststructuralism, poststructuralist anarchism, political philosophy, ethics, and metaethics. May has developed the theory of poststructuralist anarchism along with Saul Newman and Lewis Call. He brings anarchist thought, poststructuralism and politics together in his book *The Political Philosophy of Poststructuralist Anarchism* (1994). His other prominent books are *Between genealogy and epistemology* (1993), *The Moral Theory of Poststructuralism* (1995) and *Reconsidering difference* (1997).

Saul Newman

Saul Newman is Professor of Political Theory at Goldsmiths College, University of London. He earned his B.A. degree in Government, Philosophy, History from University of Sydney and his Doctor of Philosophy in Political Science from University of New South Wales in 1998. He specializes in contemporary and poststructuralist political philosophy, in particular, sovereignty, desire, identity, ideology, psychoanalytic theory, and current political problems. His research interests include contemporary political and social theory, continental thought, and radical politics. He teaches the following courses: Modern Political Theory, Discourse Power Politics, Continental Political Theory: The politics of violence. Some of his books are *From Bakunin to Lacan: Anti-Authoritarianism and the Dislocation of Power* (2001), *Power and Politics in Poststructuralist Thought: New Theories of the Political* (2005) and *The Politics of Post Anarchism* (2010).

Lewis Call

Lewis Call is an American philosopher that is seen as a post-anarchist thinker. He is known for developing the theory of post anarchism together with Saul Newman and Todd May from its source in French postmodern and classical anarchist thought. He completed his B.A. at University of California, San Diego and his M.A. at University of California, Irvine. In 1996, he received his Ph.D. in Modern European History from the University of California, Irvine. Call serves as a professor in the History Department of California Polytechnic State University. His fields of expertise are intellectual history, science fiction studies, anarchism, and history of sexuality. He is the author of *Postmodern Anarchism* (2002), *BDSM in American Science Fiction and Fantasy* (2013) and *Sexualities in the Works of Joss Whedon* (2020).

Introduction

Justice is a notion that humanity has perpetually pursued and yearned for since the inception of our adventure on earth. The desire for justice has surrounded us with a passion we cannot stop pursuing. It has manifested in both efforts to theorize about justice and in the demands for justice that emerge in cases of injustice. In other words, although the desire to ensure justice revealed by injustices presents itself as a strong demand, the need to reveal what justice is through theories has been just as crucial. However, despite an intense emphasis on justice, no other notion lacks consensus on its definition as much as justice. A meaningful investigation into justice begins with accepting that the concept cannot be precisely defined. It is, therefore, comprehensible that justice is regarded as a call and a promise – even if it cannot be reduced to this.

On the one hand, we must never allow the limitations of the status quo to constrain our aspirations and horizon of hope for justice; on the other hand, we should not accept anything that masquerades as justice. Justice cannot be accomplished by what it says it has done or what it claims is just, no matter how urgently it is required. Justice has to include an openness to the future and the constant need for improvement. Although justice is a critical and imminent necessity, it remains an unfulfilled promise. As Derrida argues, "the future" is more important than democracy in the context of the democracy to come (la démocratie à venir), "the future" is more important than the current horizon of justice. Because the emphasis on the future points to a demand for justice that disturbs the present and calls the present beyond itself. Because the most unjust thing would be to close the future by saying that justice exists and that the present is just.[1]

Justice is something we strive for and pray for. Prayer is an intense desire for what is to come. One prays for and believes in something that does not exist at the moment but that one desires to be realized, but one does not know precisely what will be realized. The emphasis here is always on the need to keep our hope for a future that can be better, even if we are short-sighted. Praying for the coming of justice is to address injustices so that justice can haunt us as much as possible, like a spectre. To call for justice in a world overwhelmed with injustices, to believe in justice as something that famulate the others and to wait for its coming, is a forthcoming that we cannot see what is coming. Still, it is also something that we cannot quit waiting for. In this sense, justice is a

1 John D. Caputo, *The Prayers and Tears of Jacques Derrida; Religion without Religion*, Indiana University Press, Indiana, 1997, p. 81.

 | DOI:10.1163/9789004732902_002

passion for the impossible. When we imagine justice, we are, in fact, imagining the impossible, yet we keep hoping and praying for the impossible to be possible. Here, hoping for the impossible to become possible should not be considered a simple logical contradiction. Instead, it is about continuing to hope and pray for something that we cannot see coming. In Derrida's terms, this is an aporia, an impasse. Because if we have a rational reason to hope, it will not be hope but a reasonable expectation.[2] However, hope does not derive from a rational basis but from an absolute future that we cannot see coming and from the open-endedness of the future.[3]

In this sense, justice is a love for the future, but it is a love for the future that impels one to action. Because "what is to come" implies an agentship. Therefore, praying for the coming of justice, witnessing and shedding a tear for the suffering of others must be seen as strengthening the weak call for justice, not as a simplistic demand. This also refers to actual prayer, which entails taking an active rather than a passive stance by assuming responsibility and risk. *The disappearance of God from our vision is always a matter of justice*, Levinas says, because justice should be thought of in the context of the human endeavour to fulfil justice by acting as if God does not exist for the poor, the vulnerable and the oppressed or as if God has placed all responsibility on human beings.[4] In this respect, justice must be considered in the context of both the past (as a promise to remember the victims of injustice) and the future (as a promise to realize justice). So justice is something we owe to the unborn as much as we owe to the dead. This is precisely why Derrida's approach to justice with the metaphor of the spectre, which is irreducible to the existent and does not have a particular time, is intelligible.[5] The spectre is a figure of someone else who is more than we know, outside of us, who is other than us.[6] The other's demand for justice haunts us like a spectre and imposes on us the responsibility of responding to that demand.

Justice is a call, the call of the other and the responsibility to respond to this call. The other's call obliges me to hear and respond to it. In other words, to respond to the other's call is my responsibility, which is to act in response

2 Jacques Derrida, "Epoché and Faith: An Interview with Jacques Derrida" *Derrida and Religion: Other Testament*, ed. Yvonne Sherwood and Kevin Hart, Routledge London-New York, 2005, pp. 30–31.

3 John D. Caputo, *In Search of Radical Theology*, Fordham University Press, 2020 USA, pp. 84–85.

4 John D. Caputo, *On Religion; Thinking in Action*, Routledge, 2001 New York, p. 137.

5 Jacques Derrida, *Specters of Marx; The State of the Debt, the Work of Mourning and the New International*, (UK: Routledge, 1994), p. xviii.

6 Colin Davis, *Haunted Subjects*, Palgrave Macmillan, New York 2007, p. 76.

to the other's call. Considering the close relationship between the concept of response and responsibility, responding to the other's call or request emerges as the most apparent manifestation of responsibility towards the other. This responsibility requires deciding the experience of undecidability to be unconditionally hospitable to others, give a gift unconditionally, forgive unconditionally, and be just to others. This is precisely why everything happens impossibly. As Derrida emphasizes, hospitality manifests not when we invite friends into our homes where they are always welcome. However, when we receive the unwelcome when a foreigner visits us, we have no assurance that it will do us no harm.[7] A gift is a gift when it is given without entering into any economic cycle, without expecting anything in return. Forgiveness is forgiveness when we forgive the unforgivable, not the forgivable, the repentant and those who have made amends.[8]

Admittedly, justice does not and will not exist without the exclusion of others, which means that every state of justice can be questioned and criticized. Justice -if it is done- is done singularly, at the moment of justice, when justice is demanded, when we do our best or our least worst to respond to what the singular situation demands. Because justice is revealed not in the universality of the law but in the singularity of the event, law is about the language of universality; justice is about the singularity of the situation in which justice is done. That is why we can never say that a law, a rule, or even a behaviour is entirely just. Because this would represent a kind of rigid framework, and therefore injustice, that is reduced to the existent and holds the possibility of closing the openness of the future. As Lyotard reminds us, this is precisely why it is crucial for justice to consider whether a particular course of action was just after each decision it makes in pursuit of justice.[9] Because justice does not have an essence situated in the given moment; on the contrary, its essence is that it never has an essence. It never exists in the present because it has no essence. It is always calling, demanding an answer, but it never exists, and the call of justice can never be completed.

This ambiguity and elusiveness of justice will also render all efforts to explain and define justice on the axis of absolute meaning and ground in vain. When justice is tried to be addressed within a definition with defined boundaries, it will exceed that boundary and will not be confined within it. In this respect, it can be said that the very judgments and actions that we consider

7 Giovanni Borradori, *Philosophy in a Time of Terror: Dialogues with Jurgen Habermas and Jacques Derrida*, University of Chicago Press, 2003, pp. 162–163.

8 Jacques Derrida, *On Cosmopolitanism and Forgiveness*, Routledge, 2005, pp. 32–33.

9 Jean-François Lyotard – Jean-Loup Thébaud, *Just Gaming*, University of Minnesota Press, 1985, p. 29.

to be just distort the notion of justice rather than define and describe it. To be sure, associating such an undecidable situation with a concept that urgently needs to be fulfilled, such as justice, will not prevent us from taking action. On the contrary, it would function to prevent our judgments from being used as an instrument of epistemic violence against others and thus from falling into injustice. What will ensure justice is the acceptance of an experience of otherness that cannot be reduced to human epistemic categories, the ability to establish an ethical relationship with otherness, and the responsibility to respond to its demand for justice.

Based on these concerns, this book was conceived as a small contribution to the demand for justice and was structured in this manner. Interviews on justice is the product of an effort to compile the different opinions of the leading philosophers about justice based on their work. Even though many different subjects were discussed in the interviews in this book, one common theme was the notion of justice. Topics such as ethics, metaphysics, God, politics, anarchism, human rights, and the refugee problem were debated concerning their relation to justice. In this context, I would like to expand on the interviews included in this book. First, I created a pool of questions dedicated to each one of the professors before conducting the interviews. I asked them to answer the questions of their choice, and sometimes, I picked them. Though I tried to focus on a specific subject while asking the questions, I thought it would broaden our horizons to discuss various issues during the interviews.

For this reason, I entitled each interview based on a prominent theme mentioned in the respective interviews, even though the discussions were not limited to that specific theme. In this sense, the titles do not imply the whole content of the interviews but rather point out a prominent theme in the interview. In addition, I annexed some works of each philosopher at the end of the interviews. The mentioned works comprised the basis for the questions posed in the interviews. Therefore, I included the list of the works that can be of help to the readers. I also asked the same question, which I found significant, to every one of the philosophers at the end of the interviews. I aimed to determine whether humans focused on justice or injustice by posing this question. In other words, what was the best way to achieve justice? Was it developing theories of justice or detecting and eliminating injustice in the real world? Even though thinking begins with justice, life is unjust from the start, for we feel the injustice when we encounter it without needing a theory in the first place. My final and common interview question was raised within this scope to find an answer to these concerns.

This book comprises twelve interviews carried out with twelve philosophers. The first interview, "God and Justice", was conducted with John D. Caputo, who tackles religious belief and experience about philosophical thought and is known for his concept of weak theology. In the interview with Caputo, we touched upon the relationship between justice and concepts such as God, belief, and religion, as well as how Derrida's deconstructionist approach can provide a perspective for dealing with these concepts. The interview revolved around the ethical responsibility for the other, deconstruction as radical hermeneutics, and the concern for justice in this respect. In the interview "Ethics and Justice" with Simon Critchley, whom I learned from his book The Ethics of Deconstruction, Levinas' understanding of ethics, deconstruction as an ethical demand, and thus the relation between ethics and politics were among the themes that stood out. We discussed many topics ranging from refugee policies to Critchley's argument that philosophy begins in disappointment, not wonder. In the interview "Hermeneutics and Justice," we explored Richard Kearney's diacritical hermeneutic approach, how to differentiate right and wrong as well as good and evil, radical hospitality, responsibility for the other, and the immigration problem. Justice has been tackled more extensively, but its legal aspect has always been significant. As Derrida argues, law is not justice, yet the realization of justice depends on the law.

For this reason, in the following interview called "Law and Justice," I discussed the legal aspect of the matter with Michel Rosenfeld, who is a Professor of Law at the Benjamin N. Cardozo School of Law, where Derrida gave his famous speech "Force of Law: The Mystical Foundation of Authority" about the relation between law and justice. We exchanged views with Rosenfeld on the relation and the tension between justice and legal practices within a wide range of topics. In the interview with Christopher Norris, who has done extensive research on deconstruction, we reviewed different subjects such as Derrida's deconstructionism and his conception of justice, modern and postmodern philosophy, analytic philosophy, and continental philosophy. Furthermore, we discussed various topics related to his recent interest in poetry and music. I interviewed Samir Haddad, my advisor at Fordham University, on Derrida and the legacy of democracy. We touched upon the notions of legacy, deconstructionism, democracy and friendship, ethical-political issues, radical hospitality and the September 11 attacks, among many others, in the interview.

In the interview "Human Rights and Justice" with Seyla Benhabib, we handled a vast array of topics, including the justification of human rights, the Enlightenment, the relationship between reason and violence, the relation between justice and good life, immigration problems around the world, and the concept of the nation-state. Richard J. Bernstein has great importance in this project. We lost Bernstein in July 2022. I conducted the first interview of this project with Richard J. Bernstein. My first interview was perhaps his last. That is why I would like to commemorate Bernstein here. In the interview "Pragmatism and Justice" with Bernstein, a leading figure in pragmatism, we began with questions about the relationship between deconstruction and pragmatism. We moved on to elaborate on different topics ranging from the notion of radical evil to Levinas and Heidegger.

Todd May, Saul Newman, and Lewis Call have laid the foundations of post-anarchism based on the connection between poststructuralist philosophy and classical anarchism. In this regard, we discussed poststructuralist philosophy, anarchism, justice, and various philosophers such as Lacan, Deleuze, Foucault, and Derrida in the interviews titled "Post-anarchism and Justice." Within this scope, I conducted the interviews where the philosophies of the poststructuralist thinkers were debated in depth and some of the problems that arose from the philosophies mentioned above were discussed within the frame of the concern for justice. I interviewed with Noam Chomsky, who has researched a wide range of areas, including his opinion about anarchism and poststructuralist anarchism, the relationship between violence and justice, and the responsibility of intellectuals.

Undoubtedly, every research has challenges, but there is help and support to smooth the path. At this point, I think it is crucial to point out the support I received while conducting this research. I would like to express my gratitude to The Scientific and Technological Research Council of Turkey (TUBITAK) for funding the project. I am deeply indebted to Samir Haddad, my advisor at Fordham University. His support, help and patience helped me have an easier time. Moreover, I am incredibly grateful to the philosophy department at Fordham University, the professors and the university library for providing me with a fantastic work environment while I was there as a visiting researcher. Thanks should also go to each philosopher who helped me complete this research by supporting me and the project idea and showing me tolerance. They kindly helped me during this period. Furthermore, John D. Caputo's and Richard Kearney's support was unmatched. I would like to express my deepest gratitude, especially to both.

Lastly, I would like to acknowledge two people. The first one is Volkan Atilla, my husband, who motivated and supported me continuously. The latter was Abraham, my son, with whom I became pregnant just before the project started. Therefore, I conducted these interviews with my son when I was pregnant with him and after he was born. It was a challenging time. I hope that I see in his life the manifestation of this period where he was exposed to the concept of justice and that the notion of justice stops being an abstract concept for him and starts guiding him throughout life.

Sema Cevirici Atilla
2024

CHAPTER 1

God and Justice: John D. Caputo

John D. Caputo is an American philosopher known for his work in postmodern theology, continental philosophy, and hermeneutics. His philosophy centers on the concept of "radical hermeneutics" and the exploration of religion without fixed dogmas, advocating for an open, interpretive approach to faith and ethics. Deeply influenced by the ideas of Jacques Derrida, Søren Kierkegaard, and Martin Heidegger, Caputo's work focuses on the notions of "the weak" or "undeconstructible" force of religion, ethics, and justice – emphasizing humility, openness, and vulnerability as essential to a meaningful life.

One of Caputo's core ideas is the concept of radical hermeneutics, developed in his book Radical Hermeneutics: Repetition, Deconstruction, and the Hermeneutic Project. Here, Caputo argues for an approach to interpretation that embraces uncertainty, ambiguity, and the absence of ultimate foundations. Radical hermeneutics rejects the idea that meaning can be fully grasped or conclusively defined; instead, it views understanding as an ongoing, open-ended process of interpretation. This approach challenges traditional views of religious and philosophical certainty, inviting individuals to live with an openness to the unknown and a recognition of the limits of human understanding.

Caputo's philosophy also delves into the concept of "the weak force of God" in works like The Weakness of God: A Theology of the Event. In this book, he proposes a theology centered not on an omnipotent, commanding deity but on a "weak" God – one that calls for compassion, justice, and love rather than absolute power. Caputo's "weak theology" suggests that God is best understood as a call or event that inspires ethical action rather than a force that imposes rules or control. This approach sees the divine as an invitation to embrace humility, empathy, and responsibility, rather than obedience to authoritarian structures. By focusing on this "weak" dimension of faith, Caputo opens up a space for a more inclusive, non-dogmatic spirituality that resonates with modern, skeptical perspectives.

Another significant work, On Religion, expands on Caputo's vision of faith as an open-ended, interpretive journey rather than a system of fixed beliefs. Here, he critiques traditional religious institutions and explores the idea of faith as an existential experience – a relationship with the unknown that

 | DOI:10.1163/9789004732902_003

drives individuals toward ethical engagement with others. For Caputo, religion is less about doctrines and more about the ethical demand to respond to the needs of the world with compassion and justice.

In The Insistence of God: A Theology of Perhaps, Caputo introduces the idea of "perhaps," advocating for a theology that embraces possibilities rather than certainties. This notion of "perhaps" speaks to Caputo's broader philosophical outlook, which seeks to honor the mystery and unpredictability of existence, encouraging individuals to live with openness and readiness for the unforeseen. John D. Caputo's philosophy offers a radical reinterpretation of religion, ethics, and faith in a postmodern world.

Sema Cevirici Atilla [*SCA*]*: You have adopted a distinctive approach to religion which is called weak theology. When did this idea occur to you? What were the questions and problems that led you to investigate this subject further?*

John D. Caputo [JC]: It has always been true for me that writing one book leads to the next and that is exactly what happened here. When I was working on *The Prayers and Tears of Jacques Derrida*, the idea struck me to follow this up with another book, one on God, not Derrida, which would draw out the implications of what Derrida was calling "religion without religion." Writing *Prayers and Tears* led me to realize that there was another way of thinking about theological questions, one that is inspired by deconstruction, and another way of thinking about deconstruction, one that is inspired by religion – one which cannot be identified with a "death of God" atheology, which was the received account of deconstruction in those days. So instead of the "death of God," I proposed "the weakness of God." It should not go unnoticed that after writing *Heidegger and Aquinas*, I did not spend a lot of time talking about religion. I had in my own mind given up on it. I had grown up steeped in Catholicism, including entering a Catholic religious order, and then, at a certain point in my life I just decided it was all mythology and I basically dropped it. In the 1980s I immersed myself in hermeneutics and deconstruction. I identified myself as a philosopher and would have smiled at the idea that I was a theologian. I spent most of my academic life in a philosophy department, not a religion department. It was only when I started working on *Prayers and Tears* that I decided that there is actually something interesting about religion, after all, something that Derrida was bringing up, something that could go somewhere. I think Derrida himself had a similar experience. He rediscovered his Jewishness but it was a Jewishness without Judaism, beyond the Judaism he grew up with as a child in Algeria. The key analysis in Derrida, the crucial link, what led me to formulate the idea of weak theology, was his analysis of justice in "The Force of Law." He is saying, in effect, that justice does not exist, that justice calls, and the only thing that exists is the law. Accordingly, since we can't make justice stronger, we have to make the laws just. Then it hit me. I thought, if you substitute the word God for justice, that actually makes for an interesting way to think about God. God does not exist, God calls, and since we can't make God or the call stronger, then we have to make the world look more like what God is calling for. That, in turn, would prove to be the sense in which God does exist, in the same way justice exists. Justice only exists in just laws and just deeds. The same thing would hold with God. God only exists insofar as God's call is answered in our lives. Our response fills up what's missing in God. So whatever day that was, whatever month, when I saw the analogy between justice and the name of God, between the event is harbored in the name of justice and the event is harbored in the name of God, that's when I started developing the argument found in *The Weakness of God*.

SCA: *Can weak theology be a solution to the problem of evil? Does the problem of evil turn into a human problem rather than being about God, especially considering that God is defined as a non-coercive force or invitation and that people take responsibility for evil?*

JC: Yes, that is right. This solves the problem of evil by dissolving it. This robs the problem of evil of one of its basic premises, which is that God seems somehow responsible for evil, and the job of "apologetics" is to let God off the hook. But in weak theology you don't have to get God off the hook because God is not a being who does things or doesn't do them. God is not a being who intervenes in things or fails to intervene. As Dietrich Bonhoeffer says, it is time we behaved like adults and assumed responsibility for our lives. The name of God is the name of a call, which it is entirely our responsibility to answer. The problem of evil is our problem. It is we who have gotten ourselves into the mess that we're in, and it is we who have to get ourselves out of it. That means that we have to pay attention to the better angels of our nature. We have to rise above our selfishness and our narcissism and listen to something that calls us out of ourselves to be something more than we are. I don't think there is a supernatural being behind that call, or a supernatural intervention on the part of a superbeing called God who can save us. The name of God is the name of a promise, an aspiration, an injunction, of something we desire with a desire beyond desire. We are dreaming of an event, of the coming of what we can't see coming, of an opening to the future that's inscribed in our heart. I think this injunction is irreducible but I do not think this it is of supernatural provenance. I think the supernatural is religion's worst enemy. The reason why nobody trusts theology is that theologians, classical theologians, at least, claim to have supernatural resources, to be the beneficiaries of a special revelation, in virtue of which they are somehow plugged into something beyond the human, beyond the world. But we are not plugged into anything that's beyond the world. I think there is just one world, in which we sometimes behave maliciously and sometimes nobly. Either way, we're responsible. This is not anthropomorphism. On the contrary, it is asking us to overcome our narcissism, not because some supernatural authority demands it and will reward us if we do and punish us if we do not, but because the better angels of our nature are pleading with us.

SCA: *In your article called "The Return of Anti-Religion: From Radical Atheism to Radical Theology," you state that "I re-imagine and reinvent God, so my radical theology is considered radical atheism and the 'death of God'." According to Jean-Luc Marion, every "evaluation," even if it is positive, actually expresses a subjective construction, which is an idolatry. He defines idol as a limited function of man in which man actually creates an image of the divine, rather than an incorrect or inaccurate image of the divine. In this context, what do you think saves your imagination and reinvention about God from idolatry?*

JC: I think that what I am saying about God is "iconic" not idolatrous, but not exactly in Marion's terms. In my view, Marion entertains the fantastic idea that the alternative to a human construction is something that, as he says, comes to us *à partir de Dieu*, from God on high, which I think is a supernaturalist illusion; it is like believing in magic. In my view, there is no bypassing human constructions, but we should distinguish between human constructions that are open-ended and evocative (iconic) and human constructions which are closed and rigid (idols), like the dogmatic constructions of the confessional religions – biblical inerrancy, say, or papal infallibility – or like nationalist idolatries of the "fatherland." The notion of God that Derrida himself identifies, an idea I think really does get very close to what we mean when we speak of God, is "the possibility of the impossible." The Abrahamic God can do things that are impossible for human beings. In my mind that's a very elemental notion of God, but the crucial thing is not to mystify it with a theology of omnipotence but to appreciate it as a work of theopoetics. The name of God is the name of an open-ended aspiration for something beyond the horizon, beyond the pale, which shatters our horizon of expectation, of what is possible. There is nothing idolatress about that. Quite the opposite, it is an extremely iconic figure. In deconstruction, we do not get trapped inside the name itself. We do not confuse the name of God with the *event* that the name of God harbors. We do not confuse something that has been constructed in history with the undeconstructible. In the name of God, we are being drawn by the God beyond God, by a desire beyond desire, by the more-than-possible, beyond the possible. The name of God is the name of the "always more." Whatever we desire, there is something more that we don't foresee. Anything we say about God would be deconstructible. Anything we would say about the unconditional or the impossible would be deconstructible. The name of God is a construction of human language to give words to something which is greater than anything we construct. It is aporetic – a concept of the inconceivable, imagining the unimaginable – but it is not supernatural. Who knows? Maybe we are ultimately talking about the mystery of the universe. The more we discover in contemporary physics about the universe, the more awesome and inspiring it is, the more it looks like the *mysterium tremendum et fascinans*. Whatever it is, there's something we desire with a desire beyond desire. So there's nothing idolatrous for me in any of this, whereas the idea of something *à partir de Dieu* is a transcendental illusion, a fantasy. Deconstruction reminds us that we are always dealing with contingent, historical constructions, and nothing that we ever construct will be undeconstructible. Not so long as we are living in space and time. I think one of the Jewish inspirations for Derrida's work is the critique of idols in the Hebrew Bible. He was not religious in the conventional sense. He hated Hebrew school, he hated studying Hebrew for his bar mitzvah, he used to cut classes so he could play soccer, He was never an observant Jew but he grew up in a Jewish home, had Jewish parents, lived in a Jewish world, and so he had what we could call a Jewish memory. There are figures and images in his head from the Bible, and the critique of idols is one of them. I think that is part of the reason he is came up with something called deconstruction. He is acutely sensitive to the instability of anything that we say or do, but unstable does mean worthless. It's unstable because it's not the finished product. So, I would say deconstruction is a very good theory to protect you from idols, not to get you caught up in them, whereas ultra-conservative Catholicism is rife with idols.

***SCA:** In* The Prayers and Tears of Jacques Derrida, *you comment that "I cannot say whether God is a translation of 'justice,' so that whenever I pray and weep over justice I am praying and weeping over God, dreaming and desiring God, with a deep and abiding passion for God. Or whether everything I mean by the passion for God, by loving God, by the desire for God, by 'my God', is a way of dreaming of justice." Do you think the passion for justice has replaced the passion for God in this regard?*

JC: I don't think justice replaces God in any final and decisive way, but I think it's one of the substitutes. I think the name of God belongs to a chain of substitutions, one member of which would certainly be justice. And there are others – forgiveness, hospitality, love, joy. There are many ways in which to affirm something of unconditional value to us. For an artist it would be the beautiful, for a scientist, perhaps, an exquisitely perfect mathematical formula. There is something of unconditional import in our lives, and in the Abrahamic tradition, we tend to call that God. If we were born somewhere else, some other time, some other place, that word might not be part of our vocabulary. We might have a completely different way of thinking and speaking about things. But there would be a way to affirm something of unconditional value, of unconditional importance. So I posit a chain of substitutions that we would never be able to stop, an endless chain. History is the proof that there are always other ways to think about the unconditional. My wager is, if we knew all the languages and all the cultures in the history of the world, we would find a long list of things assigned unconditional importance, depth, and value, things that would also be considered mysterious. Various cultures, various traditions will valorize different things. In the Hebrew tradition justice does seem to function as a synonym for God. In the Christian tradition love is a synonym for God. I think in each tradition those words are doing pretty much the same thing. Different vocabularies, different paradigms, different forms of life, but all playing analogous roles. So, yes, justice is a substitute for God, but that raises the question, how can we determine which is the substitute for which? If you ask Derrida – and I have asked him questions like that several times – he had a favorite answer. "If I knew that," he would say, "I would know everything!" So that's the right answer.

SCA: *Would calling God absolutely just be treason against God or justice?*

JC: In order to avoid treason – that is an interesting way to put it – in order to avoid betraying the name of God or the name of justice, I would rephrase your question and instead of "absolutely" I would say "unconditionally." The name of God is the name of unconditional justice. When you speak of something as being "absolutely just" in deconstruction, you want to be careful. Nothing would ever be absolutely just. Justice would be contextual, an effect of *différance*, which means it would be at this time, in this place, the right thing to do, or maybe merely the least bad thing to do, because sometimes we are only given bad choices. So in weak theology "absolutely just" would be too strong. When someone manages to do something just, to do something well, we can call that action just for that moment, not "absolutely just". So in deconstruction, while justice in itself, if there is such a thing, is undeconstructible, unconditional, we avoid speaking of something absolute, which suggests something absolved from or outside of its context. In deconstruction everything is relational, contextual, so things are more or less just, they are never absolutely. God is not absolutely just because God does not exist, and God is not an agent who does things, just or unjust. God calls, and we are the ones who are called upon to respond justly. So, I would say the name of God is the name of a call for unconditional justice, but not that God is a being who is "absolutely just". That is how I would avoid treason, avoid betraying the name of God or of justice. Nothing will ever be "absolutely just," not if it exists. I agree with Derrida on this point.

***SCA:** Do you think your own view of God is open to deconstruction as well? How would you proceed if you were to deconstruct your own understanding?*
JC: Yes, of course, it is deconstructible. Whatever is constructed in space and time – and what is not? – is deconstructible. At the present moment, in particular, I think we are entering upon a seismic shift which will change everything I am saying, that we all have been saying. I'm thinking about the promise and the threat, the cure and the poison, the *pharmakon,* which we now call "posthumanism." This is the notion that ultimately at some point – we can argue with how long it will take – science will be able to "upload" consciousness into the cloud, a computer, acquiring a kind of virtual existence, digital existence, shedding our corporeality and eventually our life here on planet earth. Now that would be a real challenge to philosophy and theology. I think that almost all of the classic discourse on God would be transformed, and maybe even just evaporate, in a situation like that. I sometimes wonder – supposing my books are not ignored or lost – what someone would say who reads *The Weakness of God* a hundred years from now. Will it make any sense to them? Or will the person reading it actually be on some other planet, a being of digital consciousness, and this book will look completely obsolete and quaint to them – the way the doctrine of the "four humors" or "bloodletting" look to us today. There are people who maintain that the world we live in may be a "virtual world," having been constructed by a superintelligence somewhere. This is absolutely a serious consideration put forth by David Chalmers, who is a well-respected philosopher. Maybe what we are doing is going to look hopelessly primitive in the future compared to what's ahead. Everything I am saying may come completely undone. Then my question is, would there be still some sort of *mystery*? I hold that even then, in that world, yes, there would still be mystery, but then it would be a cosmic mystery. It would be the mystery of the universe or of the multiplicity of universes and perhaps that will become the subject matter of theology and philosophy.
***SCA:** While Derrida associates justice with undecidability, he emphasizes that "justice cannot wait, because it must be done immediately." Is there not such an urgency in religion? Can one delay matters of faith or leave them unclear? Can we conclude that faith does not wait like justice?*
JC: Yes, I think that undecidability and the demand for urgency go hand in hand. Undecidability does not mean endless indecision. I am comfortable speaking of the urgency of justice and of faith, but when it comes to "religion" I hesitate. I'm inclined to say that is a more deconstructible notion. Some words are more evocative of justice, more open-ended, more suggestive of what we desire with the desire beyond desire than others; some are better than others. The word faith is evocative and open-ended, whereas the

word "belief" is more deconstructible, more contingent, which, I think is also true, and I do not know if you agree with this, of the word religion. Religion is a more thoroughly sociological, historical construction. It's actually a quite Christian word, which is why Derrida will speak of the "Christian Latin word religion" (Lat. *religio*). When I was lecturing in the Sultanate of Oman, I was accompanied by a translator whom I asked about how he was translating the word Anglo-Latin word "religion." He said that he was using an Arabic word *Din* which, when I asked him, meant literally something like judgment or debt. So to answer your question, I would say faith, which is also a Christian Latin word, and also deconstructible, is more open-ended than religion, and perhaps justice even more so. So yes, faith cannot wait; we need faith; we need it now. The same thing is true of justice. Justice deferred is justice denied. But I'm less confident about religion. I sometimes think religion has no future. The word has been taken over by right-wing extremists, and I often find myself thinking that it can't be saved. I like to say religion isn't going to save anybody, it's up to us to save religion from itself. So, I don't know about you, but I myself wonder if we can fix it this word after all the damage that's been done to it by right-wing religious extremists, all over the world. Not just in rural America but, all over the world. But, I agree, faith and justice are urgent, and that the undecidability does not destroy its urgency; it magnifies it. That's the mistake that I think people make with what Derrida is saying. I think the "to-come" character of justice or democracy, of whatever the event is, does not leave us despondent, apathetic, in a position of listless waiting. It is more like a white light that shines on the present and warns us against complacency, reminds us that nothing should dare call itself justice or democracy or hospitality, not yet, not here and now, because these things always demand more. The just are the last ones to think themselves just. So, the to-come puts pressure on the present, making the present situation urgent. In "The Force of Law," that's the third of the three aporias of justice – the urgency of justice now. Deconstruction does not somehow undermine action and the present. I don't think so. The opposite is true.

SCA: *In* Deconstruction in a Nutshell, *you bring up the relationship between justice and knowledge. You explain that "justice precedes knowledge, is older than knowledge, and belongs to another order – something more actual than knowledge, if this distinction is valid." In this sense, can we say that there is a tension between justice and knowledge? Does justice exclude knowledge or does it require performative knowledge? How would you evaluate the relationship between justice and knowledge? Can they be reconciled in any respect?*

JC: I was speaking of Derrida's view that, even when we have time to deliberate, which is not always the case, an ethical choice is ultimately a free decision in a singular situation which we make in the night of non-knowing; it is not the conclusion of an argument which follows logically and shines the light of a universal principle upon a particular case. It belongs to the performative order, not the constative. In language of the middle ages, it is a movement of the will, not the intellect. We remember the debate in the Middle Ages between the intellectualists and the voluntarists. The intellectualists, like Thomas Aquinas, held that we need to know something in order to love it. The voluntarists, like St. Augustine, held that we need to love something in order to know it. This is a complicated debate and it requires making many distinctions, and of course you cannot neatly separate two different "faculties" like that. But that aside, I agree with St. Augustine and voluntarists on this point, and I think so do Derrida and Levinas. Love is a kind of commitment to something, where you don't know what you are getting into. It's the love that makes you commit and continues to hold you fast, not the fact that you know what's going on and you can see what you are getting into. I wonder if, in a certain sense, we might even say that if we completely and totally knew and understood something, we couldn't love it. The transparency, the knowledge, would eliminate the commitment. It would all be completely clear, it would be like a contract where every single item is completely clear, or a bet made in a situation where we know the outcome is assured – there's no risk. Love is not a contract, nor is it transactional. Love is about risk and risk is about not knowing. I think love drives knowledge, we seek knowledge, we want to know as much as we can. But when you love something, you're also committing to a part of the thing that you don't know, and you cannot see coming, and you are ready for it, willing to take the risk. That's why one might object that in the classical notion of God, God can't love anything because God can't suffer risk and rejection. The God of omnipotence cannot be put at risk. But we cannot love without risk, without making ourselves vulnerable. To say "I love you" is to take the risk that the person on the other end doesn't reciprocate, and then there is a terrible moment, an awkward silence. To say "I love you" is to take a leap of faith, a leap of non-knowing. So, too, with justice. I think that justice holds, that it calls upon us to respond, that we are not excused from this call, whatever the state of knowing or non-knowing, whatever ultimate account we have of the world. The call of justice does not wait for knowledge to come in and back it up and make everything clear, which why Kant said that he was willing to limit knowledge to make room for his faith in ethics. I think Levinas is following Kant on this point – the call of justice which puts me in the accusative, *me voici*, originates in the invisible face of the other – and Derrida is following Levinas. So, I think love precedes knowledge, drives knowledge, is deeper than knowledge, prior to knowledge. I hasten to add that I do not want to denigrate knowledge. We want to know everything we can, the more the better – but that is what we want, what we desire, what we love.

***SCA:** Derrida endorsed and praised your reception of him. In addition, he stated that such a reading required courage and that it was difficult for you and added, "His success will be the success of the one who transforms the picture in the United States and the English-speaking world into a picture of the relationship between religion and philosophy." When you look retrospectively at your intellectual journey, do you see what you are doing as something difficult that requires courage? Would you call this passion of yours a passion for the impossible?*

JC: I think that when Derrida said that, he was thinking of two things. First, he was aware of how thoroughly Anglo-American philosophy is dominated by British analytic philosophy, and he knew that there is a terrible rift between the analytic and continental philosophers, something he experienced when he was nominated for an honorary degree at Oxford. Continental philosophers have a difficult time in the United States, as you probably have already learned. Only a dozen or so Ph.D. programs specialize in continental philosophy. A lot of the time, in the United States, if you want to study continental thinkers, you have to go to a comparative literature department or to a religion department. So, he was thinking of that. The second thing he had in mind is was what they call in France *laïcité*, secularity, the separation of the religious and the secular. In western Europe, in France in particular, religion is a much more taboo than it is here. Paul Ricoeur, for example, tended to keep his religion out of his philosophical work. But as it happens, neither of those things demanded much courage on my part. When I was working on *Prayers and Tears*, I was a tenured full professor with an endowed chair. My professional position was completely secure. I was in not vulnerable. By and large, my work, like that of most continental philosophers, was simply ignored by the analytic establishment. Only very recently was a book of mine – *Cross and Cosmos* – reviewed by an analytic philosopher, who also happens to be a right-wing Christian, in *Notre Dame Philosophical Reviews*, and he judged the book badly, thought it to be foggy obscurantism, cloudy nonsense; the only thing clear to him was that it was clearly heretical. What do I care about reactionary ignorance like that? I also taught at a Catholic university for most of my career where continental philosophy has traditionally enjoyed a welcome reception. Catholic universities like Villanova, Duquesne, Fordham, Loyola and Boston College have played a large role in establishing a beachhead in the United States for continental philosophy. So, no, I don't think I represent a profile in academic courage. I think, based on his own experience, Derrida thought that anybody who was interested in him was going to get into trouble, because he was always getting into trouble. I think one of the reasons he traveled a lot was that he was visiting places where he would be made welcome, where he was actually a celebrity. At Villanova, he was treated like Elvis. I might add that I have been criticized for something that Derrida did incite in me, which is to write in a more playful way. I have had people advise me against writing like that, warning me that I was going to ruin my reputation. So I try to maintain myself on the border of academic propriety and a professional insouciance which tests those borders, working both inside and outside the university. But I have always thought was a matter of good judgment, not courage.

SCA: *You describe deconstruction as a more radical hermeneutics. When you compare hermeneutics and deconstruction, which one do you think is more sensitive to justice?*

JC: The idea behind radical hermeneutics is that there is a point where hermeneutics and deconstruction merge into one, a point where if we pressure hermeneutics strongly enough, and understand deconstruction amply enough, we see that hermeneutics is a kind of deconstruction and deconstruction is a kind of hermeneutics, albeit more radical one. Derrida himself would never talk like that but that's because when Derrida uses the word hermeneutics he is thinking of Paul Ricoeur, not Heidegger's hermeneutics of facticity. Derrida and Ricoeur were friends, and Ricoeur even supported Derrida to be his successor in a chair of philosophy at Nanterre, which never happened because of French academic politics and not a little jealousy of Derrida's celebrity on the part of the establishment. So, for Derrida hermeneutics means Ricoeur; it is a theory of meaning, whereas *différance* is found on a level prior to meaning. Derrida says that while hermeneutics allows for what Ricoeur calls "polysemy," the multiplicity of meaning, deconstruction is a theory of the "trace," and it is exposed to "dissemination," to chance convergences and divergences, to homonyms and misspellings and the like, which is more than just polysemy. That I think is the basic distinction. Now in those terms, to get to your question, the deconstructive side of radical hermeneutics is more open to chance inventions, and the hermeneutic side is more bound with the tradition which is to be reinvented. Of course these two things cannot be separated and radical hermeneutics means keeping both together, all with the aim of keep the future open while reserving a memory of the past, both those things at the same time. The hermeneutics side is more oriented towards preserving, keeping the memory of the past alive, whereas openness to the future is the more deconstructive side. But remember, we owe justice to the dead, which Derrida calls mourning, as well as to the future, to the children, which Derrida calls the messianic, so there can be no choosing between them. But if we say justice lies in recognizing the singularity of the other one, the unforeseeability of the other one, that sounds more like deconstruction. Deconstruction is a little more impious, a little riskier, whereas the historical origin of modern hermeneutics is in theology and piety. Hermeneutics has a more traditional, edifying source. Deconstructionism is more of an outsider, a rogue. Gadamer and Ricoeur were respected university professors, Derrida a bit of a renegade. If you think justice is always a matter of trying to acknowledge something *tout autre*, which shatters the horizon of expectation, if you think justice is a matter of dealing with the coming of something that you didn't see coming, that's deconstruction, probably. But this is complicated. I have good friends, like Richard Kearney, who studied with Ricoeur, and Jim Risser, who is very close to Gadamer, and we have been arguing about this for years.

SCA: *In your book* Against Ethics, *you maintain that "people who produce victims are not the other to whom we owe everything. The other as Levinas says are always the orphan, the widow, the stranger that is the victim not victimizer." Levinas was subjected to serious criticism after his statements about the Sabra and Shatila massacre in a radio interview. In this connection, is it possible for us to decide whether the other is the victim or the victimizer by getting rid of our beliefs and ideologies?*

JC: You are raising several important issues here. First of all, that interview with Levinas was not one of his better days. I don't know if you've ever heard the expression "weasel words," meaning failing to step up and say what you should say. I think this interview was a personal failure on Levinas's part. But beyond a personal failing, there is a more difficult philosophical question. I am no longer satisfied with the way I formulated this point in *Against Ethics*. If we say what we mean by the other is the victim not the victimizer, we are making things easy for ourselves. Then openness to the other is trivially true. It obscures the ambiguity and the risk of welcoming the other and it puts off the problem. For – apart from the fact that we cannot simply write off the victimizer as beyond help – we can always ask, how can we tell the difference between the two? The answer is, we often cannot, not with any kind of real certainty. This is the source of a long-standing disagreement between me and Richard Kearney concerning what Derrida called unconditional hospitality. If there is an axe murderer knocking on my door, someone who is coming to my house to do me harm, Richard objects that Derrida's idea of unconditional hospitality would require me to open the door. I deny that. I think that in deconstruction, nothing, including unconditional hospitality, would ever result in an unbreakable rule – like "always open the door, no matter what." *Against Ethics* means against unbreakable rules. Deconstruction is the deconstruction of rules which dictate "always do this" or "never do that." The notion of a rigid rule governing our actions is the very "ethics" in "*against* ethics." This means it is the singularity of the situation which should govern a decision, not a rule.

So, Derrida says, sometimes the best way to keep the future open is to say no, to keep the door closed. As we speak, we can say, unconditional hospitality does not require the Ukrainians to let the Russians overrun their country, just as his critique of the concept of "sovereignty" doesn't mean that the Ukrainians don't have the sovereign right to rule themselves independently of the Russians. The ultimate principle is to keep the future open. An axe murderer or Vladimir Putin or an evil doer is closing off the future. So, in the singularity of the situation, the question is what keeps the future open, here and now. That's a kind of rule without rule. It is not a rule in the sense that you could simply "apply" it, universally. It's not a univocal rule, it's an ambiguous, undecidable axiological desire, and it is often far from clear what we ought to do. The "unconditional" does not translate into a universal rule but into ineliminable risk. Suppose, for example, someone tells us something and we have to decide whether to trust them. We have known them for a long time, we suspect something is out of joint in what they are saying, but we trust them. There is always an element of risk, and if we could eliminate the risk – which is the unconditional element – then, as Derrida says, a computer could do it. If it's risk free, if there is a rule that we can apply, a computer can do it. But what we are doing in ethics is making judgments which require discretion, which is what Aristotle called *phronesis*. The *phronimos* knows what to do in a *new* situation, not because there is a rule for it but because there is not, because he can discern what to do when the rules fail us; he a cultivated seasoned judgment that can assess something that we never saw before. If we follow Richard Kearney, we have to have criteria and rules, but if that were so, we would never have a paradigm shift; we would be left helpless before something radically new. A paradigm shift occurs the moment when the rules and criteria go limp because we are dealing with an anomaly. Even when there are rules, we are at a loss to know how they apply in a situation this unique. Once we figure out how to deal with it, we can make up new rules, but they'll be good only until you hit the next anomaly, when again there won't be any rules. Rules don't go all the way down. Ethics as rules doesn't go all the way down. When it comes to discriminating the victimizer and the victim, sometimes it wouldn't be too hard to tell the difference, but sometimes it would be. When we are making a judgment, we ask ourselves, is this a good idea or a bad idea? The problem is that a lot of good ideas turn out to be bad ideas.

***SCA:** Both Derrida and Levinas associated metaphysical thought with a kind of violence, totalitarianism, and oppression. Can metaphysical thought be deemed as a philosophy of injustice considering their criticisms in this regard?*

JC: That would be too strong. It is true, on the one hand, that metaphysical theories lay behind the monstrous totalitarian systems on both the right and the left, that they spawn metanarratives that reinforce colonialism and oppression. In modernity metaphysical thinking has a totalizing tendency which treats the individual as a cog in a wheel. But, on the other hand, we don't want to make metaphysics itself into a monster because metaphysics is, in a way, basically the subject matter of philosophy. It's the tradition that has been handed down to us from Plato to Hegel to today. We don't want to treat it in a reductionistic or dismissive way. Remember that Heidegger moved on from talking about *überwinden* ("overcoming") metaphysics to *verwinden*, coming to grips with it, wrestling with it, wresting something from it, which is more in line with his idea of "retrieval" (*Wiederholung*). As Derrida might say, a metaphysical theory has an identity – Plato is not Hegel – but it is not identical with itself; it is full of internal disturbances and openings. The cracks are how the light gets in, as Leonard Cohen says. Even Kant, after criticizing metaphysical illusions, said that reason has deep "interests" at stake in metaphysics. We might think of the major metaphysicians as people with great imaginations, who come up with these striking visions of the world, interesting and compelling insights into the human condition. But if these vision are universalized and canonized, turned into comprehensive and rigid systems, they become destructive. So we should take them instead as works of creative imagination, flights of fancy in the best sense. Nicholas of Cusa talks about God as *posse ipsum*, the matrix of pure possibility, of everything that is in any way possible. Nietzsche describes a stunning and unsettling play of forces that has no regard for our tender hearts. Hegel unfolds the spirit as that runs through all things. If we think of metaphysicians as novelists telling us eye-opening stories, or as imaginative phenomenologists, then we can take them to heart without turning metaphysics into a heartless system, into a monster. I grew up in a world where St. Thomas Aquinas was treated like a supernal being who dropped out of the sky in order to communicate to the rest of us the absolute truth. I knew someone who had read just about everything St. Thomas wrote. As a professor, he expected his students to memorize Thomas's words and when it came publishing, he was paralyzed. All he could do was quote St. Thomas. Aquinas had become a monster; his writings had taken possession of this man's mind with a kind of violence that shut down his imagination. Metaphysical thinking can do that, but it can also do the opposite. So it is a *pharmakon*. Ironically, premodern systems like the *Summa Theologica* of Aquinas are *not* like that, because they are marked throughout by a deep respect for the mystery and incomprehensibility of God, and their writings – like Saint Augustine's *Confession* – were often cast in the form of a prayer. Aquinas's *Summa* is not a modern system. He calls his five "proofs" for the existence of God five "ways" (*viae*), out of respect for God's eminence. Pre-modern metaphysical systems were not "onto-theo-logical" in the way Heidegger uses that word. But in modernity it's different. With Descartes, Leibniz and especially Spinoza, where reason is thought of as a system, we encounter systems so powerful that philosophers like Kant and Schelling are left trying to figure out how you could have a system of reason and still preserve freedom. That's a problem characteristic of modernity which did not beset pre-modern philosophy and shows us why we need something called post-modern. Especially today, when we live in a "global world," in a vast system of systems – climatological, environmental, biological, planetary and astral, financial, and above all "information" systems. But the solution is not to try to get rid of systems. The solution is to keep the systems open. So the operative distinction should be made not between systems and the individual, as Kierkegaard thought, but between open and closed systems. That is another reason for my interest in Derrida. His notion of the "quasi-transcendental" is a theory of quasi – or open systems. Language is a system, but it an open-ended on-going self-revising system. His whole idea is to keep these systems revisable, deconstructible, auto-deconstructible. Then the system will not do violence and it will not be a source of injustice. It will be more like what Gadamer called, invoking a classical definition of hermeneutics, the *subtilitas intelligendi,* the subtlety of understanding. The key word is *subtilitas,* having a light touch, the right touch, as opposed to dealing with things in a rigid, rule-governed and heavy-handed way where everything is either black or white. When metaphysics goes astray, it loses its touch, lacks a light touch, and then the system becomes violent, but it doesn't have to be.

***SCA:** In the post-truth age, if there is no absolute truth, what is the basis of our ethical responsibility and fairness to the other? Why should I be responsible and fair to the other if there is no truth? What would be our epistemic justification for being just and responsible?*

JC: First of all, if we require a "basis" or an "epistemic justification" for being just and reasonable, we are already off on the wrong foot. Is the implication that, if we do not come up with a foundationalist argument which "justifies" being "just" then we will *not* be just? That seems to me a cynical view of ethical life. I think "being just" speaks for itself, that it gets along very well without an ultimate epistemological or transcendental foundation – without a God to reward or punish us, or a "Form of the Good" or a "Categorical Imperative" to back it up. Radical hermeneutics is post-foundationalist. We take things on their individual merits. That brings me to what you are asking about truth and post-truth. When we say there is no truth, we must be careful. That has a certain value in certain circumstances. In a totalitarian situation, a situation of despotism and dogmatism, authoritarianism and repression, it has rhetorical value, but nowadays, in the age of post-truth, of wild-eyed and contrived conspiracy theories, it is too dangerous to talk like that. I wrote a book which I dared to entitle *Truth* by which I meant an ongoing auto-correcting search, where truth is a process and a promise not a finished product. So we could say, there is no truth with a capital "T" truth, no absolute, unrevisable, fixed, dogmatic "Truth." But that does not mean that we promote chaos and conspiracy theories. It means that there are instead only multiple auto-deconstructible contextual truths. In the same way, I would say there's no such thing as pure transcendental reason, capital "R" Reason, but there are "good reasons," better reasons for thinking or doing this rather than that. So truth is always contextual, hermeneutical. After all, Truth and Reason can become monsters. The "reign of terror" took place in the age of "Enlightenment." People start killing each other when they think they have the Truth, capital T truth. But where does that leave us? Not with bedlam but with hermeneutics, with multiple, contextual, conflicting truths, in the plural and the lower case, competing hermeneutical judgments that have to be adjudicated. Based on what? Based on an axiom, or meta-axiom, an axiology, of keeping the future open. Instead of rigid formulae, a series of negotiations in shifting circumstances. There are no canonical truths but there is ongoing debate and exchange, openness to what diverse people are saying, fresh judgments, unorthodox opinions, novel experiments, interesting explorations, uncertain suggestions. Interpretation goes all the way down, but some interpretations are better than others, more plausible, suggestive, and some are invidious and far-fetched. The one real requirement is that this free play of opinion, this conflict of interpretations, should be conducted without violence. There is a thin line between being willing to die for an idea and be willing to kill for it – and the line is *nonviolence*. I am not saying we cannot be passionately committed to an idea, but we need to be committed nonviolently. In the civil rights movement in the 1960s in the United States, people like Martin Luther King engaged in passionate but peaceful protest. They did not assassinate anyone but they did get assassinated. They were willing to put themselves in harm's way for what they believed, but they did not put others in harm's way. So, we can believe something with all our heart – but nonviolently.

Truth seeking requires caution and modesty, a sense of fallibility, all of which are embedded in the idea of democracy, where the idea is to allow differences to flourish and then to come together and resolve these differences non-violently. The critique of sovereignty does not destroy the power to make a decision but it divides the power as widely as possible. We have beliefs, but one of those beliefs is that we could be wrong, so we advance our beliefs nonviolently. The threat posed by the idea of absolute truth, truth with a capital T, is that it inspires violence. The history of religion is a case in point. If we do not make a distinction between the religious "beliefs" that we have inside our heads because of the time and place we were born and a deeper sense of "faith," which constitutes what Derrida calls a "religion without religion," meaning a faith not imprisoned in beliefs, then the result will be the religious violence we see all around us. Beliefs are weakened by doubt but faith can be made stronger with doubt. Sometimes in order to be true to our faith, we have to abandon one set of beliefs for another – theists become atheists, atheists become theists – but we must never abandon our faith – in life, in the future, in the "event" that is harbored in the name of God. A faith in justice, which does not exist, produces discontent with what does exist, with the "law," that is, the existing arrangements currently in place to insure justice. My messianic faith in a justice-to-come is not to be confused with my beliefs in the particular ways in which we presently administer justice. Justice today is not the justice-to-come.

In hermeneutics and deconstruction we avoid capital letters. That I think is deconstruction in a nutshell! Don't go around capitalizing truth and justice, science and art – and religion! Keep them all in the lower case and in the plural, exposed to *différance*, to the undeconstructible, to the unconditional. Deconstruction is a theory that things are relatively stable and therefore relatively *un*stable. That allows us to get through today and also to be open to tomorrow while keeping the memory of yesterday alive. Rigidification and absolutization are the beginning of trouble, the root of all evil. The unconditional is always to come, but what we have to deal with, now and always, are concrete existing conditions. And they are deconstructible.

SCA: *At this point in the debate on justice, it seems that justice is merely an ideal and injustice is a reality. For this reason, can we say that the best way to achieve justice is to define injustice and eliminate the cases of injustice instead of developing theories of justice?*

JC: That's a very good idea. I had not thought of putting it that way. You should write your dissertation on that. Instead of trying to develop a theory of justice, we should just pay attention to the injustices all around us and then the theory of justice will be implicit, hovering in the background like a ghost, which it is, since justice in itself does not exist. Justice calls, but it is up to us to make it exist. I do think that for Lyotard and Derrida a lot of ethics, maybe all of ethics, is like that. With them, you get the impression that ethics comes down to choosing the lesser evil. We are forced to compromise. We have to make a decision, justice is urgent, but there are no good choices. We see things wrong with every option, so we choose the lesser evil. I think we do that a lot. We single out the greater injustice and choose to avoid it. Maybe we do not actually need a theory of justice, just an eye for injustice. I like that. You should work on that.

Suggested Readings

John D. Caputo, The Prayers and Tears of Jacques Derrida; Religion without Religion, USA: Indiana University Press, 1997.

John D. Caputo, Against Ethics, USA: Indiana University Press, 1993.

John D. Caputo, The Weakness of God; A Theology of the Event, USA: Indiana University Press, 2006.

John D. Caputo, *More Radical Hermeneutics*, USA: Indiana University Press, 2000.

John D. Caputo, *On Religion; Thinking in Action*, New York: Routledge, 2001.

John D. Caputo, *Deconstruction in a Nutshell: A Conversation with Jacques Derrida,* USA: Fordham University Press, 1996.

John D. Caputo, *Specters of God; An Anatomy of the Apophatic Imagination,* USA: Indiana University Press, 2022.

John D. Caputo, *The Folly of God; A Theology of the Unconditional,* US: Polebridge Press, 2016.

John D. Caputo, *The Insistence of God; A Theology of Perhaps,* USA: Indiana University Press, 2013.

CHAPTER 2

Ethics and Justice: Simon Critchley

Simon Critchley is a renowned British philosopher whose work spans existentialism, political theory, ethics, and the philosophy of tragedy. Critchley's philosophy is grounded in a commitment to questioning traditional notions of identity, belief, and social cohesion, with a particular focus on how individuals and societies navigate meaning in a world often characterized by uncertainty and existential angst. His thought is notably influenced by thinkers such as Emmanuel Levinas, Martin Heidegger, and Jacques Derrida, which reflects his deep interest in phenomenology, deconstruction, and ethical responsibility.

A central theme in Critchley's philosophy is the question of how individuals can create meaning and maintain ethical commitments in a secular, often disenchanted world. His book The Faith of the Faithless explores this in detail, investigating how political identity and collective belief systems can provide a foundation for shared meaning and commitment, even in the absence of traditional religious structures. In this work, he examines how figures like Jean-Jacques Rousseau and Leo Tolstoy approached political and ethical questions, using these ideas to argue that politics requires a form of "faith" or commitment, even if it is directed toward secular goals.

Another influential work, Infinitely Demanding: Ethics of Commitment, Politics of Resistance, articulates Critchley's view of ethics as a continuous and radical commitment to others. He proposes an "infinitely demanding" ethical framework, arguing that responsibility toward others is limitless and cannot be fully satisfied by institutional structures or legal systems. Instead, Critchley suggests that individuals are always called to exceed these frameworks by cultivating an ethical life marked by humility, resistance to injustice, and a dedication to empathy. This work resonates with his belief that true political engagement arises from an ethical demand that transcends the self.

Critchley's philosophical investigation into tragedy and humor offers another dimension to his thought. In Tragedy, the Greeks, and Us, he explores the role of ancient Greek tragedy in shaping Western notions of fate, suffering, and human limitation. He argues that the tragic perspective allows us to confront uncomfortable truths about mortality and the limits of human agency, fostering a kind of wisdom rooted in the acceptance of uncertainty. Similarly,

 | DOI:10.1163/9789004732902_004

in On Humour, Critchley explores humor as a means of coping with existential absurdity and as a tool for philosophical insight, noting how humor allows individuals to see the world in novel and often subversive ways.

Critchley's body of work is unified by a commitment to exploring how individuals confront the void left by the decline of traditional religious and moral systems. Through his reflections on faith, ethics, tragedy, and humor, he offers a vision of philosophy as a discipline capable of engaging life's most profound challenges, encouraging individuals to embrace uncertainty with integrity, humor, and a deep ethical sense.

Sema Cevirici Atilla [*SCA*]: *According to you, philosophy begins with disappointment, not in wonder. The disappointment comes from our difficulty in accepting our finitude. What do you think the reason behind this disappointment is? Why do we not want to accept our finitude? What is the most significant factor that led you to this claim?*

Simon Critchley [**SC**]: I suppose the reason behind the disappointment is the world, as it is awful. The idea of philosophy beginning in wonder has always struck me as a strange idea. Secondly, that idea is in Aristotle's metaphysics, but it is a view that is attributed to ancient schools, a lot of which were based on all the Ionian coasts. Aristotle says some of these people, the physiologists, believed that philosophy began in wonder. Aristotle does not have a view about it, but it is an attractive idea, yet the evidence for it is rather limited. I begin with either from the idea of disappointment and the fact that the world is a violently unjust place and questions of meaning which particularly in relation to transcendent guarantees of meaning like God and the rest are at least in doubt. What people often get wrong with my view is that they think I am just arguing for disappointment. I say philosophy begins in disappointment; it does not end disappointment. If philosophy begins in wonder for some people, that is certainly going to end in disappointment. You begin in disappointment and you end somewhere else with a kind of affirmation or knowledge. To answer your second question, we do not want to accept our finitude, because death is terrifying. There are many people who have the memory of death in a time before they had the understanding of death, perhaps when they were children, and then suddenly death comes into the world. Who wants to accept that? But it is to be accepted, because it is a fact. Therefore, I begin from disappointment, as that is the way things are. I think it is mistaken to begin anywhere else.

SCA: *You have argued that deconstruction should be understood as an ethical demand. How would you define ethics? In this context, what kind of ethical demand would be deconstruction?*

SC: This goes all the way back to my work when I was doing a PhD in the late 1980s. At that time, deconstruction was seen as a form of close careful textual reading by people that liked it and as value-free nihilism by people who did not like it. I saw something else in Derrida's work. At this point, I was very influenced by my PhD supervisor Robert Bernasconi who introduced me to the work of Levinas in my second year as an undergraduate. At that time, Levinas was not well-known at all. I found a copy of *Totality and Infinity* in a book sale for a couple of pounds and bought it. I remember reading it on the train to London and just being captivated by it as a text, as a piece of prose. At some later point when I was getting interested in philosophers like Derrida, I realized that he had written about Levinas. Then, I began to read texts such as "Violence and Metaphysics" and started to put together the idea that perhaps there was something of this Levinasian dimension in Derrida's work that had not been articulated in any of the literature. In the years between 1985 and 1987, deconstruction was beginning to be understood in more philosophical terms. For instance, Rodolphe Gasché's book *The Tain of the Mirror* was very influential, but this is where he understood Derrida's work only as a variation on transcendental philosophy in the Kantian and post-Kantian traditions. That was not wrong, but the question which I began to ask myself was: Why bother with deconstruction and engage in this activity? What is it for? What is it trying to do? I began to see this in terms of an ethical demand which was expressed in Levinas' work. I became more and more convinced that this was one of the animating motivations for what Derrida was doing. At this point, most people were not reading Derrida inside philosophy. They just thought it was some form of criticism which is fine, not very profound. In the French context, there was an awareness of Derrida as someone who had been deeply influenced by Heidegger. It was a kind of Heideggerianism, and then the Heidegger affair began in 1986 and 1987. This is very much the context for what I was doing in my PhD. The full awareness of Heidegger's commitment to national socialism became apparent to people like me and then we were trying to think about how one made sense of that philosophically. At the same time, Derrida very clearly saw the Heidegger affair, as it was called in France, as being directed at him and his work. Thus, he began to respond to that in a number of texts. We see the beginning of a shift in emphasis in Derrida's work in the mid to late 80s and into the 90s where his work is much more explicitly open to an ethical demand in a Levinasian sense, as I argued for. So that is the ethical demise and ethical demand in this Levinasian sense which I see and what most of us say, Derrida's activity as a thinker.

***SCA:** For you, politics begins as ethics, because ethics begins as a relationship with the other that questions me and invites me to the discourse of universal reason and justice. Do you think a period where ethics was separated from politics has ever been possible in the history of thought?*

SC: I would like to touch upon a couple of things. Going back to the context and into the kind of thinking that people like me were doing in the 90s, liberalism was seen by people like me following on from both Marxist traditions and thinkers on the right like Carl Schmitt as a form of the organization of society based upon ethics and a certain abstract idea of ethics, for example, rooted in a constitution with a set of rights and an understanding of economy, broadly a free market economics which was consistent with the emergence of capitalism. The political sphere on that view within liberalism had been evacuated. Liberalism was seen by people like me as an anti-political form of politics. We were trying to think about politics in a more substantial and real sense. That is one side of it. In a sense, liberalism saw itself as an ethics separated from politics, which is deeply problematic. On the other hand, there was a number of traditions of thought, for instance, within Marxism that everything is politics and ethics is just a kind of bourgeois, bourgeois deviation and a bourgeois set of values which have to be got rid of through an understanding of politics which is understood in terms of the class struggle. On the one hand, you have liberalism which is a largely depoliticized understanding of things. On the other hand, you have a very highly politicized understanding of human activity and praxis in Marxism. I was very sympathetic to Levinas' critique of the primacy of politics. In a sense, a society which understands that everything is politics and everything is political risks a kind of blindness when it comes to our actual obligations or our experiences with the other person. That is the ethical dimension; ethics is all about that relationship to the other person. In that sense, it becomes an issue of how we can look at social life not just as something which is politically administered or as part of a political struggle but where that political life is made up of an infinite network of ethical relations with particular singular beings, people that are making particular demands. Marxism was very suspicious of such an approach, and thus the approach I was taking in my early work was trying to steer a course between liberalism on the one hand and Marxism on the other and trying to do something else. Regarding universalism and justice, Levinas is a universalist and has a place for reason, yet that has to be based upon the experience of the relationship to the particular other person. If reason becomes a kind of blindness with regard to the person that stands in front of me, then reason needs a supplement or some other dimension. For Levinas, questions of reason and universalism come at a secondary level. What he tries to develop in some of his later work like *Otherwise than Being* is a theory of justice and the third party.

SCA: *You think that there is no politics without dirty hands. In this context, how can politics become more desirable, clean and fair?*

SC: I think it appears very similar to Levinas who was inspired by Martin Buber who developed the idea of the I-Thou relationship. It makes a distinction between I-Thou relations between persons and I-It relations which indicates a relation of things. He argues that the I-Thou has been lost in the world of the I-It. When we reify persons into things, this produces a mechanistic and functionalist understanding of society. So this is where I began. The first bit of writing I did about Levinas was on his relationship to Martin Buber. Levinas criticizes Buber for the purity of the I-Thou relation. He says that the I-Thou relation risks becoming an angelic relationship because of the spirituality of angels. It is as if there is a great purity to it which is then dirtied by the descent into the I-It. From the beginning, Levinas' view is that the ethical relation to the other can be seen as an I-Thou relationship, although he has disagreements with the way that Buber describes it. Nevertheless, the I-Thou relationship is always instantiated in a social and political reality which is dirty, contaminated, and toxic. What I mean by the remark that there is no politics without dirty hands is that we cannot do politics without getting our hands dirty. Therefore, the best that one can do is to have as clean dirty hands as possible and accept that any negotiation with politics is going to necessarily involve compromise and maybe even betrayal and failure. That is the reason why I am saying there is a kind of a critique of any idea of purity and any idea of ethical purity in particular.

***SCA:** If we are infinitely responsible to the other, how can we judge or question the actions of the other?*

SC: That is a good question. Eternity is a question that Levinas does not really engage with, although it does come up at the end of *Totality and Infinity* where one can see some references to eternity. Levinas said "infinitely responsible to the Other." However, his understanding of infinity is very particular. According to him, what is infinite is what resists our cognitive powers. This comes out in a text which is very important for me and which is called "Transcendence and Height" which I was involved in translating a long time ago. In that paper which Levinas gave the *Société française de la philosophie* in 1962, he makes his argument in *Totality and Infinity* in epistemological terms. The idea of infinity is the fact that there is a very clear limit to what can be known. There are severe epistemic limits on what human beings can know and know of the other. Therefore, we are infinitely responsible to the other in the sense in which we cannot lay the other under the concept that we have of him or her. We have to acknowledge a limit to our knowledge, thus an idea of acknowledgement rather than knowledge. The question of judgment is a question which Levinas hardly ever sufficiently answers. He raises the question in *Otherwise than Being* in the fourth chapter where he deals with the issue of whether one can judge the Other or whether it is infinite responsibility, so one cannot make a judgment. I can make a judgment in the political realm. I can make a judgment when I look at myself from the standpoint of that. Levinas says, "Am I my brother's keeper? What is Hecuba to me?" quoting Shakespeare. At that point, the question of judgment arises at a secondary level for Levinas. At the level of ethical responsibility, I cannot judge the other and I am just responsible to the other. That is the core experience he wants to describe. At a secondary level, there could be judgment over the other. One can see Levinas' work as a core of duty or possibly a basis for a theory of justice and a theory of judgment, but he does not actually flesh that out in his work. I have been critical of Levinas' work on that basis. We have to be able to judge others' actions, yet the judgment of others' actions has to be based on a Levinasian view and the idea of infinite responsibility which can be considered as a variant on the thought which exists in different religious traditions. For instance, Jesus says, "How can you say, 'Brother, let me take the speck out of your eye,' while you yourself fail to see the beam in your own eye?" in the sense that you are judging the other, but you cannot even notice your own faults. For Levinas, I think, the primary question is the question of me taking responsibility for the other and this is an infinite demand. The judgment has to follow from that, but this could lead to different theories of justice. You also mentioned Axel Honneth at a certain point later in the questions. In the late 90s, I worked with Axel in Frankfurt. He developed the theory of recognition that has three layers. We saw Levinas' work in terms of the first layer of recognition which can be understood in terms of interpersonal relations such as a relationship that a parent has with a child, which is an asymmetrical relationship of infinite responsibility. The second layer of recognition is the level of social recognition which can be covered by a theory of justice in the way that was put forward. So Axel was trying to show in his work that there is an "other" to justice. The other to justice would be the infinite responsibility to the Other, in Levinas' terms, and that has to be acknowledged in order to bring about the goal of a social theory which is solidarity.

SCA: According to Levinas, justice is paradoxically the limit of responsibility. If you were to give a definition of justice, how would you define it?

SC: Justice is usually conceived as a relationship between equals and is governed by law. Levinas wants to argue for this experience of infinite responsibility which is the "other" of justice or the basis of justice which should inform a theory of justice, but which is not itself justice in that sense. It is paradoxical and a very simple answer to the question would be to say justice has to begin in the relationship to the other. That is not a full definition of justice; it requires more than that. However, I think Levinas' point is that any judicial or juridical system has to be informed and shaped by this experience of infinite responsibility. Levinas believes that there is something about law and the operation of law that can make us blind to the suffering of individuals, because law can be an impersonal mechanism which overrides the suffering of individuals. For Levinas, there is something wrong about law. So can there be a theory of law or a theory of justice which acknowledges the dimension of what Levinas calls ethics? Particularly in the 1990s, some legal theorists were trying to develop an answer to this in different ways. To give an example, Desmond Manderson wrote a book on Levinas and law, which I found very interesting, where he argues that the most important aspect of law is the law of torts which is legal. It is how law operates in relation to responsibility, so rather than beginning with law in terms of the assertion of my rights as an individual, my rights being wronged and then me demanding redress to court of law, to begin law from an idea of responsibility. There are ways of reimagining law on a Levinasian criticism and some work was done on that which is quite interesting.

SCA: *Rorty disagrees with the following statement: "Deconstruction is justice and justice is the experience of the unexperienced." He says, "because I do not see the benefit of defining a commonly used term like justice as a name for an impossibility." Do you agree with Rorty on this?*

SC: At the time, I did not think he was right, but I have become much more sympathetic to Rorty over the years. In the paper I wrote on deconstruction and pragmatism, I try to show that there is a contradiction in Rorty's work between the definition of a liberal which is someone who thinks that suffering is the worst thing that there is and who is fundamentally motivated by the suffering of the other. On the other hand, he does not want to universalize that. For Rorty, that is a custom which he thinks is a feature of life in the rich Atlantic liberal democracies, as he would say rather provocatively, and it happens to be a not entirely terrible idea. In other words, he is against the universalism of saying things like deconstruction is justice and justice is experiencing the impossible or whatever it might be. He thinks that is too dramatic and too romantic. I can understand what he means. Rorty argues that in order for justice to have a chance in somewhere like America, it has to be rooted in the basic moral intuitions that people have. I think that for Rorty, if a society exists that does not in all cases murder and kill others but can actually move by their suffering and tries to help, then that is a good thing. It should be developed, but not with philosophy. It should rather be developed with the kind of sensitivity that could be found in literature, movies, and stories. Rorty is just a relativist. For Rorty, moral intuitions have to be based in the actual ways of life that people experience. I think that he found the Levinasian and Derridean formulation too dramatic and otherworldly.

SCA: *Derrida says that the concept of unconditional hospitality cannot actually have a legal or political status and that unconditional hospitality exceeds the concepts of politics and law. In this sense, unconditional hospitality is something that the state cannot sustain and inscribe in the law. For the condition of unconditional hospitality is that you relinquish the sovereignty of your home and nation. I would like to ask you two questions. The first question is, is unconditional hospitality an unrealistic concept or an ideal that encourages us to do better towards the other? Secondly, how would you evaluate the current immigration policies in the context of unconditional hospitality?*

SC: To answer your second question, the situation seems pretty bad, in particular, in the country that I was born. In Britain, there is an argument at the moment about immigration policies in relation to trying to send people to Rwanda. I think the current immigration policy is a scandalous indictment of politics as it is conducted in much of the world. I believe it is hard to be anything other than pessimistic about that. For example, we can look at the situation in Germany when Merkel was dealing with the huge population movements that followed what was happening in Syria and elsewhere. Germany said it could take 500,000 people. That seemed like a noble thing to say, yet it did not play out particularly well politically, because there is a basic problem around immigration which is that most people's relationship to foreigners is one of suspicion and even hostility. What do you do about that? If you have a religious framework, say any of the three Abrahamic faiths which are meant to be operative in society whether it is Islam, Judaism or Christianity, then you can tell people that they have to be hospitable. This is what your primary sacred texts seem to be saying, so you should act on that. Once that is more or less gone from people's minds, then it is very hard work. Therefore, unconditional hospitality is an unrealistic concept. I think the way which is argued for in someone like Derrida, I am not sure I am entirely satisfied by that, but he argues that unconditional hospitality has a moral force and then a big question of a pragmatic political question of how many, who, when, where, who paid and how things organized. I think the situation in Turkey could be an example of this issue. The EU has been offloading the immigration problem on to Turkey, since it is simply more convenient for the EU. I think it is a very ugly thing. Again for understandable reasons, Covid has given rise to new forms of nationalism, tribalism, and localism. That background suspicion that people have about other places and foreigners has just been amplified by the situation of the last couple of years, which I find terribly sad. We are in a much more Hobbesian world than we were 20 years ago. The world back then seems like a ridiculous dream. If I think back to the kind of debates that were being had particularly in the 1990s, it seems like a wonderful luxurious fantasy in relationship to what is happening politically nowadays.

SCA: *According to you, the world is facing us with a lot of difficult demands, and we need ethics to see what to do in such a political situation. Do you think ethics alone can offer a solution to these demands? My second question is as follows: In the post-truth age, if there is no absolute truth, what is the basis of our ethical responsibility and fairness to the other? Why should I be responsible and fair to the other if there is no truth? What would be our epistemic justification for being just and responsible?*

SC: I think once it becomes a calculation and we are into questions of epistemic justification, we are lost. For me, the Levinas' thinking and also the thinking that I have tried to do in relation to Levinas is much more fragile than it sounds. Levinas makes suggestions, offers recommendations and produces some guidelines which can be and are ignored. They have no force other than the force of the thoughts which is able to express them. That is the reason why people see Levinas' work and the thinking that I have done in relationship to Levinas as much more Kantian, much more universalist and self-assured than it really is. I think that we have to think about the relationship between ethics and religion. For Levinas, there is a relation and an infinite responsibility to the other person. In the early 50s, he called that prayer and religion, and then he described that relation as ethical. I think the blurring of the ethical and the religious is what Levinas is up to and that leads to the following thought. We can use the example of Christianity, because it is a compelling one. Jesus Christ made a series of infinite demands. What effect did they have? He was murdered and his followers were persecuted. Then, strange enough, a version of that religion winds up as the governing religion of the Roman Empire a few centuries later. That is the strangest thing, but I think the important thing is that this would put Levinas much more in the same company as someone like Kierkegaard. There is a fragility and weakness to Levinas' thought which is really its power. There is no secret mechanism that Levinas can find to make people ethical and make the people that are not ethical pay. In the post-truth age, it depends how we see them. In the 1960s, Levinas was dealing with his version of post-truth which he thought was the problems of relativism which were proposed as a consequence of things like structural anthropology, the colonial critique of Europe, and so on. He had all sorts of opinions, but I do not agree with a lot of what Levinas says on those issues. If anything is post-truth or there are regimes which are seriously post-truth, then what do you do with that? Russia would be a good example for a post-truth regime. Awful things are happening in Ukraine at the moment, but thankfully there is testimony thanks to smartphone technology. We can hear testimony from people who are in situations of extraordinary suffering and that testimony can be extremely moving. It can perhaps motivate people to do something or not. It does not have the force; it was never a police force. It does not have a legislative authority. It is the fragility of an ethical demand which is offered and which has to be accepted but it can also be refused. I think there is no way around that. Then, one is in the difficult business of persuasion. How do you persuade people, say a doctor, to adopt an ethics on the Levinasian model? One needs examples, testimony, cases, and things which are actually going to affect people in terms of how they live their lives and what they feel. It seems to me that it is not impossible.

SCA: *At this point in the debate on justice, it seems that justice is merely an ideal and injustice is a reality. For this reason, can we say that the best way to achieve justice is to define injustice and eliminate the cases of injustice instead of developing theories of justice?*

SC: Certainly, you could do that. We can take Rorty as an example here. The cruelty is awful. Suffering is something which we should try to avoid and revert. We should try to organize our day-to-day lives in ways which minimize suffering as much as possible. It can be as simple as that, which is very easy to understand. If we give suffering a voice, it can lead us to at least minimize injustices. I strongly believe that if injustice is given a voice and we are able to hear that, some things can be changed. There is a wonderful essay by Levinas which is called “Useless Suffering” which is a meditation on the Holocaust amongst other things. His view is that my suffering is always useless. We all suffer and our suffering is useless; it does not do anything apart from making us suffer. On the other hand, the suffering of the other is useful. It can give voice to something. For instance, if you decide to organize your academic work around giving voice to that suffering, then it can do something. I believe that profoundly and also pedagogically in terms of how one relates to individuals in a teacher-student relationship. I believe it is true in how one engages with the world on a one-to-one basis. Where I remain fervently Levinasian is just on the primacy of the one-to-one relationship. If you see society as a whole or as a totality, then you lose sight of the multiplicity of infinite relations amongst people. We all live in places, for example I live in New York. It is a heartless and soul-crushing place, yet if you attend to the experience of suffering and try to lend a voice and persuade other people to hear that as much as possible, it is the best you can do and it is what is possibly going to win. That is not for us to say, as we do not have a magic elixir which is going to solve all the problems of society. Therefore, I think that the weakness in Levinas’ thinking is its strength.

Suggested Readings

Simon Critchley, *The Ethics of Deconstruction; Derrida and Levinas*, UK: Edinburg University Press, 2014.

Simon Critchley, *The Faith of the Faithless: Experiments in Political Theology*, UK: Verso Books, 2014.

Simon Critchley, *Infinitely Demanding; Ethics of Commintment Politics of Resistance,* UK: Verso Books, 2013.

Simon Critchley, *Ethics-Politics-Subjectivity; Essays on Derrida, Levinas and Contemporary French Thought*, UK: Verso Books, 2009.

Simon Critchley, *Continental Philosophy: A Very Short Introduction*, UK: Oxford University Press, 2001.

Simon Critchley, *The Problem with Levinas*, UK: Oxford University Press, 2015.

CHAPTER 3

Hermeneutics and Justice: Richard Kearney

Richard Kearney is an Irish philosopher known for his work on imagination, hermeneutics, and narrative, as well as his explorations of hospitality, ethics, and postmodern spirituality. His philosophy centers on the idea of "the other" and the transformative power of imagination in ethical encounters, emphasizing that narrative and storytelling are fundamental to understanding ourselves and others. Kearney's thought is influenced by philosophers such as Paul Ricoeur, Emmanuel Levinas, and Jacques Derrida, reflecting a deep commitment to bridging philosophical concepts with lived human experience.

One of Kearney's most significant contributions is his concept of anatheism, which he develops in his influential book Anatheism: Returning to God After God. Anatheism, which Kearney defines as a "return to God after God," is not a return to traditional religious belief but rather an openness to the sacred and the mysterious in a post-religious age. This approach, situated between atheism and theism, encourages a stance of "second faith" – a form of spiritual openness and ethical receptivity that seeks to engage with the divine without dogmatic certainty. For Kearney, anatheism is an ethical and imaginative response to the otherness of both the divine and human beings, inviting a renewed sense of wonder, humility, and hospitality.

Kearney's interest in narrative and hermeneutics is showcased in his earlier works, such as On Stories and The Wake of Imagination. In these books, he argues that storytelling and imagination are essential to human identity, shaping not only individual self-understanding but also collective social and cultural identities. The Wake of Imagination explores how imagination has evolved in Western culture, tracing its impact from mythological times to modernity. Kearney proposes that imagination allows us to see beyond the limits of our immediate reality, enabling empathy, creativity, and ethical openness. Through narrative, he suggests, we can transcend personal and cultural boundaries, fostering dialogue and connection across differences.

Another critical theme in Kearney's work is the ethics of hospitality, which he examines in Strangers, Gods, and Monsters: Interpreting Otherness. Here, he explores how societies grapple with the presence of strangers and the unknown, urging an ethical response of openness rather than exclusion. Kearney argues that encountering the "stranger" – whether as an immigrant, a

 | DOI:10.1163/9789004732902_005

religious other, or even a feared aspect of ourselves – requires a willingness to embrace ambiguity and recognize the shared humanity that underlies difference. His approach to hospitality as an ethical imperative is especially relevant in today's globalized world, where cultural and religious diversity often lead to conflict rather than understanding.

***Sema Cevirici Atilla* [*SCA*]*: You have been in conversation with leading philosophers, literary theorists, anthropologists, and religious scholars such as Derrida, Levinas, Lyotard, and Gadamer. When did you come up with the idea of interviewing so many different philosophers on a wide range of topics? What motivated you to work on this research?*

Richard Kearney [RK]: I learned conversations at an early age in boarding school. I was educated by the Benedictines in a monastery called Glenstal Abbey in Ireland. I first learned philosophy around the age of fifteen. We were taught the philosophy of Simone de Beauvoir, Sartre, and Camus. Dostoyevsky and Nietzsche were important as well. However, in any case, almost all the philosophers were atheists, and yet I was being taught by Benedictine monks who were Christians. It was very interesting, as they believed that unless you knew the arguments for atheism as well as the arguments for theism, theism would not be a genuine intellectual commitment, because you would not have a choice. From the very beginning, I learned that philosophy was about a dialectic or a dialogue between different opinions. It was indeed a very tolerant school and encouraged us to always listen to the arguments of opponents, in this instance Nietzsche, Dostoyevsky, and Sartre, who argue that we cannot be free if God exists. Once you know the opponents' arguments, then you can have a genuine sense of recovering your own position. This is something that was confirmed when I went to Paris to study with Paul Ricoeur in 1977. In his seminar at the *Centre phénoménologique et herméneutique*, the first lesson he taught us doctoral students was that the shortest route from self to self is through the other. There is no access to truth, to understanding or to knowledge through oneself. In this sense, Descartes was wrong. He was right to start methodologically with doubting, yet he was wrong to conclude "*cogito ergo sum*." It is not "I think, therefore I am" but rather "We dialogue, therefore we are." The journey through the other was indeed very significant. To put it in technical terms, it was the primacy of heterology over egology. When Paul Ricoeur taught us about *le cogito*, he also called it the wounded cogito, the open cogito, the vulnerable cogito that was always exposed to others. In Paris, I also studied with Emmanuel Levinas. Both Ricoeur and Levinas were my dissertation directors at the University of Paris. According to Levinas, exposure to the other is how we first begin. The subject is not only a subject of knowledge but also a subject to the other. We are subjected to the call of the other, the summons of the other, the needs of the other, and the commands of the other such as "Do not kill" or "Give me something to eat." These are primary before we ever have a sense of ourselves. That led then to my espousal of a hermeneutics of dialogue and a hermeneutics of hospitality, which I learned from Ricoeur and Levinas. Certainly, Ricoeur's philosophy of translation is also very influential. I have been writing about that in my recent book *Radical Hospitality*, co-authored with Melissa Fitzpatrick. It begins with an analysis of linguistic hospitality, which says that we are always translating back and forth between self and other. That is how I would begin to answer your questions.

SCA: *In an interview, Derrida was asked, "How can you read in the dark?" He replied: "We can only read in the dark." However, you do not agree with Derrida on this point. You argue that it is necessary to turn on the light a little bit. Obviously, you think that there is no absolute light for us mortals, but a flash of light is necessary to remove some of the darkness and confusion. What should we do if the light causes violence or the dark creates injustice? How can we save ourselves from this paradox?*

RK: I think too much darkness leads to ignorance and violence. Too much light or the presumption of too much light and of some kind of absolute access to perfect truth, perfect enlightenment, and perfect illumination can also lead to violence. Therefore, I would say we are reading in the twilight, or we are reading between light and darkness. Derrida was also a very good friend and teacher of mine in Paris. We had many dialogues, and I have great respect for Derrida. However, this would be a difference between his more deconstructive approach and my hermeneutic approach. For Derrida, we are always "reading in the dark," as you put it. Understanding, to the extent that we have it, is always a sort of a blind leap. It is what he calls a mad leap in the impossible. That is indeed a very Kierkegaardian position. I believe that it is inspired by his Judaism, even though he always said he rightly passed for an atheist. As he always acknowledged, he was trained in the Talmudic tradition of thinking and was very close to Jewish poets like Edmond Jabès, Nelly Sachs or Paul Celan. In the Judaic position, we do not have knowledge of God. You do not write God's name or have images of God; thou shalt have no graven image of God. It is certainly true for Islam as well, but in Judaism this sort of apophatic negative theology meant that if you encounter the absolute, it is always in the dark. In the Bible, you only see Yahweh from behind and you never see God face to face. For this reason, I think that was part of his thinking. Obviously, Derrida was coming from Kierkegaard on the one hand, as he said that Kierkegaard was his greatest influence as a thinker. I think his Judaic background also had an impact. I would say structuralism played a significant role in the sense that it is not the human subject that can know, since we are propelled by unconscious structural forces. One can find that in Lacan and French psychoanalysis. It is the unconscious that speaks through us. We do not know what we are saying, we do not know what we mean, we do not mean what we say, and we do not say what we mean. Therefore, we are always caught in this contradiction where it is the unconscious and the structures of the unconscious and language that speaks through us. We are caught up in this web, this text of language and there is nothing outside of the text. That is where Derrida is coming from. I understand all that, but I would tend towards with Ricoeur and hermeneutics and Gadamer, and towards more of a sense of the phronetic, what Ricoeur calls a narrative understanding or a phronetic understanding, whereby we are instructed by stories, the wisdom of stories, and tradition, as Gadamer would say. So we do not start in the dark; we start from a position of being already in a conversation. It is not total light, but a certain amount of light and always striving for more light through dialogue. A matter of provisional, transitional, approximative direction, of limited guidance, one step at a time, 'muddling through', but not nothing, not nowhere. Not a blind leap in the night – or when it comes to religion, irrational fideism. That is my difference with Derrida and with Caputo, and even Levinas, for whom understanding the other is *too* impossible and there is too much of a rupture. Pure interruption, pure madness and invasion, even to the point of 'persecution' and 'trauma'(for Levinas). It is a philosophy of rupture rather than of translation. Translation always acknowledges that when you are dialoguing with another person or reading a text, something is always lost in translation. You never have the perfect translation and you must renounce trying to get the perfect translation. As Ricoeur says, the story of Babel was the attempt to reach perfect knowledge. In the end, the Tower of Babel falls, because they cannot have divine knowledge, Adamic knowledge, that is, perfect knowledge. We can only have approximations. In other words, we are always going through hermeneutic detours. There is no direct access to truth. That would be a critique of Heidegger, Hegel or even Husserl: in their different phenomenologies, they did seek some kind of access to truth. For Heidegger, it is *Dasein*, questioning of being, which is the short route to being, whereas the kind of hermeneutics that I am more interested in with Ricoeur's narrative hermeneutics and narrative imagination always works through mediations in culture, in nature and in our relations with other human beings. It means that we are always reading signs and never get to some perfect signified, transcendental signified of pure illumination, pure knowledge, yet we get intimations, little epiphanies, hints, and guesses. That is my difference from Derrida. I would say it is a difficult hermeneutic of truth rather than an impossible hermeneutic of truth.

***SCA:** Do you think that deconstruction is monstrous?*

RK: Not at all. I think deconstruction is a wonderfully critical tool of reading that is absolutely indispensable. I have personally learned a huge amount from Derrida and from Caputo himself who is a great friend and a great colleague. Far from being a monster, deconstruction is indeed a great ally and a reminder that we never know completely or absolutely and that we never know enough. Still, I think sometimes it goes too far in the direction of subordinating the self so much to the other that the self is humiliated and incapacitated. If forgiveness, justice, and translation is impossible, then you would ask what is there to be done and why we should even bother. I know Derrida struggled with that, for he was very committed to a progressive politics and ethics, as is Caputo, both profoundly moral ethical beings. However, sometimes I find the philosophy is so dark, apocalyptic and impossible. I know Derrida would say that it is impossible, but you must keep going. It reminds me of Samuel Beckett who says, "I can't go on. I'll go on." Thus, I do not believe deconstruction is at all monstrous, but I think that sometimes it does not sufficiently distinguish between *Strangers, Gods and Monsters*, as I put it in my book of that title. When Derrida talks about hospitality in his books, he says that when someone knocks at the door, you open unconditionally. You do not discriminate, decipher or discern between different kinds of strangers; you just let the other in. You do not know whether it is the Messiah or a murderer, as Derrida states. I think that is going too far in terms of an unconditional openness to the other, even if Derrida says it is impossible. The impression is that if we were really hospitable, having pure, absolute and unconditional hospitality would mean letting the other in without asking questions. Whereas I believe that you let the other in, but you also ask questions. That is the difference.

Now if you are God then you do not ask questions, because God accepts everybody. I think that is true of the Abrahamic God for Jews, Christians, and Muslims. God is all-forgiving and can do the impossible. It seems interesting that when Jesus Christ is on the cross, he does not say, "I forgive my enemies who are crucifying me." Rather he says, "God forgive them" because as a human being, Christ cannot forgive the human being. We human beings cannot forgive unconditionally. We do not have access to absolute hospitality, absolute justice, and absolute bargain. We wish we did and it would be wonderful if we had it, but we do not. We live in a world of finite limits and we have to accept that. Derrida and Caputo accept that too, of course, yet the aspiration, the dream, and the desire for absolute hospitality is impossible. And if it is impossible and we are not God, then we are always in a position of being somehow diminished, humiliated and contaminated. It's almost a throw-back to the Augustinian position that we are all fallen creatures, desiring god but incapable of reaching God. A sense that we are always falling short of the mark. And this ontological humility can sometimes feel like humiliation, abasement, a certain sense of impotence. A sense that there is nothing to be done. That is the reason why Derrida and Caputo – Derrida in particular – were accused of nihilism and cynicism, which I think was unfair. The right wing denounced deconstruction as a secret agent of postmodern relativism and nihilism, saying that deconstruction is about undermining family values, traditional pieties and so on. That seems very wrong to me. The ultra-conservative critics ignored the fact that Caputo and Derrida are actually engaging in micro-logical critical readings of texts on justice, law, and rights. The reason they criticize deconstruction is because deconstruction can give the impression that there is no access to truth or the other, no way of knowing where we are going, and that we are always reading and walking in the dark. Thus we are lost, and then the right wing jumps on this, saying that they are misleading us into some kind of pessimistic apocalyptic nihilism. I think that is one of the reasons why there was a big controversy about Derrida getting a doctorate at Cambridge – with many academics saying they could not give it to the cynical nihilist. And they were educated academics, not right-wing fundamentalsits. It was actually distinguished scholars saying this. Some of them do believe that deconstruction is monstrous and Derrida is a monster. Nonetheless, I would consider Derrida and Caputo not monstrous at all but scrupulous close readers of texts invigilating our 'impossible' access to truth.

SCA: *If the other transcends all our categories of interpretation and representation, then how can we tell the difference between the good and the bad? You must have some kind of critical hermeneutic to make this distinction. How does this hermeneutic make a just differentiation between the benevolent and the evil?*

RK: One can never do it absolutely. We have no absolute access to the absolute. Therefore, it is always a matter of negotiations, navigations, narrations, and mediations. We are always doing the best we can to translate a situation that we confront into as just and fair a judgment as we can. There are no absolute criteria, but there is a plurality of signposts. One of them is the Aristotelian tradition of phronesis, of practical wisdom. That is available for us in the philosophical tradition. It is not absolute, because phronesis as practical wisdom is not *sophia* or *theoria*, as Aristotle says. It is not perfect analytic transparent knowledge or absolute knowledge. It is provisional knowledge where you try to do your best. He compares it to the architect who might have a good model or a good idea, say a blueprint of the building that they want to make. Still, they have to contend with the structure and the quality of the soil, the climatic conditions, whether it is on a mountain or in a valley, whether there is water available or not, whether it is dry or moist. All of these circumstances and conditions inform the ultimate making of the building. In other words, you can set out with an ideal, but that is not always what you will end up with, since the ideal has to be translated into the limits, the conditions, the circumstances, and the contingencies of the real. So, one is always translating. The Aristotelian notion of phronesis would be one model which you learn through habituation and through responding as wisely as possible to the situation, given the fact that you bring a certain number of presuppositions from your tradition, as Gadamer would say. However, your presuppositions and ideals, whether they are religious or you get them from your spiritual tradition or the Abrahamic biblical tradition, can be values that you bring with you. You can bring with you the Greek and Roman values of law and justice, and so on. Those are signposts that I am taking from Aristotle. There is also the tradition of the Enlightenment which emphasizes the rights of man – that is another set of signposts. Unlike Descartes, I do not personally believe in innate ideas, such as that we have an innate idea of God or the good. As a hermeneutic thinker, I do not appeal to innate ideas as such, yet I think we do have experiences phenomenologically, which all human beings share to some degree, of exposure to other people who call to us in their need. For that, it does not matter whether you are Christian, Jewish, Islamic, Buddhist, Hindu, Zoroastrian or atheist. The appeal of the other person that says, "Do not kill and give me food," in Levinas' words, is something that calls us to justice phenomenologically. Thus, it is not just a question of us in our own minds saying, "How do I know what is the right thing to do?" or "How do I judge between good and evil?" There is somebody who is telling me to do good. In other words, that person is saying, "Share your food with me, give me shelter. I am a widow, an orphan, a stranger at the door." When that happens, every human being is summoned and called to be. We can also refuse that, as we are free to say yes or no. Still, it is a phenomenological summons that comes to us in that moment. They do not mention, "as Jesus says, as the prophet says or even as Aristotle says." They just say, "Do not kill me, give me food." That is a phenomenological appeal that comes to us irrespective of traditions or our hermeneutic presuppositions.

SCA: *Levinas says the other is always the orphan, the widow and the stranger that is the victim, not the victimizer. As you well know, Levinas was subjected to serious criticism after his statements about the Sabra and Shatila massacre in a radio interview. In this regard, can we arrive at a decision about whether the other is the victim or the victimizer by getting rid of our belief systems and ideologies?*

RK: That was probably Levinas' political Zionism or his moral commitment to Judaism and the Jewish people. However, he was wrong in that statement, which to me is just a reminder of how difficult moral judgments are. Even somebody like Levinas in that situation was not able to hear the cry of the victim in the camps at Sabra and Shatila. He was deafened by the cry of his own people, whether it was in the Holocaust or elsewhere, such that he was not able to listen to the cry of the stranger. He was listening to the cry of the victims in his own tradition. It is a good reminder of how somebody who has devoted his life to moral philosophy, as in *Ethics as First Philosophy*, and who has contributed arguably more than anybody in the 20th century to a phenomenology of justice, hospitality and goodness, which claimed God is the absolute goodness, could make a mistake when it came to the Palestinian-Israeli situation. That is just a reminder to me that no moral philosophy has the truth and is impervious to error. In fact, I would say maybe Levinas was too lacking in hermeneutics, because he appeals to the phenomenological call of the other that breaks through all my previous oppositions, hermeneutic interpretations, narratives, memories, and traditions. Hermeneutics is not a good word for Levinas. With regard to the Palestinian-Israeli situation, he was not aware of his own hermeneutic prejudices in that instance. So that answers the second part of your question. He was not really aware of his own hermeneutic ideologies, as they work unconsciously. Therefore, that is where phenomenology needs hermeneutics to support it and give it a certain distance from a primary sensibility. Apparently, Levinas was working from sensibility, which, as he says, is the primary source of morality. If sensibility is the primary source of morality, it must be careful not to become removed from phronetic and narrative understanding, which would be much more aware of how ideologies inform the way we make our judgments. I agree with you that Levinas needs more hermeneutics than that.

I would say Gadamer and Ricoeur sometimes need more phenomenology of the flesh. I have critiqued Ricoeur and hermeneutics in that regard. At times hermeneutics can become too textual and can forget the flesh. For instance, Ricoeur's early work on the phenomenology of the will was very based on a phenomenology of the body, passions, the flesh, and so on. In 1960, with *The Symbolism of Evil*, he turned more towards a textual hermeneutics. He always said that hermeneutics needs to be grafted onto phenomenology and phenomenology always needs to ground hermeneutics. I think he was right about that, but in his later work at the very end, he was coming back to more of a balance between a hermeneutics of the text and a phenomenology of the body. I think that is right and I try to create that balance in my own work as well.

SCA: *You said in an interview, "I learned a lot from deconstruction, but I am closer to hermeneutics." Do you agree with Caputo's definition of deconstruction as radical hermeneutics? How would you evaluate the relationship between hermeneutics and deconstruction in the context of a concern for justice?*

RK: In the first instance, I appreciate John Caputo's work on hermeneutics and his embrace of what he calls *radical hermeneutics*, which for Jack is another name for deconstruction. Jack does not see any difference between deconstruction and radical hermeneutics. So, I do see a tension between deconstruction and hermeneutics. Therefore, I propose *diacritical hermeneutics* as opposed to radical hermeneutics, although myself and Jack are very much in dialogue. It is a very robust creative friendly dialogue that has been going on for more than 20 years now. You could put it in simple terms as: Jack is representing Jacques Derrida and I am representing Paul Ricoeur. Actually, we both occupy a position somewhere in the middle between those thinkers. My preference for diacritical hermeneutics over radical hermeneutics is that as a linguistic term, diacritical comes from diacritical signs, which are inflections such as diaeresis, accents or umlaut that create a slight difference in meaning by virtue of accents. That is, I am using that as a model or even a metaphor for a certain way of reading that is not a reading in the dark, as Derrida and Caputo would say all reading is. That was actually a phrase used by Derrida in a response to me at the Villanova Conference organized by Jack Caputo about 30 years ago. Then, I said to Jacques Derrida in the presence of Jack Caputo: "Is deconstruction always a reading in the dark?" To which he replied: "Yes, it is always a reading in the dark." My response to that would be no. Sometimes it is written in the dark, and that is deconstruction or radical hermeneutics, where one deals with impossible meaning, aporias, contradictions, undecidabilities, and so on. That is important and necessary. It can be seen as a philosophical equivalent to negative theology. It is what you cannot say and trying to speak the unspeakable, but I think it is unthinkable. Thus, that is significant and there is definitely a role for that. Still, it is only one aspect of hermeneutics. It is hermeneutics at the edge, hermeneutics at the limit, hence radical hermeneutics, whereas I have been trying to develop a hermeneutics which operates in a gray zone. It is not pure light and it is not pure dark. It is in a gray zone. That's why it calls for diacritical reading, or reading between the lines, as it were. In my hospitality project *Guestbook* and my book *Radical Hospitality*, I discuss intermediary meaning, mediated meanings, double meanings, covered meanings, symbolic meanings, mythical meaning, unconscious meanings, ulterior meanings, all of which call for interpretation. I do not believe that we always have to read in the dark or take blind leaps of faith as Derrida talks about ultimate justice, ultimate alternatives, and ultimate forgiveness. We can dream of these impossibilities and desire them which is kind of a madness, as he says. I believe that is important, yet that is the language of the prophet Jeremiah. We also need Isaiah and we need to bring some light to the dark and have this gray zone, as I call it, where diacritical hermeneutics works. I can point out the example of hospitality. The word *hostis* is at the root of hospitality and hostility. We need to discern, decipher and read between the lines to be able to distinguish, discriminate, discern, however modestly and provisionally, between the *hostis* as enemy and the *hostis* as friend. *Hostis* as in the instance of somebody who is directing a missile into your local school, supermarket or apartment block, that is, a stranger who is an enemy trying to kill you, versus somebody knocking at the door. When you open it, you welcome that person into your door, because that person seeks shelter and food. We have to be able to tell the difference between the two. Derrida says, and this was a dialogue we had together in Dublin, that when somebody knocks at the door, you do not know whether it is the Messiah or a psychotic murderer, and you cannot tell the difference. That would be pure hospitality or absolute hospitality. Derrida accepts, as does Jack Caputo, that real hospitality is always a compromise. You need certain parameters, yet most of the time within a series of parameters, guidelines, indications, and signposts which we need, we never get pure light, but we are not in utter darkness, either. That is the diacritical move of always trying to discern and interpret according to very subtle fluctuations and modifications of meaning, as when we relate to somebody having a conversation. We do not really know the other person, yet we know something about the other person. This goes for all our relationships to people, to God and absolute others. In everyday life, we are always in a gray zone of mediated meanings in our relationship with all three others. That is true of human beings. It is also true of our relationship to other species and to the things of the earth in our ecological age. That's why you have to be able to interpret and, as I put it, read between the lines.

SCA: *In your book* Strangers, Gods and Monsters, *you state that Lyotard rejects any attempt to express the horror of the Holocaust because such an effort would undermine the uniqueness of the Holocaust by comparing it with other genocides or other atrocities in history. Therefore, for Lyotard and other skeptics, no analysis of the memory is possible, and only what cannot be remembered is just. You do not agree with this view, because you think if representation reduces the horror of Auschwitz, as Lyotard puts it, then we might be taking a wrong path by rejecting representation. Can we say that your definition of justice differs from what is unrepresentable, incomparable and indeterminable, and is closer to an area of representation that preserves differences? How would you define justice in this context?*

RK: I understand what Lyotard is saying in light of Adorno's famous question: "after Auschwitz who can write poetry'. It is so horrible nothing can be said. The only appropriate response is silence. I resist this position, however, because, as Levinas once said, if we are silent about the Holocaust the Nazis have won. So it's one thing to make a hyperbolic statement with Adorno and Lyotard, that the evil of the Holocaust is unsayable, unthinkable, unimaginable, unrepresentable

– which is true up to a point. But only up to a point. We shouldn't stop there. If anything, that is where we should *start,* insisting that in spite of its unspeakability we still have to try to say something that records the horrors and the trauma, albeit in traces and charged signs. We are ethically obliged to remember what happened, the horror which took place, and to do so in two senses: in the sense of history and in the sense of story. First, as history, we need remember the Holocaust by counting the bodies, thereby resisting the deniers and 'negationists'. And the same goes for the ethical duty of narrative memory when it comes to other genocides and unspeakable crimes which many wish to deny – the Armenian and Rwandan genocides, the Irish or Ukraine famines and so on. And it's also important to be able to compare and contrast different genocides and collective traumas. Each one genocide is utterly unique, but its suffering must also be shareable. If we cannot imagine what another people suffers, we cannot empathise. It is crucial to be able to bear witness and sympathise with the horrors that other people endure, to experience a solidarity of sufferings across racial, cultural and historical divides. There are no exclusive victims of evil or victors of good. 'Nous sommes tous des juifs allemands', as Daniel Cohn-Bendit said in 1968. In narrative imagination, we are all Armenians, Rwandans, Ukrainian and so on. So basically, what I'm saying is we need to remember historically that this happened and tell it as it happened. That's the duty of history – to tell it as it happened. And then, second, comes the duty of story: to represent and reimagine it 'as if' if happened like this and 'as if' we were there to experience that suffering. So, whether it's Art Spiegelman's comic strip story about Nazi cats hounding Jewish mice or whether it is Claude Lanzmann's film, *Shoah,* or Stephen Spielberg's film *Schindler's List,* or the multiple stories and *Memoirs* written by Primo Levi or Milena or other survivors of genocides, it is crucial that such stories – using powerful narrative imagination – be told so that we can not just know the facts (which is the crucial function of history) but also feel the horror, be moved and struck by the pain, so that we say 'this must never happen again'. We need powerful literary, as well as empirical-forensic, testaments to the Holocaust. So that can remember both what happened and how it happened. Both the telling it as and telling it as if, are necessary for a full account.

SCA: *Can you say more about this double hermeneutic duty to remember horror by both history and story?*

RK: Let's come back to the Holocaust, about which so much has been written. The crimes and the sufferings of the concentration camps need to be remembered lest the Nazis win by history consigning it to silence and allowing the possibility that it happen again. Let us not forget the infamous Wannsee Convention of 1942 where Hitler and Himmler gathered the SS leaders to discuss the 'Final Solution' in Berlin and had them all swear a vow of total secrecy. Regarding the liquidation of Jews, all empirical or logistical evidence was to be removed. Nobody must record or represent it. The Nazi order was clear: don't speak about the Holocaust under any circumstances. Then along come Adorno or Lyotard after the war and repeat the injunction, albeit for very opposite reasons, namely – representing or writing about the holocaust is to betray its unspeakable and unimaginable horror. The only appropriate and respectful response being 'silence'. But what we all need to say about the holocaust is what Daniel Cohn-Bendit (a German Jew) said about all those taking part in the 1968 revolt (in France and US and Prague and Northern Ireland and elsewhere) – 'nous sommes tous des juifs allemands!'. We must all empathise and imagine ourselves as each other and with each other. That is what solidarity with the oppressed and the suffering throughout the world demands. There is a recognition of the uniqueness of the Jewish shoah but also an awareness of the quasi-universal character of all human suffering and horror. Without diminish the singularity of any particular people we can sympathise with the pain of all peoples. Uniqueness of unspeakable trauma does not mean exclusiveness or exclusion from fellow suffering, from fellow solidarity with everybody else suffering evil and injustice in the world.

It is crucial that we continue trying to represent the Holocaust or other unspeakable genocides and historical traumas. While acknowledging that such acts of representation can never be complete or even adequate – there will always be something lost (even perhaps 'betrayed') in the translation from unspeakably to speech or image. There are limits to what and how evil can be communicated, but to refuse to communicate it at all is to give into it. It is to risk making evil irresistible, totally incomprehensible – to succumb to its demonic and deranging mystique, so to speak. We have to keep on trying to represent the unrepresentable, to speak the unspeakable so that, as Primo Levi says, it may never happen again. It's a huge ethical problem that we have to confront if we want to resist the dehumanizing lure of radical evil. Let me give you an example from the story of Schindler's List. I was giving a talk on Stephen Spielberg's film on the subject at McGill University in Montreal about 30 years ago and at the end of my talk a little old lady came down who'd been sitting at the back and she said to me: "I was one of the survivors of the Holocaust, I was on Schindler's List. I escaped the camps thanks to Oscar Schindler and managed to emigrate to Montreal where I've been living since. And for fifty years I never spoke to anybody about my experience. I couldn't. I never spoke to my husband, my children, my doctor, my Rabbi, my psychiatrist – nobody – until I saw the film made by Spielberg and when I saw myself being played by a fictional character I suddenly was able to return to the death camp, to return to my inexperienced experience through the detour of representation, vicariously, by proxy, through the mediation of imagination – an historical fiction with actors and imaginary scenarios depicting the original horror. Then and only then was I able to speak of it all to my family and friends about what had happened'. In sum, she needed the hermeneutic detour of imaginary mediation, so that she could see herself again through the eyes of another, re-member herself so to speak, rejoining the two separated parts of herself, namely, her past traumatized self (frozen in time) and her present living self. This is the greatness of story when it comes to history, of art when it comes to pain, of narrative when it comes to trauma (what Freud called the transition from melancholy to mourning through the 'talking cure'). But imagination is not of course always on the side of the angels. There can be bad representations too – that distort, disable and dishonor the pain of the past. There are many examples of propagandistic or abusive representations used for distorted ideological purposes, or simply for cheap soap opera sensationalism and Hollywood escapism of facile frisson and *Schadenfreude*. So to serve memory well, we need – I repeat – to observe: 1) the historical recording of reality (the 'hard facts' of empirical forensic evidence which gainsays the Holocaust deniers and negationists); and 2) the art of good storytelling which supplements and complements historical truth with affective and imaginative truth. We need to both tell it as it actually happened in the past and relive it as if we are experiencing that past (through imagination). There's a double duty of representation, of just memory – to tell the past as both history and story.

SCA: *You say that making a choice between Chora and God is a necessity for believers. Because, for believers, this cannot remain ambiguous, otherwise you rightly say that the God of religion would have turned into an absurdity. Do you think deconstructionist indeterminacy and undecidability turn into a problem rather than a functional one when it comes to belief? Is faith, like justice, a state of urgency that cannot wait?*

RK: I would say that deconstruction has an indispensable role in making us vigilant. Deconstruction teaches us to attend to micrological nuances of reading and the tacit undecidabilities of meaning. So, it definitely has a role in the work of interpretation; but I repeat – it is not the last word. At best, it is the beginning, it exposes the limits and parametres of what we can know, say and believe. You start with the impossibility of belief but you don't stop with the impossibility of belief. When Mary tells Gabriel that what he is announcing is impossible (*adunaton*), he replies that what is impossible to humans is not impossible to God. In genuine acts of faith, you go from the impossibility of belief to the possibility, but that possibility is not an easy or immediate possibility. It's a possibility beyond the impossibility of belief. A belief after disbelief. Or what I call anatheism as a movement beyond theism and atheism to a second moment of belief (see *Anatheism; Returning to God After God*). Deconstruction provides the atheistic moment of disbelief, atheism, impossibility. As Derrida says, "I rightly pass for an atheist'. Deconstruction is a-theism. And this can be read, from a religious standpoint, as opening up the possibility-beyond-impossibility of a 'religion without religion' or what Derrida and Caputo also call a 'messianicity without messianism'. I see this as a salutary and preparatory moment in the life of authentic faith. A sort of preliminary or purgative atheism equivalent to (but not identical to) what the John of the Cross and other mystics called the dark night of the soul – a moment of doubt, unknowing, abandonment in the very midst of one's journey towards or back to God. What the Patristic fathers called 'negative theology, a via negative which opens a way towards the possibility of a god beyond or before or beneath 'God'. It is what Keats calls 'negative capabiliity' – the ability to 'be in the midest of mystery, uncertainty and doubt without the irritable reaching after fact and reason'. It is why Eckhart prayed to God to rid him of God. And it is that feeling of abandon and abandonment which even Christ experienced on the cross when he cried out, in a moment of terrible darkness – "my God my God why have you forsaken me". An indispensable prelude to his ultimate leap of anatheist faith: 'Unto thee I commend my spirit'. The 'Thee' here being the God beyond the the old God. The God of new life and rebirth after the death of the old God of triumph, power and theodicy (who did not rescue him from the cross or turn all stone to bread during the famous temptation of Christ in the desert). The God after the God of the Grand Inquisitor (so brilliantoy portrayed by Dostoyevsky). Reconstructive anatheism may (or may not) follow from such a moment of deconstructive atheism. But it cannot exist without it. Otherwise religion can remain at the level of dogmatic certitude, a naive childish passive faith in a Alpha-Mega-Omni God of power and might, magic and manipulation – so powerfully exposed by Freud, Marx and Nietzsche – what Ricoeur calls the three great masters of the 'hermeneutics of Suspicion'. To which list we could add Derrida and the deconstructionists.

Which raises the old problem of evil and theodicy, going back to Voltaire's critique of Pangloss in *Candide* or more recently, Elie Wiesel's claim that 'God died in the hangman's noose in Auschwitz'. The old question: how can God be good when we look around us and see evil everywhere, to which theodicy replies that evil is all part of the hidden will of God. Ins pite of all the earthquakes and genocides and wars and violations of man against man, we are still living in the 'best of all possible worlds'(Leibniz). We are all actors in the secret plot of divine redemption through suffering. Against such perverse and pathological theism, we need a good dose of atheist deconstruction – all the hermeneutics of suspicion we can get. So that a possible God may be reborn, may return after (*ana*) the death of God. It's not necessarily a different God, it can be the old God returning as new wine in new wineskins, the promise of a former god or gods – as announced in the Quran, the Torah, the Gospels, the Upanishads – but now recovered, reimagined and retrieved in new ways after atheistic deconstruction. A radical deconstructive hermeneutics of religion is not just an act of destruction (as it is often misread) but an invitation to re-read the sacred scriptures and re-engage with traditional inheitied ceremonies and rituals but in a new diacritical way. That is what the Greek prefix 'ana' means, as defined in the Oxford English History: again, back, after, up in time and space. It is a moment of return which, if faith is authentic, takes the form of a spiral (repetition forward) rather than a vicious circle (repetition backward).

SCA: *As you know, Levinas, referring to the example of Cain and Abel, states that all immorality begins when we lose our sense of responsibility. When God asks Cain where is your brother, Cain says, "Am I my brother's keeper? According to Levinas, with this Cain's answer, all kinds of immorality had begun. Levinas continues, "of course I am my brother's keeper. I am a moral person, if I don't look for a special reason to be a moral person. Because my brother's responsibility is what makes me an ethical being." Add to this, there is a passage in your book* Strangers Gods and Monsters: *"The world belongs to everyone, but within the borders of nation-states it is more important to some. Therefore, immigration law is inevitable, and deconstructionists accept it. But they keep insisting that there is something beyond the law. That thing is justice." In the context of both examples, how do you see current immigration policies of countries, "who are our brothers" and what are our responsibilities towards them as their keeper? To be fair towards our brothers and sisters, should we go beyond the law?*

RK: That is a great question and it is where deconstruction and hermeneutics need each other. It is where Caputo's radical hermeneutics and my diacritical hermeneutics may complement each other. The world does belong to everybody and it is unfair that certain people – those in Western Europe, the United States or the Northern Hemisphere – have plenty of resources while those who live in certain countries in the Southern Hemisphere are starving or living in appalling circumstances of war, poverty and disease. It is unfair that one part of the world has everything and another does not, which is a fact. Radical hermeneutics would say the world belongs to everybody, therefore unconditional pure absolute hospitality should have no borders. Nobody should need a passport to ask for bread and shelter. It should be an unconditional welcome. In a way, that unconditional welcome is what gods do. It is what Allah would enjoin, or Yahweh or Christ. You accept everybody. But we also live in a world where we are not gods. It would be ideal if we could practice divine justice, divine hospitality and divine forgiveness everyday of our lives. But we do not alas. Yet we do our best in spite of everything, and perhaps trying to respond to a divine call in the face of the other. We do our best to discern, discriminate and read diacritically the faces of strangers at our borders and in our midst. We live in that tension – which is often tragically limited and disappointing. So we need radical hermeneutics to say everybody is welcome, and then we need diacritical hermeneutics to say, "Unfortunately, we do not have enough housing at the moment to take on a million people, but we can take a thousand. We do not have enough food to take a thousand, so we can take a hundred." That limitation is our finitude. It is the fact that we live in a finite, not an infinite, world. The absolute is the divine. But humans can aspire to be divine and we can be called by the divine to always be more just, always be more forgiving more hospitable. That is the call of the absolute which Levinas and Derrida have done so much to foreground and emphasize. But then we have the hermeneutics of our everyday situations with limits, finitude and tragic shortcomings. There we are faced with the difficult task of dialogue and negotiation, of trial and error, of risk and wager. How is justice possible while safeguarding or respecting the civic rights and resources of our own community?

Let's take a classic example from Kant. If somebody knocks at the door and asks you if you are hiding someone, Kant says you have to tell the truth whatever the circumstances, which seems ridiculous to me when it comes to reality. Because if you are hiding Jewish children and a Nazi comes to the door, you should not say "Yes, I'm hiding the Jewish children." Instead, you should tell a lie in order to protect them. Sometimes one has to compromise and accept the lesser evil in a world of tragic limits. Moving from Kant to Dorothy Day, the Catholic worker, activist who used to run hospitality houses in rundown areas of New York, Detroit, and Chicago. When she was running shelters for battered women, the homeless and the hungry, she would have a real dilemma sometimes when there would be a knock on the door at midnight and somebody would ask to be taken in. This is where diacritical hermeneutics comes in: she had to weigh up her responsibility to decide who to welcome and who to refuse. To decide to take in someone who genuinely needed help, food, and shelter as opposed to someone who was coming in to violate a battered woman whom she had let in one hour earlier. She was responsible for trying to discern, however difficult it might be, whether this is Jesus knocking at the door ("I am standing and knocking at your door") or whether it is Jack the Ripper wanting to come in and violate the women and children that she is protecting. So that is a terribly difficult moment, because when the door opens and you see the stranger, you do not know whether it is Jesus, Jack the Ripper or a combination of both. You have to make a call, which is definitely not a blind call. It is discernment, an interpretation, a reading, even though it happens instantaneously. You cannot go and have a philosophy seminar about it. You have a couple of seconds or minutes to decide, to talk to the person, look at them, weight them up. You try to discern diacritically the inflections at the level of word, body, mood, and gesture to decide whether that person is a violent threaet or somebody who genuinely needs help or, sometimes even a mixture of both. These are the hard cases encountered by a hermeneutics of hospitality. Another example one might give is *Les Misérables* by Victor Hugo where Monseigneur Myriel takes Jean Valjean into his house and gives him food and shelter. It is a discernment that he makes. Though Jean Valjean is a criminal and nobody else in the village of Digne would welcome him (he wears an identity marker designating that he is a criminal), Monseigneur Myriel can discern diacritically that maybe there is something in Jean Valjean that is inherently decent and redeemable. A wager that if he is received as a guest by a host and given food and shelter he will actually change and become a better human being. The possibility of transformation through grace and hospitality.

These are the kinds of diacritical interpretations and readings that we perform all the time. They are difficult, and there is a reason for that. It is not only about reading texts but also reading people's faces, actions, tones, as I try to show in recent works such *Carnal Hermeneutics*[1] and *Radical Hospitality: From Thought to Action.*[2] Therefore, we need to supplement radical hermeneutics that says everybody is welcome with a diacritical hermeneutics that says everybody is welcome under certain conditions. We acknowledge that there are certain limits, and we cannot but be sad about those. As Derrida once said, you cannot feed every cat in the street but you should feed some. Derrida admits that we have to make compromises. Nevertheless, my point would be that those compromises are actually very common, and it is what we do the ninety percent of the time when we are making those qualifications, modifications, ponderings, mediations in order to have as much peace, justice, forgiveness, and hospitality as possible.

SCA: *It seems that the problem of evil will not come to an end as long as humans exist, yet the end of evil would also depend on human existence. How hopeful are you for humanity, the future and our current world politics with regard to justice?*

RK: I'm hopeful because the alternative is too awful to contemplate. I believe in a hope without hope – similar to the notion of God without God, beyond God, after God of anatheism. There's also a hope beyond hope, without hope, after hope understood as false hope. Buddhism and Albert Camus have very

1 Edited by Richard Kearney and Brian Treanor, Fordham University Press – 2015.

2 Richard Kearney and Melissa Fitzpatrick, Fordham University Press – 2021.

keen critiques of illusory hope which offers facile consolations and cheap grace, refusing to face up to the tragedy of reality. To that extent we need to deconstruct and surpass what Kierkegaard calls the facile hope of Prometheus without succumbing to apocalyptic pessimism or nihilism, namely the passive quietism that says there's nothing to be done. Therefore, we need a real hope beyond naive hope. And this usually requires some passage through a moment of hopelessness, just as anatheism requires an atheistic purge of dogmatic theism. It is the same with hope. It is one of the three great virtues – faith, hope and charity. We have talked about faith and love (mercy) earlier. I think the same process needs to be undergone with regard to hope so that we can move from a facile infantile hope – "I hope Santa Claus will come", "I hope I'll be a millionaire in the morning" which in adults can express itself as an escapist denial of reality – to a deconstructed hope. However, this deconstruction should not be seen as the last word but as a necessary prelude to a renewed hope after the journey through hopelessness. T.S. Eliot talks about 'waiting without hope', so as to make way for a new hope beyond hope, after hope. Look at the current nature of our ecological crisis, our climate emergency, the rise of totalitarianism in so many parts of the world, the threat to democracy and freedom as well as global pandemic. When you look around you, there is so much suffering, and yet as a Christian I would look again here, while taking on board the Buddhist critique of illusory hope, at Jürgen Moltmann's *Theology of Hope*. Moltmann was was a Protestant, German theologian of the 20th century who had a big influence on the theology of liberation in Latin America, which struggled for justice against the totalitarian dictatorships and regimes. But the moment in Christianity already mentioned – and you can also find similar ones in Islam, Judaism and, other religions – is when the crucified Christ says, "My God, my God, why have you forsaken me?" He has given up hope, and that is a moment of absolute hopelessness, but then he moves on to what I would call an anatheist hope when he says, "Father, into thy hands I commend my spirit." He feels abandoned by the Mega-God of power and might, a God who does not come to save him, anymore than he saved the Jews in Auschwitz, or the dying and starving in Somalia or Eritrea or Syria or Ukraine. We have to give up hope in a God who will come down and rescue us on the cross, in the gas chambers, in the killing fields of Cambodia or the famine fields of Somalia. And then we are free to hope in spite of everything, after hope, beyond hope. We can hope in the God of little things, of 'the least of these'(*elachistos*), namely a God without power, a God of impossible possibility, a God who may be in every moment, however impossible it may seem, suffering and acting with us in our darkest moments (*Emmanuel*). I think the hope in the impossible becoming possible is fundamental to genuine faith. This is the opposite of the God triumphant, as witnessed in the triumphalist Christianity of the Inquisition and the Crusades, those who support the likes of Donald Trump or Vladimir Putin. We know about the perversions of religions, yet we still hope in the alternative 'power of the powerless', a *potestas* of divine *potentia* (translating the Greek *dunamis*) which Cusanus calls 'God as *Posse*' and we call the God who May Be. A *Posse* which has nothing to do with *imperium*. Here we hope anatheistically that love can still exist and prevail in spite of all. This is what Etty Hillesum discovered when she was in a concentration camp: even in the most appalling circumstances, there was the possibility of sharing your bread, comforting somebody on the way to the gas chamber or just putting your hand on another person's hand. That can happen in spite of everything. This is what I would call a second anatheist hope beyond both naïve hope and despondent hopelessness.

The same anatheist dialectic applies to a hermeneutics of love. Love, as we all know, is often naïve – a sort of infatuation or obsessive attachment. You are not really in love with the other person; you are in love with the idea of love. In Kierkegaard's *Diary of a Seducer*, we can see his description of Don Juan, and we see the theme of the erotic aesthetic in several of his other works as well. For Kierkegaard, as later for Freud, we need a radical hermeneutic deconstruction of that notion of love as an aesthetic unconscious projection that is all about ego fantasy and really nothing about the other person. It is neither attentive nor receptive. As Kierkegaard says, that aesthetic project undergoes what he calls *taedium vitae*, that is, weariness of life. The aesthetic project burns out and then the person trapped in the aesthetic stage has a choice between giving up altogether on love and becoming a cynic, or moving on to what he calls a choice for the ethical or the religious. If one chooses the ethical, then it is a return to love in terms of serving your neighbor through human affection, service, welfare, marriage, and family, all of those commitments to other people beyond the ego fantasy of the aesthete. Or one can chose the religious where we commit ourselves to an impossible love in the absolute. I would say that love after love, after the first infectious love, is ethical-religious. It occupies a position between our moral-social-political need to help our fellow humans and the desire for an absolute impossible love. And though Kierkegaard separated ethical and religious love, I think (with Levinas) that the two are often fundamentally mixed. When we are called to share bread with someone, we respond to both an ethical need from particular unique men and women in the here and now and what I would call a quasi-messianic appeal to all men and women, to humanity as it were. A fundamental solidarity with everyone. In other words, genuine love is both singular and absolute It involves mercy for the suffering hungry person in front of me and a compassion with all suffering humanity.

Dostoevsky touches on something like this when he writes (in the person of Zossima) that 'Everyone is responsible for everyone else, but I am more responsible for everyone else than anyone else'. When you are confronted with the suffering of others in an earthquake, it does not matter whether you are Christian, Muslim, Hindu or Jew, you dig the bodies of the children out of the rubble and you turn to your neighbor and say, "I know you are suffering, because I have lost a child and you have lost a child." Love here is absolute in that it absolves itself from obstacles and division, it works across borders and boundaries, in spite of all particular differences of race, color or creed. The Hebrew word for mercy is *racham* which shares the same root as recham, meaning womb. It comes from the stomach, the belly, the core of your being. That is where love for the absolute comes from, for all fellow human beings (who for Levinas are traces of God). In fact, the Buddhists would go further – and I agree with them – and say that it is a compassion for all living sentient beings. Coming to the third term of the trinity of faith, hope, and love, this is the root of absolute love. It is actually what many call God. Mercy for the widow, the orphan and the stranger. A messsianic love beyond ID papers, rules, regulations, borders, and passports. It is that movement beyond ego projections or fantasy attachments that may first seem impossible, but then becomes possible in an act of radical hospitality of the heart – a loving possibility beyond the impossible. That is what I mean by a carnal hermeneutics of the heart which makes the impossible possible.

SCA: *At this point in the debate on justice, it seems that justice is a horizon that can never be reached, and that injustice is a reality. For this reason, can we say the best way to achieve justice is to define injustice and eliminate the cases of injustice instead of describing justice and developing theories?*

RK: A theory of justice will never do full justice to justice. Justice is ultimately about responding to the call of the other in the immediacy of the moment – "Where are you? Share your bread, Do not kill" (Levinas again). It stems from the primary summons from the other person in need. Then, we make laws which are necessary for a greater distribution of goods, universal healthcare for as many people as possible. Laws govern the moral-political-social operations of justice. But our human laws and conventions, however just, will never be just enough, and therefore there is a justice beyond all our laws. Derrida and Caputo would call that messianic or absolute justice, which I sympathize with, because even if it is summoned in the here and now of suffering people it is always in part still to come. So, justice is ironically something that is always already there, for it is in our everyday acts, however simple, of being kind, good, generous and just to those in our world and at the same time, always still to come. A justice that can never be fully grasped, realized or defined, but that calls us to act more justly all the time and to never stop acting thus. Like Samuel Beckett's unnamable narrator who says "I can't go on. I'll go on." It is i performative contradiction in that I cannot achieve justice for all, or even enough justice for anyone person here and now, but I will keep on trying. Or like Camus' Sisyphus raising the rock to the top of the hill, though never getting to the top of the hill, because absolute justice is God and human mortals are not gods. Still, you can always desire God, work and struggle towards God, all the while and thinking as best you can theoretically and hermeneutically, trying to imagine more what justice would be like by writing works of philosophy and theology, of literature and art. In other words, I am not against the theory of justice – whether it is John Rawls or Hannah Arendt or anyone else – but the theory is always inadequate and is never sufficient *vis-à-vis* the fullness of justice. That's why, any theory of justice needs to be supplemented by imagination – the desire to always imagine new kinds of possibilities for justice in the future. For example, if we do not think about the possibility of ecological justice for our world, if we do not plan for it and imagine what the extinction of the world would be like or what a response to that threat might entail, we will just slip into paralysis. Thus, we need a theory and a project of justice, an imagining of justice, which can move from dream to praxis, from text to action. You don't give up because you do not have full absolute justice now. You keep going. I think the answer to the question of what is to be done is always more just thinking, more just imagining, and most importantly more just action. The model of diacritical hermeneutics suggests we move from action to text then back to action. In other words, we move from trying to be just in our everyday actions – of sharing bread and not killing our neighbor – to texts where we write, think, theorize and discuss (as you and I are endeavoring to do in this dialogue) so we can be hopefully more just afterwards. We do philosophy and make literature, we read the scriptures and classics about love and justice, and then return to action in the ordinary universe. The return to action is hermeneutically and diacritically mediated by the passage through thinking, writing, and imagining. It is what Ricoeur calls the movement from prefiguration (our every efforts to transform our world) to configuration (the hermeneutic writing and reading of texts) to refiguration (the return from text to action). Thinking begins and end in action. What I call anacarnation. And the end of it all is peace.

Suggested Readings

Richard Kearney, *Strangers, Gods, and Monsters; Interpreting Otherness*, UK: Routledge, 2002.

Richard Kearney, *Poétique du possible: phénoménologie herméneutique de la figuration*, Paris: Beauchesne, 1984.
Richard Kearney – Melissa Fitzpatrick, *Radical Hospitality: From Thought to Action*, USA: Fordham University Press, 2021.
Richard Kearney, *Anatheism: Returning to God After God*, USA: Columbia University Press, 2011.
Richard Kearney, *Debates in Continental Philosophy; Conversations with Contemporary Thinkers*, USA: Fordham University Press, 2004.
Richard Kearney, *Anacarnation: Returning to the Lived Body with Richard Kearney* Edited by Brian Treanor, James L. Taylor; UK, Routledge 2023.
Richard Kearney, *The God Who May be; A Hermeneutics of Religion*, USA: Indiana University Press, 2001.
Richard Kearney, *Imagination now: A Richard Kearney Reader*, Edited by M. E. Littlejohn, USA: Rowman & Littlefield Publishers, 2020.
Richard Kearney, *The Wake of Imagination: Toward a Postmodern Culture*, Routledge, 1988.
Richard Kearney, *Carnal Hermeneutics*, USA: Fordham University Press, 2015.

CHAPTER 4

Law and Justice: Michel Rosenfeld

Michel Rosenfeld is a distinguished legal philosopher whose work centers on constitutional law, democratic theory, and the philosophy of justice. As a leading figure in comparative constitutional studies, Rosenfeld has made significant contributions to understanding how diverse legal frameworks can address pluralism, human rights, and the challenges of modern democracy. His philosophy is characterized by a deep commitment to the ideals of justice, equality, and the reconciliation of diverse cultural and ethical perspectives within constitutional democracies. One of Rosenfeld's major contributions is his theory of "constitutional identity," which he explores extensively in The Identity of the Constitutional Subject: Selfhood, Citizenship, Culture, and Community. In this work, Rosenfeld argues that constitutional identity is a dynamic and evolving construct that reflects the unique values, beliefs, and historical experiences of a society. This concept is essential in pluralistic democracies, where conflicting cultural and ethical views often need to coexist within a single constitutional framework. Rosenfeld examines how constitutional identity allows diverse groups to maintain their distinctive identities while adhering to common principles of justice and democratic governance. His work underscores that legal systems must be adaptable, allowing societies to reflect changing cultural norms and values within their constitutional structures.

In Law, Justice, Democracy, and the Clash of Cultures: A Pluralist Account, Rosenfeld addresses the philosophical and practical challenges of achieving justice in a multicultural world. Here, he offers a pluralist theory of justice that seeks to balance universal human rights with respect for cultural diversity. Rosenfeld argues that while human rights must be upheld as universal standards, democracies must also accommodate cultural differences, recognizing that various communities may have unique conceptions of justice, equality, and autonomy. This pluralistic approach to justice, according to Rosenfeld, is critical for fostering peaceful coexistence in diverse societies. By engaging with the ethical and cultural dimensions of legal systems, Rosenfeld's work promotes an inclusive view of justice that respects both individual rights and collective identities.

Another significant aspect of Rosenfeld's philosophy is his analysis of the relationship between law and democracy. He has written extensively on the role of constitutionalism in protecting democratic values, even when societal

 | DOI:10.1163/9789004732902_006

pressures challenge these principles. In Just Interpretations: Law Between Ethics and Politics, Rosenfeld explores how legal interpretation can mediate between ethical obligations and political realities, offering a nuanced approach to the challenges of judicial decision-making in democratic societies. He argues that the law should be understood not as a fixed set of rules but as a living, interpretive process that responds to the ethical and political contexts within which it operates. Rosenfeld's philosophy is ultimately rooted in a commitment to reconciling justice and pluralism, recognizing that legal systems must evolve to address the diverse ethical, cultural, and political realities of contemporary societies. Through his extensive scholarship, Rosenfeld provides a framework for understanding how law can promote justice while respecting cultural and individual diversity, shaping constitutionalism as a bridge between universal principles and particular identities.

Sema Cevirici Atilla* [*SCA*]*: Firstly, I would like to ask you a question related to Derrida's famous speech on justice at Cardozo Law School where you are still a member. As a lawyer, how do you evaluate Derrida's statement that deconstruction is justice? In other words, is deconstruction justice or is justice an ideal that transcends deconstruction?

Michel Rosenfeld [MR]: Justice is an ideal that certainly transcends any individual view or philosophy. Aristotle is the first at least Western thinker that we focus on when we talk about justice. And he knew nothing about deconstruction. Now of course, Derrida deconstructed and, in some ways, reconstructed Plato and Aristotle, but reading Aristotle on justice is not the same as a reading of Derrida on the same subject. Derrida gave his paper on law and justice at Cardozo, and I was present, in a fully filled room where a lot of those you have talked to, including the late Richard Bernstein, were present. Many times, that Derrida came to Cardozo and to the New School many of the people that you have been engaging with have had personal experiences with Derrida. Moreover, I want to point out that the second time Derrida came to Cardozo which I think was 1990 or 1991, I wrote a very short piece in the Cardozo Law Review in which I compared him to Aristotle. And the one key distinction between the two is that Aristotle has the idea that the justice is expressed in general maxims and there are some exceptions. Sometimes a general rule needs some exceptions to remain equitable throughout. Derrida took that and turned it into every instance of justice has to be *at once* a general rule and an exception which makes justice impossible. To my best reading of Aristotle, and I can only read him in translation, he would not at all agree with that. Aristotle really thought that you could achieve justice and that you had to be sensitive to the fact that some exceptional cases cannot be encompassed within a general rule. That I think, underscores a key distinction between Aristotle and Derrida.

***SCA:** Derrida used to visit Cardozo Law School frequently. At one of his visits, you conducted an interview with Derrida in which you asked him why philosophers had been interested in legal issues and legal justice for the past 15–20 years. Derrida answered this by stating how significant the independence of justice for democracy is and that the philosophers should address justice and law with the globalization of democracy. What are your thoughts on this subject? Has the problem of law and justice now become a problem for philosophers to solve?*

MR: I think that the philosophers and lawyers have overlapped in their concerns over justice. One of the key debates in legal theory and legal philosophy is about law as a field that stands apart. It is a normative field that is self-contained. Legal positivists agree with that, but others want to tie law to morals and to justice and have even said that laws that are immoral and unjust should not be followed. This is a key debate within law, and it is a key debate within philosophy. And philosophers who take justice seriously must address the question of what's the place of law in achieving justice. If you read Hume, if you read Mill, if you read Rousseau if you read Kant or Rawls, all of whom wrote about justice, they all refer to law. The basic point is that both lawyers who are thinking about law and not just applying laws that they learned – that is, anybody that thinks about law and engages with what is known as jurisprudence or legal philosophy has to deal with the issue of justice. And philosophers that deal with the question of justice have to at least somehow address questions of law. In this sense, I think it is inevitable that many philosophers speak about law in the most abstract terms and don't know much about it. Similarly, a lot of lawyers speak about philosophy and know very little about it and are quite superficial. But it's an important subject about which you hopefully have enough competent people on both sides of the question.

***SCA:** In the same interview, Derrida said that "Cardozo is for me the place I learn, where I can discuss what interests me in the law." What do you think separated Cardozo from other law faculties for Derrida?*

MR: Let me give you a two-part answer. The first part is the attitude toward Derrida in French law schools with which he had virtually no contact because French law – at least during his generation and this may be changing now – was very formal, deductive, and rigid and hence not open to a deconstructionist. He was viewed by many influential in law as a controversial and destructive force against the prevailing order in France. I have taught for many years in French law schools. I was a recurring visiting professor for many years in French law schools and one of the leading French legal academics asked me: "Why do you engage with Derrida? The only good thing about Derrida is his cousin who happens to be a professor of business law. That was the prevalent view in the legal academy in France during the 1990's when Derrida increasingly focused on issues pertaining to law. In contrast, The American part of the answer is quite different. Although Derrida was by no means well known in the American legal academy, as I have written in one of the books that I published a long time ago, called *Just Interpretations,* deconstruction as an interpretive methodology works well with the common law which is the system used in the United States and which originated in England. Within the common law, the law is based on precedent – meaning on what courts have said in the past about analogous legal issues. Accordingly, as a judge you have to interpret judicial texts from the past and then you must project what you draw from these texts into the future. This very much looks like the deconstructive approach. Because they rely much less on deductive thinking and are mainly based on inductive and empirical thinking, the American, the English the Australian and the Anglo Canadian approaches to law are more open-ended to deconstructive backward and forward looking dynamic interpretive maneuvers. . With that in mind Derrida, as far as I know, had besides Cardozo only one other experience with a United States law school, and that was namely Yale. For many years, Derrida had very strong bonds with the literature faculty at Yale, and in particular with one of its most prominent members, Paul de Man. This became subsequently very controversial because it was discovered that Paul de Man had an unbeknown to Derrida and many others extensive Nazi past. Derrida was very marked by that revelation and did not cut off his links with de Man while at the same time accepting these revelations. This turned into a very bitter experience for Derrida. But as he used to go to Yale all the time Derrida was once to the Yale Law Faculty. As Derrida told it to me, he was treated very politely by the Yale legal academics, but he could see that there was no connection there. So that leads me to why Cardozo? In the late 1980s when I joined the Cardozo faculty, there were many people at Cardozo that went into teaching with dual degrees. So, the typical American law professor only had training in law and only in American law. In that context, French theory was probably as far as you could get from their daily concerns. But Cardozo had many professors that had PhDs in various fields. I myself have a PhD philosophy. A colleague prominent in feminist philosophy, Drucilla Cornell, played a very important role in bringing Derrida over to Cardozo and we had a relationship working with the New School which was not only across the street from Cardozo but at the time had in addition to Richard Bernstein, Seyla Benhabib and Andrew Arato – and much later Simon Critchley. So, there were many people at the New School who were in other fields and notably Richard Bernstein who was the person who brought Derrida to the New School. So, every year Derrida would come to lecture for two or three weeks at NYU in the comparative literature department where his sponsor was, one of close American collaborators, Avital

Ronell. Derrida had nothing to do with it with the NYU law school, however, which could then be characterized as being even more American-centric than the Yale law school was. Typically, Derrida would give one or two lectures at Cardozo, and he would give a series of lectures at the philosophy department at the New School. So that's the context in which there were many people at Cardozo who interacted with Derrida and some of the meetings also involved NYU literature people and New School philosophy people and political theory people. Regarding my personal relationship with Derrida, I became his principal Cardozo liaison after a few years as Drucilla Cornell left law teaching and took a position in political science at another university. I also met Derrida at least once or twice a year in Paris where we were together at certain conferences and used to meet at times for coffee. and he started discussing with me certain legal questions he had in relation to a lot of subjects that in la in his later career he was concerned with. One area where we had a long discussion particularly because the United States is unique as compared to Europe was the death penalty. He wrote on it and he came to Cardozo to have exchanges with our faculty on the death penalty as well as on immigration about which he took very strong positions against the anti-immigrant positions taken by the French government at the time. So, then there were things that he wrote about in relation to which we engaged in discussions, and he seemed really interested given that he obviously had outstanding originality and insight, but I was more knowledgeable when it came to legal theory and technical details.

SCA: *Derrida asserts that there is an unbridgeable gap between justice as the law which should always preserve its universality and justice as giving everyone what is their right which includes an irreducible element of individuality. How can this paradox be resolved which is created by the necessity of law and justice to be both universal and exceptional at the same time?*

MR: I do not think this could be resolved. In this sense, although you deserve a much fuller answer, and obviously we can't do this in a short time. I do address this issue in my book *Just Interpretations* (1998) Derrida's position as I view it is tragic in that it is a little reminiscent of the myth of Sisyphus. As Albert Camus recounts, Sisyphus carries the rock up the mountain, but it always falls down before he reaches the top. For Derrida we must pursue justice as an absolute moral imperative, but we are condemned to never achieving it. This raises a question which became particularly acute in the context of the aftermath of the terrorist attack on New York on 9/11/2001. Derrida commented on that attack the year before he died. If there is no possibility of justice, how do we distinguish with between something that is relatively more just and something that is relatively less just? My own view and – unfortunately Derrida is not here to refute me – is that Derrida doesn't give us an answer. What is very striking about Derrida is that at the beginning of his career as a deconstructionist philosopher he was accused of in fact being a relativist and an amoral thinker, because to the extent that every discourse can run into every other discourse you could deconstruct anything with the result that nothing can remain stable. You could reinvent the past, you can figure the future in multiple different ways, and you can shift your focus on the present through certain analogies that lead to one conclusion or other analogies that lead to the opposite conclusion. Derrida had brilliant analyses of particular philosophers but was accused of philosophically ignoring morals or ethics. Whatever the merit of this accusation, it became obsolete by the time that Derrida delivered his Cardozo conference in 1989 where for well over an hour Derrida focused on the nexus between law, justice and violence. Some of Derrida's American interlocutors (perhaps we were being parochial) have claimed that his turn to ethics represented American side of Derrida. He came to the United States gave this big lecture on law that raises both ontological and ethical questions that he had not addressed before. And if you look at his output from the late 1980s until the end of his life it is much more concentrated on ethical issues and on the relationship between the singular and the universal and between what some people to others, such as the nature of friendship or that of democracy. So, I think that he was in this sense a very important figure, because in the United States there was a movement called the critical legal studies movement in law that basically attacked all law as being merely power relations that judges, and lawyers could manipulate and come up with the result they preferred, which almost inevitably favored the rich and powerful. In contrast, ordinary lawyers think that in most cases there are determinate and unambiguous legal answers. Sometimes these answers are just and sometimes they are unjust. That depends on the nature of the law, but if you tell me, you did this and then you are legally protected or not legally protected, but and the answer does not depend on politics. As against this, the Critical Legal Studies school of thought comprised of a group of leftist professors – in the American sense of leftists, so I mean nothing like the communist party in France or Italy – contended that all law is primed for manipulation given its being indeterminate and left in the hands of judges and lawyers who come for the most part from the ruling class. They speak in this abstract beautiful terminology, but in fact what they are doing is reproducing the interest of the ruling class. And what Derrida did – in relation to these legal theorists who were attracted to deconstruction because they saw it fitting their theory without looking deeply into its intricacies – was to open a path beyond these theorists' relativist or nihilist bent by introducing and ethical ontological dimension to law's quest for justice. We have an obligation to the other which consists in never overlooking the latter's singularity.

We must acknowledge that singularity and give the other his or her due as a singular human being. I think that it is out of the confrontation with the other's singularity that Derrida concentrated on the dichotomy between law and justice. Then there is the whole discussion embodied in the second part of the presentation that Derrida presented at Cardozo, namely his paper on Benjamin where he discusses the latter's linkage between law and violence. The law is institutional violence and is that violence different than the violence in the state of nature world that Hobbes portrays as pitting everybody as a constant threat to kill everybody else. Derrida, I think, leads us to a different conclusion because of his focus on the obligation to seek justice. In seeking justice your violence is not as arbitrary as the violence of let's say a thug or a mafia leader who establishes his own law, but the violence of let's say a thug or a mafia leader who establishes his own law. Nevertheless, a serious problem remains in that one can never reach justice and thus no violence through law can ever be fully justified. Does that set up a scale to separate less just legal outcomes from more just ones? Or does the unbridgeable gap between law and justice make any legal coercion ultimately amount to unjustified violence against those subjected to law?

SCA: *You compare Derrida's understanding of the relationship between law and justice to that of the common law, for legal rules in common law are shaped by the implementation of precedent decisions. Faced with the conflicting arguments of opposing parties, the judge seeks a fair resolution of the concrete case at hand making a judgment in line with similar judicial decisions of the past. In this respect, what other common denominator do you think the Derridean conception of law and justice and the common law have in common?*

MR: I would say that what is in common with a common law in the first place is methodology. And it's the idea that you have to deal with intertextual realities and that they are never settled. If you take – and this is an oversimplification, but a productive one – the idea of the civil law which consists of codes calling for resolution of individual cases through the use of syllogisms, then you are led to a single solution that all reasonable people ought to concur in. For example, you have no right to hit your neighbor. Accordingly, if you took an oar and smacked the arm of your neighbor, you are unmistakenly guilty of hitting your neighbor. This is a logical result and any person who can reason in a syllogistic way will get it. Deconstruction has nothing to do with this as we are not interested in hearing any controversy on, or elaboration of, the interplay between to hit and not to hit. Now of course in law there may be some type of factual questions such as did you miss your neighbor when you swung your oar at him. Regardless of factual issues, there is supposed to be a fairly a logical process providing some linguistic conventions and so forth and rules that we can refer to, such as, say for example, section six of the code, which provides the rule to be applied and the first premise of the syllogism. Now, in sharp contrast, the common law relies on precedents – that is past judgments on relevantly sufficiently analogous cases. For example, you are my neighbor and if your horse destroys my flowers and then a judge decides that the horses should not be allowed loose by their owners to destroy the property of their neighbors. What happens if subsequently your dog destroys some of your neighbor's property? Does the horse case apply or not? And there are arguments in favor and against relying on the horse precedent. You shouldn't treat horses the same way as you treat dogs, or vice versa in terms of destruction of your neighbor's property. So, you see from this one example that it opens up a whole series of possibilities, and you cannot capture or give a resolution in one simple procedure. So, in this sense the Derridean approach, the deconstructive approach to text is more akin to what happens in the common law. Now of course if I gave a common law judge the text of Derrida and said what you're doing is the same as what Derrida is doing, the judge might become very upset at me because there is re legal techniques and conventions suggesting a contrast with the Derridean analysis that really flows much more widely. So, I'm just speaking of an analogy not a correspondence between deconstruction and the common law. And my thesis is that Derrida is more relevant to the common law than he is to the civil law, but this does not extend to justice. Indeed, there are theories of justice in the common law that are quite different from Derrida's. For instance, the common law comes from England where it was developed starting in medieval times. The judicial body of common law decisions in are justified in terms of the common sense and widespread notions of justice of the British people. So, supposedly the British people all see certain legal issues and their implications for justice the same way. Now we can certainly mount a deconstructive critique of that, but if you speak to the judges issued from the English people, they sound are very proud of their more than a thousand years of continuity in law. There is this shared belief that if you have common sense if you have a pragmatic approach, and if you have the good values of English people, then you will have no difficulty in determing what amounts to a just result. This attitude is even reflected indecisions of the Supreme Court of the United States that refer to the principles of justice of the English-speaking people. Obviously, the United States is not England and even had a revolution against England, but remains part of the tradition of the English-speaking people and of its corresponding conception of justice. So, in this sense Derrida's sense of justice as being ultimately impossible and the English language lawyer's countervailing sense of justice remain very different.

SCA: *Do you see a close relationship between the interpretation practice of Derridean deconstruction and Ronald Dworkin's Herculean judge? Do you think Judge Hercules is a good role model for fair decision-making?*

MR: The answer is no and no. I have an article on the famous Dworkin thesis, in which he relies on Hercules, that there is one right answer to every hard case. My article appeared in the Revue Internationale de Philosophie in 2005. Dworkin's approach is based on his very adamant belief in a particular moral and political philosophy which I would characterize as liberal egalitarian, which is not exactly the same as, but close to that elaborated by Rawls. Dworkin argues that ordinary judges often make mistakes because they are unable to capture the full picture and he introduces Hercules as the superhuman judge who has a full grasp of all the ramifications of actual cases. When ordinary judges reach the wrong result, it is akin to someone who is not gifted in Math getting the wrong result while attempting to solve an equation. But just as that doesn't mean that there isn't a right answer in that a gifted mathematician will have no trouble reaching, so too the ordinary judge is limited in ways that Dworkin's Hercules is not. However, what Dworkin's Hercules doesn't take into account is that in real society we don't all agree on the same theory of justice, the same morality, and the same political philosophy. So, you can have right answers that are different because you have different moral codes or different ways of interpreting legal texts and a whole other series of variants. In this sense, Dworkin is the anti-Derrida. Judges come to different conclusions because the very idea of multifaceted intertextuality usually precludes a single right conclusion. Accordingly, it makes little sense to claim that I got the right interpretation because I am smarter than the others. Derrida would not philosophically preclude that you or I could not in a genuine way try to draw different implications from the same series of textual connections. So, in this sense Derrida and Dworkin are completely opposites.

SCA: *Since rules of law are general and events are particular, interpretation is inevitable. What possibilities can deconstruction offer as a way out from the crisis of interpretation of legal rules considering the fact that deconstruction is a logic of interpretation?*

MR: Well, I have tried to deal with this question in the first chapter of that book that I mentioned to you called *Just Interpretations* which was published in 1998. My interpretation is that deconstruction never leads to a single answer, but when applied to law in a authentic way – as opposed to pre-deciding the outcome and then claiming that because deconstruction allows me to make many moves I can work backwards and claim a victory for justice – then some interpretive paths are open while others are closed. I give an elaborate explanation, which you may or not find persuasive, as to why deconstruction can be usefully used not to find a single answer but a range of answers that seem much more plausible than alternative ranges of answers. In this sense, in a common law system there often are no predetermined answers because judges in the present have to read the decisions of past judges, given facts that are not exactly the same. A precedent can be very easy to apply if the same fact pattern is replicated – so if your horse eats my flowers and then my horse eats your flowers, then the cases are exactly the same case so the results should be the same. In real life very rarely do cases coincide so neatly as there are likely to be trivial differences even in the absence of substantive ones. What if a murderer wears a blue shirt and the next murderer wears a green shirt, does the precedent with a blue shirt apply to the murder with a green shirt? Obviously, no serious judge would say that the color of the shirt has anything to do with the guilt of the murderer. On the other hand, differences that are not as easily dismissed may well not lead to the same result. So, you always have an openness but what that does in terms of deconstruction would be the opening of certain paths of connections and the closing of others.

SCA: *In some recent news, a claim was made that robot judges can make fair decisions to a large extent. Do you think the current studies in artificial intelligence can make it possible to produce robot judges that can make fair decisions? If this is possible, how do you view the ethical dimension of it?*

MR: I am not an expert in artificial intelligence (AI), but I have had discussions about this hypothetical with people immersed in the subject. And some of them say artificial intelligence will never replace the human brain and will never make intelligent decisions. But others claim that AI will make intelligent decisions. Could AI therefore become Dworkin's Hercules? There are certain matters in relation to which the function of the judge is not mysterious. We want to punish murderers, but we have lots of problems with facts and putting together documentation, testimony and DNA tests and all kinds of other things. So, the ordinary judge or the ordinary juror may lack a precise way of deciding whether or not the person on trial is the murderer. I can imagine that AI could somehow distill all this information and putting it together might be a better a better way to do it. There are many things we do today that we didn't do 40 years ago because the computer is better equipped than a human being for certain purposes. I want to find a good restaurant near where I live, and a computer is likely more efficient than reliance on memory. When it comes to theories of justice, however, then it seems to me I don't see how AI does more than whatever you feed it. If you feed a whole theory of justice into your computer, maybe it'll come up with a better answer than you could acting alone. This seems analogous to playing chess with a computer that can be better than a living person in as much as the computer can analyze a million moves where even the best chess player has no equivalent skill in this regard. Having said that, I do not see how AI could systematically decide among competing conceptions of justice.

SCA: *What would you say if you were to evaluate the hospitality of deconstruction in terms of the immigration problem and its reflections on the law?*

MR: The one problem I find with deconstruction is its inability to provide answers to specific questions like that. In my book that is coming out next month (A Pluralist Theory of Constitutional Justice) I address this, and I once discussed it with Derrida. Derrida has been influenced by existentialism and in particular by Heidegger, but importantly for present purposes, also by the existentialism of Sartre. Sartre speaks about authenticity, and you cannot be authentic if you look to the past. Each time that you have a moral decision to make you have to jump into it based on your immediate intuitive assessment and for Sartre this was a very easy task, because the omnipresent enemy of the times was a Hitler and those who collaborated with him. But if you read Sartre's philosophy, it does not give you any guidance in a world that is not as black and white as Hitler versus all the people that fought him. There is some degree of similarity in Derrida who very strongly argues for justice and for ethical behavior. But because he regards the link between law and justice to be inevitably broken, there cannot be a properly grounded philosophical answer to a specific question such as the one under discussion. I know that Derrida was a passionate and committed supporter of immigrants in France and he even defended breaking the law to register his moral outrage at the fact that the laws of the time in France were anti-immigrant. I also know what he said about the al-Qaeda 9/11 attack on the US, namely that it amounted to pure violence that remains beyond any meaning as it cannot be integrated it into any text. I have taken issue with him on that as Al Qaeda's attacks do have meaning and its terrorist endeavors sended certain unmistakable messages. These messages were extremely destructive and morally repugnant morally resisted but they highlighted grievances – some of which were justified some of which not – and they communicated an ideological stance suffused in violence against the Western way of life. Accordingly, we cannot say that global terrorists are outside of human communication or of human interaction no matter how violent they may be. In this sense I cannot agree with Derrida that there are actual answers that global terrorists are to be unqualifiedly condemned *because* their violence remains beyond the realm of any meaning.

SCA: *As you know, we have been facing a judicial crisis since Kant. The basis of our judgment and the question of how we judge are the issues that have been seriously debated. Lyotard introduces the idea of judgment without criteria. Do you think it is possible to judge without criteria with respect to law?*

MR: There will be people who will claim that, but I think that law has a systemic core that can be invoked through use of Wittgenstein's metaphor by characterizing law as a language game. This language game is plainly deployed in contemporary constitutional all democracies. Thus, for example, a judge must provide an explanation for his or her decision. If the judge would just say, is it the person wearing a blue shirt or the person wearing a green shirt who wins, then it would be completely without foundation other than the subjective whim of the judge. But a judge has to find some way to articulate a reason for the decision. And the reason has to fit within the language game of law. Because law and justice are not necessarily coordinated, there may be very unjust laws and they may be more just interpretations of certain laws than others. Achieving justice is a different story and depends on what your criterion of justice is. But in terms of the right result in the purely legal sense – for example, what is the correct result of this contractual dispute – the judge has to find some justification within the language game of law. There may be disagreements within the language game of law and judges may interpret the pertinent law and facts in a case in somewhat contradictory ways leading to dissenting opinions, but all interpretations at stake must remain within the language game of law.

SCA: *Do you think phronesis can be applied in the current law and in fair decision-making processes?*

MR: The problem with that is that as I read Aristotle (and I'm not an expert on Aristotle) he assumes that there would be consensus on what phronesis requires. And I think we live in pluralistic societies in which there is no such agreement. To be sure, for certain matters Americans tend to turn to pragmatism. From within pragmatism certain things are obvious. If medical science says that you must take this medicine to get rid of this virus and out of 100 people that took this medicine, 100 got cured, then you would say as a pragmatic matter that you're better off taking this medicine for this virus. There seems to be no valid argument against this conclusion because we all agree on the purpose at hand which is to make you healthy again. But pragmatism is very tricky when there is disagreement about ends. Let us consider an issue that is currently very much in conflict in the United States, namely abortion. What's the pragmatic answer to the legalization or prohibition of abortion? If you think that abortion is murder the pragmatic thing to do is to forbid it and to police every woman and every doctor to make sure they don't engage in it. Conversely, if you think abortion is a health and mental health related issue that a woman should decide alone or maybe sometimes in consultation with her doctor then pragmatism would counsel widespread legal permission to have an abortion. In short, pragmatism doesn't help with ends, but only with means provided there is no disagreement on ends. means. Accordingly, Aristotelian phronesis projected into a country like the United States where the population is very divided on moral issues, religious issues, policy issues, and economic issues does not appear to have much potential.

SCA: *I would like to address the paradox between justice and violence. When a person imposes his rights on the other in the name of justice, he inflicts violence on the other. However, if the person renounces his rights to be fair to the other, he inflicts violence on himself. In this situation, can we say that justice or the pursuit of justice leads to violence inevitably?*

MR: Law and justice are inseparable from violence and that is because unless you speak of justice in very abstract terms or we live in a just society where everybody loves everybody else, there is no avoiding violence within and against the law. In a real society what the law may do is to allow you to complain about me and the judge will say that you win resulting in violence against me in the sense that I'm coerced let us say to pay damages to you. Conversely, if I win then there is violence against you because in your mind you have been injured by me, and the law says I owe you nothing. So even in a simple civil dispute, the law seems bound to force people against their will and thus always comprises a measure of violence. Now of course if we believe that justice can be fully achieved, then violence that is linked to justice is justified and violence that is linked to injustice is not justified. So, if I stole 100 dollars from you and the court says I have to pay you back, there are many instances of violence that come into play. First, there was violence when I stole from you. The second violence occurs as I have these 100 dollars in my hand, and I am ready to buy myself a good dinner when the court forces me to return it to you. This latter violence is just because you are entitled to compensation, and the court order restores justice. In this sense, even though there is violence it is legitimate violence against me whereas not to order me to compensate you would be illegitimate violence because not only have you been violated first by me taking away the money from you. But if the court refuses to award you any remedy, you end up suffering two acts of violence, one illegal and one legal. Consistent with this, returning to Derrida, if there is an infinite gap between law and justice then either every application of law is equally violent or we may have gradations in the gap between law and justice making some laws more unjust than others.

SCA: *You claim that deconstruction does not support the idea that law is reducible to politics. Could you expand on this subject?*

MR: I mean that by introducing an ethical and ontological dimension deconstruction cannot lead to exclusively political interpretive outcomes. The ontological dimension is that the other is equally important as you are, but you cannot completely figure out the other because you can never absorb the other in her full singularity. But you still have an ethical obligation to try as best as you can to accommodate the other singularity as that is what justice requires. You have a universal rule that you understand but that leaves open to what extent you can try to accommodate the singularity of the other. You will never succeed completely but you have the moral obligation to keep trying and that is not political. Moreover, I mean political in whichever way you understand the term, whether in an Aristotelian sense or in a more cynical way that reduces politics to power struggles to maximize power in order to impose one's vision of society and of its needs or goals. I think the deconstructive ethical dimension transcends the purely political. That is why, as already mentioned, in spite of common elements, deconstruction and the American critical legal studies movement remain distinct from one another. Derrida's insistence on an ethical obligation departs from the American movement's approach to deconstruction as a methodology but not as an ethics. In contrast, Derrida refuses to yield on the ethical obligation to seek justice even though one is ultimately bound to fail.

SCA: *At this point in the debate on justice, it seems that justice is merely an ideal and injustice is a reality. For this reason, can we say that the best way to achieve justice is to define injustice and eliminate the cases of injustice instead of developing theories of justice?*

MR: Yes, but the two are connected. Now there are certain things about which we all agree or at least that all people in good faith agree. And that is for instance that torture is an intolerable injustice. In this sense we know what justice means, you have to completely abstain and end all torture. We may not achieve that because you could keep defining torture in different ways. But at least to the extent that we agree that certain practices do not amount to torture we could find a significant common ground. Now of course there are horrible or crimes against humanity, such as what Putin is doing in Ukraine, by gratuitously bombing buildings, hospitals, and maternity wards. We can all agree on that, but he does not. Putin has a "vision" and a different point of view, but the means he uses are obviously utterly repulsive. However, in more complicated situations in which reasonable minds can disagree you both have to make a claim as to what justice would be and articulate a vision indicating how you could claim to have diminished injustice. Now in some cases it's very obvious. When somebody starts killing children, it is an obvious injustice, and we can all agree that it is a terrible thing that should stop immediately. But once you get into more philosophical nuances in areas in which people disagree morally or on the basis of different religions and different lifestyles, then I think you are almost in a situation in which it is impossible to proceed unless you have some notion of what justice would look like. Consistent with this, you can claim that you are gradually eliminating injustice without ever coming close to fully succeeding.

Suggested Readings

Michel Rosenfeld, *Just Interpretations: Law Between Ethics and Politics*, USA: University of California Press, 1998.

Michel Rosenfeld, *A Pluralist Theory of Constitutional Justice: Assessing Liberal Democracy in Times of Rising Populism and Illiberalism*, UK: Oxford University Press, 2022.

Michel Rosenfeld, *Law, Justice, Democracy, and the Clash of Cultures: A Pluralist Account*, UK: Cambridge University Press, 2011.

Michel Rosenfeld, *Affirmative Action and Justice: A Philosophical and Constitutional Inquiry*, USA: Yale University Press, 1991.

Michel Rosenfeld, *The Identity of the Constitutional Subject: Selfhood, Citizenship, Culture, and Community*, UK: Routledge, 2010.

CHAPTER 5

Deconstruction and Justice: Christopher Norris

Christopher Norris is a British philosopher whose work in deconstruction, literary theory, and epistemology has been instrumental in advancing a rigorous understanding of Derridean thought. Norris has written extensively on the challenges of interpreting deconstruction, presenting it not as a form of relativism but as a disciplined approach to exploring language, meaning, and truth. His careful, scholarly work on deconstruction makes a compelling case for its philosophical relevance, particularly in relation to ethics and epistemology.

One of Norris's most influential contributions is his work on deconstruction, where he stands out as a strong advocate for Derrida's approach to reading and interpreting texts, countering many misconceptions about Derrida's philosophy. In his book Deconstruction: Theory and Practice (1982), Norris provides an accessible yet nuanced analysis of how Derrida's ideas challenge traditional views of language and truth. He argues that deconstruction, rather than denying objective meaning, reveals the complexities of how meaning is constructed, encouraging a careful engagement with language. Another significant work, Derrida (1987), delves into Derrida's philosophical project, emphasizing that deconstruction requires intellectual rigor and should not be mistaken for an "anything goes" approach to interpretation.

Norris is also known for his criticism of relativism, arguing that deconstruction does not imply an abandonment of truth but a deeper understanding of its contextuality. He suggests that by recognizing the instability of language, deconstruction offers a way to address ethical issues without resorting to absolutism. His writings have contributed significantly to debates in philosophy, especially regarding the boundaries of knowledge and the ethical responsibilities of interpretation. Norris's philosophy evolved to encompass a robust defense of epistemological realism, which is evident in works such as Against Relativism: Philosophy of Science, Deconstruction, and Critical Theory. Here, Norris critiques the relativistic trends in postmodern philosophy, arguing that skepticism toward absolute truth should not equate to an outright rejection of rationality or objective knowledge. Drawing from critical realism, he contends that while knowledge is fallible and shaped by social contexts, it is still possible to make justified claims about reality. This realist stance distinguishes Norris

 | DOI:10.1163/9789004732902_007

from many postmodern thinkers, positioning him as a philosopher committed to balancing critical inquiry with a belief in the possibility of objective truth.

Sema Cevirici Atilla **[*SCA*]*:*** *You are interested in literature, poetry, and philosophy. Is there any connection between your poems and science and philosophy? If so, what kind of connection are you trying to establish?*

Christopher Norris [CN]: Well, many of my poems are directly political – they are activist, directly interventionist, and they have to do with current affairs in the UK and the world. So, those really form a separate category, and they are written generally in ballad form, or in satiric mode, or as verse-polemics – they are supposed to be hard-hitting and to get people thinking and protesting out on the streets. But I also write a lot of philosophical poetry and it's inevitably based on, or grows out of, my past academic interests. I don't write very much academic philosophy nowadays, at least not regular prose philosophy, academic books or essays. But I've published a collection of poems about Derrida, based on specific passages from his texts which I have treated in a range of verse-forms, fairly traditional forms with often quite complex rhyme schemes, and a collection of verse-essays inspired by Adorno's wonderful book *Minima Moralia.* These are basically commentaries, glosses, creative engagements with Adorno's thought which come at it from various, often oblique angles and tease out further implications of his already remarkably complex and many-sided project. What I try to do is bring the two halves of my life together, the academic interests (including the interest in analytic or Anglophone philosophy and continental philosophy in the German and French lines of descent. I suppose in a way it was the result of thinking about what I was going to do when I retired from university teaching; I couldn't stop writing but I did want to do something different, not carry on producing more articles and monographs, so that's really how it started.

SCA: *In* Platonism, Music and the Listener's Share, *you remark, "I take music as a highly problematic but, for just that reason, a revealing test-case with regard to the current debate as to whether truth can be conceived as always potentially transcending the scope and limits of attainable knowledge or accredited best judgement." In this context, can you explain the relationship you have established between music, knowledge, and truth?*

CN: In the discourse of analytic philosophy the realist/anti-realist debate has to do with whether one believed in the existence of objective, mind-independent, verification-transcendents truths or whether one believes that truth is relative to attainable knowledge, or 'truth at the end of enquiry' (a weasel phrase!). I have written quite a lot about that. In musical terms, as discussed in my book, the issue has to do with whether musical works have structures, attributes or qualities that exist – not so much objectively as inter-subjectively across wide differences of individual response – and thus transcend mere individual taste or the vagaries of pure subjectivity. I push my version of the musical-realist case pretty hard and a lot of readers have resisted my arguments. I think it is it's good for a listener to music or a performer, you know, an instrumentalist or a singer to understand something about music theory in the traditional sense: what makes a melody beautiful or haunting, how counterpoint works, how keys relate to other keys, how works develop over a long span within symphonic movements or, beyond that, in whole works; and I think that understanding our responses is the best way to respond more actively and become more deeply engaged with music. So I'm talking about knowledge in that sense, a well-informed knowledge of how music works, how musical works are put together. But also, generally speaking, the more we understand about our cognitive, emotional and ethical responses – the more they're rendered conscious, so that they're available for critical reflection – the better for our lives as a whole. It's important to get the human brain to work as well as possible and to be as actively aware of its own workings as possible. So, there's a way of thinking about music which says music is 'transcendent' in a different sense, that it takes us into realms beyond rational understanding or reflective knowledge, and that I think is bad because it's defeatist, it's effectively giving up on the whole enterprise before you've even started. Musical attributes and values are 'transcendent' in the sense 'transcending the limits of individual or idiosyncratic response', rather 'transcending all human grasp'.

***SCA:** I would like to ask you a question based on this quote by Hölderlin: "Man is a god when he dreams, a beggar when he reflects." If you were to make an evaluation between philosophy and poetry within the framework of the quote, what would you like to say?*

CN: It is strange in a way that Hölderlin should have said that because he was a very reflective poet, and he was a philosopher of poetry as well as a practising poet and he brought the two things together and scarcely wrote a line that wasn't deeply pondered and that reflected the intimate relationship he saw between philosophy and poetry. So, a strange quote in many ways, but what he probably meant is that when we philosophize or theorize about poetry, we're beggars in the sense that it's very difficult to bring to conscious reflective knowledge what is more intuitive for the poet. In other words, we're comparatively beggar-like when we try to have a theory of poetry, because as poets or responsive readers of poetry we are pushing ourselves against the grain to understand more than what our intuitive responses tell us. So, we're God-like when we write poetry, or when we read it in a mood or a state of mind maximally receptive to what the poet felt as he wrote it. And this is of course a very central part of the romantic poetic creed especially the German romantic creed. The idea that poetry is a gift – not like a 'talent' or 'genius', not a gift in that sense, but something that is given to you, whether by the muses or by language, the possibilities of language which, as it were play, into your hand. I think it's a strange quote, but I think you can make sense of it in those terms.

SCA: *Does justice have a poetic dimension from your point of view?*

CN: Depends what you mean by 'poetic'. If you take it back to its etymological sources, the word 'poetic', then it has to do with making, creating, shaping and there's an element of that which comes into legal or judicial philosophy, well, into legal judgments. But the analogy can't be pressed too far, I think. I mean there are philosophers of law who say that law is an evolving story and it's a constant series of narrative reinterpretations of previous law. This would apply more to case-law than statute law, for instance, in the American context or the UK context. But that seems to me to go too far. I think there have to be guiding principles of justice which can't be directly analogized with the writing of a poem or the fashioning of a narrative. There's always that danger when you aestheticize ethics – taking philosophy of law to be a branch of ethics or at any rate to involve ethics – a danger that if you aestheticize it too far, then it becomes simply a set of fictions, or simply a performative speech-act, one that responds more or less creatively to other performative actions. So this approach, whether among analytically-trained or continentally-inclined theorists of law, can be highly reductionist in its way and can become a means of evading the ethical issue about what legal principles should be.

SCA: *You also have undertaken significant studies of deconstruction. How do you define deconstruction based on these studies? What do you think is the most essential function of deconstruction?*

CN: I think I'd have to fall back pretty much on Derrida's characterizations and he describes it in very different ways in different contexts depending on the immediate issue. But his basic idea, at least in his early works, is that it involves the very careful close reading of texts trying as far as possible to suspend traditional prejudices. In other words, not taking it for granted that the passages in a text that are often highlighted in orthodox or mainstream interpretations are necessarily the crucial, the most significant or revealing passages. It might well be that there are other, apparently marginal or less important passages like parentheses or footnotes or stray metaphors that the authorized commentators routinely pass over. And those are exactly the things you should be looking at because there may be reasons why they've been kept in the background or pushed into the margins. They may create problems with the main line of argument. They may not be what the writer wanted to say but was forced to say by the logic of his or her argument. So that's a pretty standard definition of deconstruction, but it's as good as any for introductory purposes and covers most of what Derrida does in the major texts of his early-to-middle period. What differs in the later texts, in those short books he wrote later on in his career, is that very often it's single words and concepts that he's deconstructing – words like 'justice', 'hospitality', 'forgiveness', and 'rogue' – whereas in an early, much longer work like *Of Grammatology* what you get is a very close-focus detailed deconstructive reading of how a word like 'supplement' functions across numerous contexts in the texts of a writer like Rousseau. So, there's that change of scale and approach but the basics are still there, I think, early and late.

SCA: *Do you think that Derrida's concept of deconstruction can be seen as a contemporary reading of Plato's ideas of good and justice which cannot be taken as absolute, transcendent or universal values any longer?*

CN: Well, as you know there's that famous (or infamous) statement in the essay 'Force of Law' about laws or legal discourses being eminently deconstructible but justice – the idea or concept of justice – being the one thing lies beyond reach of deconstruction. But of course he engages very early on – in the great essay 'Plato's Pharmacy' as well as other places – with Plato on truth, justice, beauty, all the big Platonic concepts, and hence with all the big unresolved issues around Platonist metaphysics. And then in his later work he returns to those questions, especially the question of justice which preoccupied much of his thinking in the wake of his encounter with Nelson Mandela. Those initial oppositions and concepts are still very much in play. But they take a different form, they tend much more toward a kind of decisionist approach to ethics and questions of justice, the idea that, in the end, we're always going to be dealing with incommensurables, with aporias, if you like, or with strictly irreducible paradoxes. Some of those texts have created problems for his interpreters and given rise to a decisionist conception of ethical choice or commitment with, I think, undesirable consequences, as seen in the current rather modish fascination with the Nazi juridical philosopher Carl Schmitt.

SCA: *The problem with deconstruction is the irreducibility of the other. Indeed, it completely obscures the distinctions between benevolent others and evil others, thus making it impossible to distinguish between good and evil. Do you think this situation that is left ambiguous by deconstruction which aims to be open to the radically "other" actually betrays the other? Is there a way out of this paradox?*

CN: I very often feel there's no way out in the way Derrida frames it in his later work. I think if you go back to his earliest essay on Levinas (well the earliest published or well-known essay 'Violence and Metaphysics'), you'll find that it's often been taken as endorsing the idea of radical otherness – an absolute otherness such that, in principle, we cannot claim to understand or comprehend the other person. That's what you find in Levinas, or at least you find a view that moves very strongly in that direction. But Derrida in 'Violence and Metaphysics' raises very serious questions about the possibility of having an ethics that is grounded in that kind of radical otherness, and this for a very simple reason. I mean, he finds the counter-argument in Husserl whose works he was studying very deeply at that time. He points out that, for Husserl, it cannot be a question of radical otherness: the other has to be an alter ego, has to be another self with equal emphasis on 'self' and 'other'; we can only understand other people's situations, their problems, their perplexities, and their injustices from the point of view of a sympathetic understanding of what it is to be like them. In other words, there's got to be some element of community, of mutual understanding, before the ethical question of responsibility to the other even arises. So, that essay of Derrida, which is very long and very meticulously argued, is in fact a far-reaching critique – not so much 'anti-Levinas' (because he professes great respect for Levinas as he does for everyone whose texts he deconstructs) ... but a critique aiming to show that this emphasis on the extreme singularity of the other, the utter impenetrability of the other from our point of view, goes beyond any humanly comprehensible ethics in its sheer extremity. It doesn't leave room for that necessary first moment of mutual understanding and sympathy that must go toward any kind of ethical judgment or relationship. So in some of my later work on Derrida, I tried to redirect people's attention, the attention of commentators like Simon Critchley, for instance, to that early essay of Derrida on Levinas which I think is a very necessary antidote to some of the later work.

SCA: *Referring to the essay "White Mythology" in one of your works, you express that Derrida is modern rather than postmodern and that deconstruction is more closely related to the issues of epistemology and philosophy of science. To what do you attribute Derrida's being classified under the category of "postmodern" philosophy in this regard?*

CN: I think I will have to be unkind and say I attribute it to readings that are not close, detailed, or rigorous enough. I mean, when you approach a text you judge, or ought to judge, what level of engagement this requires and in Derrida's case it requires very close attention, the kind of attention he gives to the text he reads. And I think a lot of people from the mid-1980s on, people who'd read Lyotard, who'd read Baudrillard, or at any rate read a number of postmodern cultural theorists tended to go off with the idea that Derrida was basically a postmodernist, that basically he was saying there is no truth, everything is textuality, everything is representation, everything is a simulacrum, language (or rhetoric) goes all the way down, etc., very much as in Richard Rorty's neo-pragmatist reading of Derrida. So a kind of neo-pragmatist, all-purpose, anti-disciplinary (or 'post-philosophical') reading. What they missed out were all the elements in Derrida's work that show him to have been, among other things, a thinker of extraordinary analytic powers and well up to stretch on all the aspects of logical discourse – including modal logic, tense-logic, and deviant, non-bivalent or many-classical logic – that engage the interest of analytic philosophers. I mean, he may very well create problems for those not *au fait* with such developments, postmodernists (and some analytic philosophers) among them, but that's no reason for people like John Searle to call him irrational or a muddlehead! His arguments are themselves meticulously logical at a sentence-by-sentence or overall structural level. If you look at the detailed argumentation of *Of Grammatology* or any of the essays in *Margins of Philosophy*, he's doing philosophy in a very traditional, a very recognizable sense and engaging deeply with philosophy of logic.

To be sure, he's talking about – deploying – deviant, non-bivalent, or dialethic (aporetic) logic of a kind that has problematical implications for any proponent of classical true-false logic. Nevertheless, Derrida's arguments are themselves meticulously logical. I think a lot of people relied on second-hand sources, my little 1982 book included, to be honest, because I went in for that sort of reading during the heady days of deconstruction's arrival in this country when there were lots of idols, especially in the sleepy quarters of academic Eng Lit, that cried out for toppling. I won't disown the book – *scripta manent* – but there are lots of things in it that I soon came to think were just plain wrong. So, I think those ideas were floating around, and they received a kind of popular-cultural interpretation which got into the national newspapers and radio programs and the assumption was that deconstruction was just a kind of sub-branch of postmodernism.

SCA: *Again in the same work you remark, "Especially if you look at 'White Mythology,' you will see that he does not say what postmodernism wants him to say, on the contrary, he says the opposite." What do you think is the theme that places Derrida opposite to postmodern philosophy in this study?*

CN: Well again, I think it's a question of readings that didn't go far enough. In this case they didn't go far enough into the essay, which is, admittedly, a long one! But the first part of it says pretty much what the post-modernizers are saying about metaphor, following Nietzsche or at any rate following one line of Nietzschean thought: that everything is metaphor, you know, that truth is a metaphor, that metaphor is a metaphor (from 'carrying over' from one context to another), so that you can do a kind of wholesale Nietzschean job on the concept of metaphor. Thus 'concept' is a metaphor from grasping-together, as in the idea of grasping-together, or comprehension. So that's what you get in the first 20 pages or so of 'White Mythology'. But then, beyond that, Derrida turns right around and says 'but we can't leave it there'. He says we have to recognize that, if we just say in a kind of breezy way, 'everything is metaphor', then we don't recognize that the concept of metaphor is itself a philosophical concept and it's one that has been worked over and reformulated and refined and developed and applied in various ways by philosophers as well as by rhetoricians and literary critics over the centuries. And he says it has to be thought through very carefully, so he spends the rest of the essay, 80-or-so pages of it, unpacking the conceptual resources available within definitions of metaphor and pointing out the problems with various traditional definitions from Aristotle down through the Medieval and Renaissance traditions to the present, to present-day philosophers of science like Bachelard and Canghuilhem.

It's a very analytic, very closely and carefully worked-over essay, but I think people have been misled partly by the first 20 pages and also by the way that he occasionally goes into what one can only call poetic prose where he exploits in a performative way the suggestive powers that metaphor exerts on the discourse of philosophers and theorists of metaphor. And I think they've taken that to finally confirm what they thought about the first part of the essay, that Derrida is somehow performatively demonstrating – like Nietzsche before him – that everything is metaphor when you come down to it. I spent quite a lot of time trying to get analytic philosophers, especially philosophers of logic, interested in Derrida. Some of my writing got into fairly complicated technical areas of modal logic where I showed that his logics of supplementarity, differ*a*nce, the parergon, and so forth, were valuable and far-reaching contributions to philosophy of logic which they'd find both challenging and highly productive. I still think that was worth doing, if only to make the point that Derrida is not saying what so many commentators make him out to be saying.

SCA: *Do you think we need a convergence or correlation between "analytic" philosophy and "continental" philosophy? If so, why is that the case?*

CN: Well, in the simplest terms, because they're like two ships in the night, you know, passing by each other without even noticing but partly because some continental philosophers do need a bit more grounding in typically analytic subject-areas like philosophy of logic, philosophy of language and epistemology. I mean there's room for a great deal of mutually beneficial exchange on both sides. Analytic philosophy has become an extremely specialized, highly self-insulated group of philosophers talking only to themselves on rather trivial topics. Of course this doesn't apply to all of them. I mean, there are some analytic philosophers, the more open-minded of them, people like Adrian Moore and Simon Glendinning, who are doing really valuable work, often under the aegis of metaphysics because that gives them something to work with in an area which is recognizably central to both traditions – that's to say, it keys into analytic concerns but also means they can talk about Deleuze for instance, or

Derrida, if they want to, or even talk about Foucault under the capacious heading of metaphysics. I think some of those more adventurous souls are doing very useful work here.

So the benefit to analytic philosophy would be more speculative freedoms of the kind that a postmodernist philosopher like Richard Rorty claimed to bring, but then threw away because he said, in effect, let's dump all that technical stuff that we called 'philosophy' and make it more like literary criticism, cultural criticism, poetry, or something. Let's make it more liberal, creative and free-ranging, he urged, but on his view that meant pretty much giving up philosophy *tout court*. The result would be the kind of wholesale anti-realism and 'strong' linguistic constructivism that counted truth and knowledge concepts best dumped in the rush for new inventive horizons. And of course this fitted in with 'continentally' inspired movements of thought like post-structuralism and postmodernism. Hence all the excitement – and the frisson of scandal – around the emergence of so-called speculative realism in Quentin Meillassoux's 2009 book *After Finitude*. Thus you find continental philosophers and people who call themselves continental philosophers in Britain and the US getting very worked up because here, all of a sudden, you have this strange beast slouching towards Paris to be born – a continental realism, of all things, and the odd thing is their not seeming to realize that there's a lot of really useful realist philosophy of science and epistemology on the analytic side, really refined and sophisticated work. So they all say my goodness, there's objects out there, not just mental constructions or linguistic constructions or textual constructions – we can actually believe in objects again!

***SCA:** Derrida asserts that deconstruction can be deconstructed, because it enters the academic repertoire. What do you think about this remark? Should deconstruction be deconstructed now? If you were to deconstruct deconstruction, how would you do so?*

CN: Well, its procedures can be criticized and refined, and certain readings can be faulted on certain details. I take issue with some of Derrida's later work, in particular with his decisionist stance with regard to ethics, as I mentioned earlier .... Years ago there was quite a craze for deconstructing deconstructors, not the kinds of downright hostile attack which very often came from ill-informed quarters, but attempts to up the ante by going even further in a deconstructive direction. I suppose the most striking example is the whole debate around 'The Purloined Letter', you know, the Edgar Allan short story, Lacan's psychoanalytic account, then Derrida's deconstructive reading of that, then the essays by Barbara Johnson and others, so it all became a question of who is the most truly, rigorously textualist deconstructor. This debate led on to some really brilliant work, for instance Shoshana Felman's essay on Henry James and her later book on J.L. Austin and Emile Benveniste. But it was a kind of ultra-purist exercise in going one better, going one step further than the previous reading. Quite apart from deconstructing deconstruction, you can criticize deconstruction or you can point out problems that have been artificially induced, as for instance – to make the point again – by taking a view of ethics where it's either conceived as a system of rules, constraints, directives and maxims or whatever, or it's conceived as infinitely open-ended, undecidable, aporetic, and so forth. I think that's very much the kind of pseudo-dilemma that tends to capture ingenious minds with a taste for paradox but which doesn't have any useful application in ethics or in jurisprudence.

SCA: *Starting from Levinas, you state that ethics now invalidates the epistemological project conceived as a search for grounds of certainty, knowledge or truth. In this context, you express the view that our epistemological assurances are shaken in the encounter with the face of the absolute other. Do you think our understanding of ethics has outstripped our understanding of epistemology or has ethics made the understanding of epistemology obsolete? In other words, should epistemology be silent when it comes to ethics? Is it possible to imagine a situation where ethics is linked with epistemology?*

CN: No, you've got me quite wrong there. In my early work I made it clear that I took very seriously Derrida's criticisms of Levinas in his essay 'Violence and Metaphysics', reprinted in the book *Writing and Difference*. Derrida is immensely civilized and generous in his treatment of Levinas, as always, but he does bring out the impossibility of an ethics that would so totally reject the ethical salience of shared humanity, or empathy, or the other as in some sense an *alter ego*, and instead regard the other as absolutely, utterly, incommunicably other. I'm referring to the last part of your question: is it possible for there to be a situation in which ethics and epistemology come together? I would hope so in the sense, quite simply, that we can't make informed ethical judgments in specific cases, perhaps really vital decisions in our own lives or in the sphere of politics, without evidence and without assessing the situation or without taking realistic account of people's motivations along with their needs and their aspirations. Ethical decisions have to be well-informed, they don't take place in some Empyrean of pure thought. In that little book on deconstruction I do try to direct people back to Derrida's early essay on Levinas which doesn't actually talk about epistemology – Derrida very rarely uses that term, and mostly in the context of talking about Bachelard who was, among other things, an epistemologist of science and scientific concept-formation. But I've been saying for quite some time that we should take epistemology in the broadest sense, not as a specialized academic discipline but as the question of how we get to know things, how much we can know, what are the scope and limits of human knowledge, all of which have their place in any account of ethical conduct or reckoning. I think there we'd much better keep ethics in touch with epistemology in that broad sense which is exactly what Derrida is doing in the early essay – he's professing great admiration for Levinas up to a point and he's saying, again up to a point, that we have to allow for maximal possible differences between human beings in order to respect their differing personal, cultural, and ethical priorities. But he's also saying that in order to do that we have to understand those priorities and those other, even if for us difficult-to-access belief systems. You can't decouple a decent respect for their alterity, their otherness, from the simple necessity that we have to do our very best to understand other people before we can even start to make informed allowance for their differences. So, epistemology in the broad sense comes in at a very early stage and never drops out altogether, I would say so.

SCA: *Do we need to have the knowledge of good and bad or right and wrong in order to be ethical towards the other?*

CN: Yes I think we do and the knowledge comes from all sorts of things; most crucially from personal experience in dealing with other people, whether those dealings go well or badly. It also comes from comes from broader contexts of historical knowledge, from ethical reflection on hugely challenging issues like war-crimes and atrocities, for instance, events that have generated much ethical discussion and continue to divide historians and partisans of various persuasion. Of course such knowledge – or such understanding – doesn't require an advanced education in philosophy but is possible for any reasonably well-informed and judicious individual. They will need to have that background of reflectively processed and critically examined knowledge if they're to arrive at responsible judgments, rather like a lawyer who specializes in case law – they have to know a lot a lot of very detailed case-histories in order to apply them. And the more they know the stronger their arguments and the better supported their judgments are likely to be.

SCA: *Taking into account the criticisms of Derrida, Levinas, and other thinkers towards metaphysical thought and their claim that this way of thinking leads to domination by reducing difference to the same, do you think it is possible to read the metaphysical way of thinking as a philosophy of injustice?*

CN: No, not without deep reservations. I think it has done a lot of harm and created much confusion, the way that the word 'metaphysics' has been used not only by continental philosophers in the last century, right up to now in fact, but also by analytic philosophers from the 1920s on. This is a problem with how Heidegger uses the word metaphysics, and also the way that – not Derrida, but many disciples of Derrida often use in a sweeping, indiscriminate and unself-critical manner. It's taken to be more or less synonymous with 'illusion', or to carry a charge of naive complicity with the Western logocentric tradition of thought – 'from Plato to Nato', as Terry Eagleton once put it – so it's taken as being an insult, or highly pejorative, to call someone's thinking 'metaphysical', and you find the same thing among Vienna Circle philosophers in the 1920s and '30s, denouncing Heidegger among others for doing 'metaphysics' or being 'metaphysical'. One might want to take issue with Heidegger – God knows there's reason enough for that! – and still recognize that that metaphysics is an absolutely essential, inbuilt component of human thinking. We categorize things, we observe the world, we interpret our own experiences, we sort our memories, we make predictions, we arrive at historical judgments in terms of metaphysical frameworks and conceptions. So, it's not some lamentable defect of thinking, some lapse into an age-old error that we should have left behind with the infancy of thought. Metaphysics is simply part of the way we make sense of things as soon as we go beyond appearances and ask how those appearances hook up together. So it shouldn't become, as unfortunately it has, a routine term of abuse, contempt or suspicion. To be sure, it is always possible that some text or line of argument may turn out to have bought into misleading metaphysical commitments, or to exhibit metaphysical assumptions that don't hold up under critical scrutiny. Derrida is notably acute in pointing these out, as indeed are many analytic philosophers, from Gilbert Ryle to Timothy Williamson. Metaphysics has long been regarded with a degree of cautionary skepticism and that's all to the good. The way that certain metaphysical categories are applied as covert justification for certain racial stereotypes – that would be one such example. There's a kind of metaphysics at work here, a malevolent and nasty metaphysics, and deconstruction is one name for the kind of thinking required to show up its errors and confusions.

***SCA:** Do you agree with Derrida's remark that the history of the logos is the history of oppression and domination?*

CN: It strikes me that many of those very generalized statements of Derrida can be taken in two ways that it's often important to distinguish. I mean the word 'domination' suggests something violently exclusive or something deeply prejudicial to the point where violence may be just around the corner. In that sense I think it's too sweeping. I mean, this happens to all sorts of terms in philosophy – as soon as they're raised into fighting or rallying calls, then they become potentially oppressive. So, for instance, a lot of the debate about truth from post-structuralism on was premised on the idea that truth, or truth-talk, is always intrinsically oppressive, coercive, or just a form of rhetorical bullying by those with the power to enforce their views. No doubt if people claim to have the truth and they promote their beliefs in such a way as to silence other people with opposite views then certainly that's an abuse of the notion of truth.

But the case is quite different with truth conceived as an object of inquiry, as a desirable end-point to the quest for knowledge, or as what provides the needful incentive to an open-minded search for better, more accurate or more reliable ways of understanding. It may sometimes be necessary in the interests of truth and justice to point out what you take to be errors in other people's way of thinking since otherwise you simply wouldn't have, for instance, any grounds for criticism of or resistance to unjust political regimes. This is what results, or would result, if you took the Lyotard view that truth regimes or regimens are incommensurable and therefore that whenever we claim to perceive a fault or an omission or injustice in someone else's worldview we are doing them an injustice or oppressing them because we are not sufficiently sympathetic or responsive to that worldview. In effect we are denying ourselves the very possibility of criticism and we're denying them the chance to engage in any kind of productive ethical, political, or inter-cultural debate. So, I think that with many of those discussions around post-modernism people tended to confuse the 'good' concept of truth that entails patient, non-dogmatic, open-minded inquiry fully cognizant of the ever-present possibility of conflicting views with the 'bad' concept that adopts a coercive, authoritarian, or monological view.

***SCA:** According to Lyotard, the question of justice cannot be separated from the question of criteria. Lyotard says, "We are always in a situation without criteria, but we have to make a decision." What are your thoughts on this relationship? In other words, how can we establish a relationship between decision-making and justice in situations without criteria?*

CN: There are no situations without criteria, I think. There are situations in which there are multiple kinds or orders of criteria in play and those are the situations that require to think hard about them and find our way forward with the utmost care. Also there are extreme situations where the divergent views are so polarized that there is little if any common ground between the parties in dispute. These are situations that can be described as metaphysically laden in the sense that the disagreements involved are themselves metaphysical. The debate about abortion is one such case because if you are a Catholic, taking the doctrines of Catholicism to constitute one set of criteria, then you will believe in the existence of the soul, you will believe that it comes into existence at the very moment of conception, and you will consequently believe that to destroy it at any point whether sentient or not is absolutely wrong and you would understandably find it intolerable to think of abortion. If you're pro-life and you reject that belief then you may – very likely will – reject any belief in the soul too. You'll tend to think, well, we have minds, we have personalities, we have characters, traits, dispositions, we have all those things about us that make us who we are, but we don't have souls. And if you get two utterly conflicting views like that then you're in a situation that's in some sense 'without criteria'. But I think there are very few situations of such an intransigent kind and that's the reason why that debate is so fiercely partisan whereas in just about every other kind of disagreement that human beings have within or across cultures there are shared criteria which can be brought out and taken as a starting-point for more constructive discussion. Of course those criteria may be far from self-evident and then the pressing need is to feel your way very carefully around all the underlying conflicts and get a better, more inclusive and, hopefully, tolerant sense of just what's involved. So I think Lyotard habitually goes for the extreme case where there is a downright irreconcilable clash of divergent criteria, then generalizes that case and calls it 'the post-modern condition' and tries to persuade us that we are in it whether we like it or not. Well, we're not – or not unless we perversely will ourselves into it – and we'll do much better if we can get our minds to work a bit harder on ethical problems and not throw up our hands in postmodernist fashion when things get messy or complicated. I have the same problem, as I mentioned before, with those symptoms of zealous aporia-hunting in some of Derrida's late, excessively decisionist essays on justice.

SCA: *If our criteria are facing a crisis, then is it possible to move from the right to the just?*

CN: I think it is possible, all the more so since I don't think the 'crisis' is anything like as deep or historically unique as you and other postmodernists believe! But we shouldn't want to conceive 'the right' as anything absolute or 'the just' as anything that somehow transcends particular processes of ethical thought or moral-evaluative judgement. We're never going to achieve a perfectly rightful or righteous order, whether in the spheres of personal, social, or political conduct. After all, Derrida is the first to concede that there is, and must always be, that distinction between absolute and particular, localized, situation-specific, or practically attainable orders of justice. I think that's where he differs crucially from Lyotard, another difference between deconstruction and post-modernism, if you take Lyotard to be a representative figure of post-modernism. That's precisely Derrida's point about the difference between law and justice, as it is in those later books about the distinction as it operates in the instances of hospitality, forgiveness, the gift, and so forth. You can deconstruct the law, you can take individual items of case law, or individual statutes, and of course American critical legal theorists have been doing just that for a long time now and showing that they are always to some extent compromised, prejudiced, based on very partially informed juridical viewpoints.

SCA: *Lyotard rejects any attempt to express the horror of the Holocaust, as such an attempt would undermine the uniqueness of the Holocaust by comparing it* *with other genocides and atrocities in history. Therefore, no analysis of the memory of the Holocaust is possible for Lyotard and other skeptics. Only what cannot be remembered is just. My question is the following: If representation reduces the horror of Auschwitz, as Lyotard argues, then perhaps we would take a more detrimental path with the rejection of representation. In this context, can we say that what is fair is not what is unrepresentable, incomparable and indeterminable, but rather an area of representation that preserves their differences? How would you define justice from your perspective?*

CN: First, I want to say that it seems wrong and perverse to say that we ought not to want to represent terrible or (in the moral sense) unspeakable events whether in graphic images, cinematic images, or descriptive-narrative-documentary accounts. I think on the contrary it's very important to convey at least something of the full horror of what occurred and try our utmost to represent the ultimately unrepresentable. It may and should strike us as morally inconceivable that human beings have done such monstrously wicked things to other human beings. We should register that there is indeed something obscene about trying to bring those horrors home to the consciousness or imagination of successive generations by means of graphic or verbal representation. But that doesn't mean that we should wholly turn away from it and not talk about it, not attempt to form an adequate conception of the suffering and the scale of the suffering. That can only be a tactic of evasion, of refusing to face up to the enormity of what was done and what it requires us to grasp about the human potential for cruelty and evil. We need to represent it as vividly as possible and I take it that's what people are trying to do when they constantly draw our mind back to it, when the Jewish survivors say don't forget about it, tell them in the schools, tell them everywhere so they don't forget. At the same time we have to remind them there have been other monstrous happenings – other outbreaks of exterminist terror – which we may not wish to compare with the Holocaust but which we have to keep firmly in mind if we're not to lose our sense of this constant human capacity for behaving in the most appalling ways toward other human beings. We do sometimes need to document, describe, narrate, discuss and represent it, and so I here again I deeply disagree with Lyotard.

SCA: *According to Foucault, the claims of universal knowledge and absolute truth are based on exclusions and hence result in the exclusion of the other. Such claims have brought along cruelty and violence. Foucault suggests that the ideal of a paradise where everything will be known has ignored the other and has been unjust. In this respect, how would you evaluate the relationship that Foucault established between knowledge-violence and justice?*

CN: Foucault did some wonderful work in reminding us of the enormous variety of human thought-systems, knowledges, discourses, epistemes, and orders of representation. I can remember being absolutely bowled over by his great book *Les mots et les choses* (*The Order of Things*) when it first appeared, as likewise by his more area-specific studies *The Birth of the Clinic, Madness and Civilization, Discipline and Punish*, and his multi-volume *The History of Sexuality*. Foucault did some hugely valuable work in coaxing us away from our culturally and historically parochial habits of belief, our common-sense ways of thinking, as in the famous passage in his Foreword to *Les mots et les choses* where he talks about Borges' fictive Chinese Encyclopedia where the animals are classified in terms such as 'drawn with a very fine hair camel brush', or 'having just knocked over the water pitcher' or 'belonging to the Emperor', or 'not included in this present classification'. The point of the exercise, he says, is to make us feel the sheer impossibility, for us, of actually thinking *that*. He was a wonderfully inventive thinker, a great delver into out-of-the-way archives, and he opened up areas of investigation that set any number of highly productive research agendas. But he also showed that fairly typical sort of 20th century French tendency to push things a bit too far, to offer sweeping generalizations and say *of course* systems of knowledge mutate so radically that no continuity is possible between them; *of course* thought-systems are totally opaque to one another; *of course* there is no making sense of talk about 'progress' from one conceptual scheme to the next. To which one wants to reply: well, Foucault, in that case you're doing a remarkably good job of describing and explaining them to us total outsiders! But you get that same leap to an unworkable or self-refuting doctrine of far-gone cultural-linguistic relativism in 'analytic' thinkers like Donald Davidson and Thomas Kuhn, the philosopher-historian of science, so Foucault's not alone on his particular limb.

***SCA:** We need to know the truth in order to be just, because decisions based on false information and judgment cannot be fair. In this case, what is the difference between the necessity of knowledge to be just and the understanding of knowledge that leads to injustice? Is it ever possible to get rid of this paradox?*

CN: It's a difference I suppose in level of self-critical awareness and the one thing you have to be aware of is the ever-present possibility of prejudice in one's own views. I mean, one of the standard conservative lines of attack against liberalism is that self-styled liberals have always been highly partial in their understanding of it – you know, it was quite possible for a liberal like Jefferson, one of the 'founding fathers' of American democracy, to be perfectly happy with the existence of slavery – they just didn't perceive that there were gaps, conflicts, tensions, or flat contradictions between abstract precept and everyday practice or belief. 'All men are equal', but that excluded slaves, just as for nineteenth-century British liberals like J.S. Mill everyone should have the vote and a democratic say in things, though that excluded women, and so on with multiple other instances of 'liberalism' narrowly, selectively, or self-interestedly defined. You can certainly hammer home that point about historically- or no doubt presently-existing liberalism. But as a general outlook or mindset it is also capable, later on, of perceiving those ideological blind-spots – those suddenly visible exceptions or exclusions – and moving on to some different, more capacious or less prejudicial view of things, even if you'll never reach the ideal that liberals have always, however incompletely or lopsidedly, envisaged. And I think that's a weakness of postmodernist thinking: that it makes a valid observation about the prejudices, blind-spots, and hypocrisies of existing thought-systems and then draws the highly premature conclusion that somehow we should never take any step beyond its own kind of far-gone cultural pluralism or relativism. After the demise of all those 'grand narratives' like Marxism, Liberalism, or philosophical (Kantian) modernity we are left with only 'postmodern pragmatist first-order' narratives by which to make sense of history, politics, science, and everything else. Because otherwise – as this (please note) rather grandiose narrative goes – we will always be overstepping the mark and imposing our beliefs on others if we don't judge them by their own criteria, which we can't do for the usual postmodern-pragmatist reasons. And this would mean that thirty years ago when we talked about South African politics we'd have had to recognize that white South Africans had their own view and it upheld the status quo – the existence of gross racial inequality – as legitimate and indeed an ethico-political necessity. It is a thoroughly wrongheaded and pernicious doctrine which leads to some absurd conclusions, though again you can find plenty of analogues in the thinking of 'analytic' philosophers influenced by Wittgenstein with his notion of 'language-games' and cultural 'forms of life'.

***SCA:** I would like to address the paradox between justice and violence. When a person imposes his rights on the other in the name of justice, he inflicts violence on the other. However, if the person renounces his rights to be fair to the other, he inflicts violence on himself. In this situation, can we say that justice or the pursuit of justice leads to violence inevitably?*

CN: It would be a sad conclusion if that was the case. But I don't think for a moment that we're forced into that kind of plainly absurd double-bind. It would amount not only to a way of inflicting violence on the person, usually from a dominant culture, who takes that view but also to inflicting an even worse violence on the other, mostly disadvantaged, person because it's placing them, knowingly or not, in position where they are likewise not entitled to raise objections when their views, interests, or beliefs are set aside as beyond comprehension from the dominant viewpoint. I have argued this case at great length in many books and essays. It is one of the big problems with Richard Rorty's version of post-modern pragmatism, his idea that we must never extend our interpretations to other cultures or belief-systems since we will thereby be doing them an injustice, a version of Lyotard's argument in his book *The Differend: phrases in dispute*. Yet he also says that *speaking as a twentieth-century American liberal* he thinks on balance that those are the best views, that he goes along with them and thinks that, on balance, it would be a good thing if everyone everywhere went along with them. But of course this would mean that you'll just have to put up with it if you're not a well-placed US liberal ('liberal' in the US sense) professor and you have no choice in how the US bullies its way around the world and bombs your country and uses the CIA to overthrow democratically elected governments. Because you belong to your own culture you can't justifiably criticize, resist or condemn the culture that's oppressing you, not in any way they could possibly understand, just as the oppressors can't get outside their own belief-set. So Rorty, speaking as a citizen of the US, this globally dominant (for now!) culture, can't be expected to re-examine or criticize his own self-disabling neo-pragmatist views. It's losers all round and a dire prognosis for the chances of human survival.

SCA: *Could you share your opinion about the recent refugee problems across the world within the context of Derrida's unconditional hospitality?*

CN: Yes, he takes these two conceptions or ideas of hospitality, one of which is unlimited, non-provisional, absolute and unqualified while the other is the practicable one, restricted to specific situations and taking account of reservations, special clauses, limits of applicability, and so on. At times the most important thing is to emphasize the unconditional, and actually I noticed just today in my email inbox that several of the charities working for refugees and asylum-seekers are saying exactly that in response to the UK government's very wicked current policy of packing refugees off to Rwanda. They, the charities, are going all out for the unlimited admission of asylum-seekers and refugees, enshrining it amongst the most basic principles, this idea that it should not – must not – be restricted. So they're coming down very firmly on the absolute side of Derrida's binary, where the other conception, the 'practical' side of it, would be a matter of ensuring the numbers don't exceed safe limits in terms of transportation, you know, properly equipped boats and vehicles, and then making sure they've got decent homes to go to over here until their cases are settled. At the moment things have become so brutal in this country that Derrida's text is very timely because he does make this very strong point; he's not dismissing the restricted idea of hospitality because we have to acknowledge that there are wise, humane, generous and refugee-friendly ways of applying certain needful practical restrictions. But they had better be geared toward the safety, well-being and safe arrival of the refugees than toward Home-Office requirements, premised as they are on narrowly legalistic precepts or downright refugee-hostile rules and regulations. These are often just a way of wasting time and preventing or discouraging applications for refugee status. So I think ethically there is no doubt about it: we need a massive swing, a massive correction of the current highly restrictive conception and a swing toward the idea of absolute unlimited hospitality.

SCA: *Do you think it is a paradox of human beings developing concepts like justice and good which were once seen as the ultimate ethical foundations based on ambiguous concepts such as groundlessness, uncertainty, and undecidability? Can we argue that this paradox is the very basis of justice?*

CN: Yes, at least in the sense that it is always good to examine our prejudices, to keep in mind, if you like, a Derridean notion of the sometimes vertiginous character of ethical choice, the element of 'ungrounded' decision. It's good because otherwise we may tend to be dogmatic, inflexible and simply unimaginative – not trying hard enough to stretch our minds around the variety of situations that people are placed in and the variety of interests, values, or principles that enter their ethical reasonings. Where it can become harmful, or become a real distraction, is when we're too insistent on the *absolute* ungroundedness, or the *absolute* undecidability, or the *absolute* aporia of justice. I think this applies to decisionist concepts of justice in whatever ethical, socio-cultural, political or wider philosophical context. I was rather disturbed around the time I retired from university teaching about how interested my graduate students were in figures like Carl Schmitt since one straightforward fact about Carl Schmitt is that he was a Nazi jurist; he was the philosophical lawyer-in-chief, in a sense, of Nazism, his decisionism had a hefty influence in Germany at that time and has continued to exert a strong appeal for far-right philosophers, especially in the US. And what fascinated those thinkers then and now was this element of decisionism, the idea of a moment of suspended judgment when no amount of evidence, no amount of reasoning, no amount of reflection on precepts, precedents, case-histories, contexts, relevant analogues, or whatever, could have any bearing because you have to decide for yourself without such non-ethical resources. That is, 'non-ethical' only if you start out from the dubious proposition that in order to count as really, authentically ethical choices must be made, as it were, on the spur of the moment, or out of the blue. Maybe that's what certain decisions feel like at the very instant of making them, maybe the process is too complex to be followed at the time or grasped soon afterwards, but it shouldn't be treated as beyond all hope of figuring out in the long run. It's like what the lawyers call 'hard cases' – cases where judgments are hard to arrive at and may not be a good 'fit' for any statute or case-law precedent but where they do eventually get decided and it's then open to debate whether that decision was a good, fair, or justified one. In ethics it involves a complicated churning of facts, details, principles, moral theories, analogues, unlooked-for complications, etc. – yes, it's difficult to unpack everything that goes into an ethical judgment, but it's not impossible and what feels at the time like a snap decision can afterwards be traced back to a host of ethically pertinent factors. If you later come to think you made a wrong decision then it's matter of acknowledging what you missed out in the process of reflection. So it is best not to raise ethics into a total mystery and it's best not to push it toward any kind of Schmittian decisionist outlook. Because you're in very dubious company if your thinking goes that way.

SCA: *At this point in the debate on justice, it seems that justice is merely an ideal and injustice is a reality. For this reason, can we say that the best way to achieve justice is to define injustice and eliminate the cases of injustice instead of developing theories of justice?*

CN: I have never fully understood Derrida's reasons for refusing to think of these themes of his like justice, hospitality and forgiveness as Kantian ideas of reason I can sort-of see why he does so because there's something free-floating, thin and insubstantial about Kant's ideas of pure reason and Derrida doesn't want to invite that charge and he also wants to keep his distance from that particular enlightenment discourse which he sees as representing certain ideals that have been badly compromised even though their conservation is vital to the discourse of enlightened modernity. (This issue is at the heart of his protracted critical engagement with the philosophy of Jürgen Habermas.) So he wants to avoid being too Kantian but at times what he's envisaging is something very like an idea of reason, something that Kant might say about democracy, about cosmopolitanism, or about the idea of universal peace. Like Kant he knows that such ideas/ideals can never be achieved, not punctually realized or brought to fulfillment – they are ideas that haunt us since still very far from attainment, though without being haunted by them we will never gain any conception of how to improve our present, highly imperfect states of justice. But they have to have a certain substance, have to be defined in terms that we can at least construe for ourselves and represent to others as a genuine, discernible improvement on the current situation. And God knows the current situation is so bad that it doesn't take a superhuman effort of thought to conceive ways in which it can be vastly improved. But those ways have to be spelled out and they have to be checked back against existing realities and subject to the kind of jointly diagnostic, critical and speculative treatment that Derrida at his best so strikingly provides and that postmodernism, in most of its forms, just as strikingly doesn't.

Suggested Readings

Christopher Norris, *Deconstruction and the 'Unfinished Project of Modernity'*, UK: Routledge, 2020.

Christopher Norris, *The Truth about Postmodernism*; USA: Wiley-Blackwell, 1993.

Christopher Norris, *Epistemology; Key Concept in Philosophy*, UK: Bloomsbury, 2005.

Christopher Norris, *Deconstruction; Theory and Practice*, UK: Routledge, 2003.

Christopher Norris, *Philosophy Outside-In; A Critique of Academic Reason*, UK: Edinburgh University Press, 2013.

Christopher Norris, *Truth Matters; Realism, Anti-Realism and Response-Dependence*, UK: Edinburgh University Press, 2005.

Christopher Norris, *The Contest of Faculties; Philosophy and Theory after Deconstruction*, UK: Routledge, 2009.

Christopher Norris, *Derrida*, USA: Harvard University Press, 1987.

Christopher Norris, *The Deconstructive Turn; Essays in the Rhetoric of Philosophy*, 1984.

CHAPTER 6

Democracy and Justice: Samir Haddad

Samir Haddad is an American philosopher with a primary focus on ethics, political theory, and the philosophy of friendship, especially as they relate to Derridean deconstruction. Haddad's work examines the issues of friendship, particularly in terms of loyalty, difference, and ethical responsibility within social and political structures. Building on Derrida's idea of friendship, Haddad's philosophy suggests that true friendship necessitates an openness to difference, resisting simplistic views of identity and solidarity.

In his book, Derrida and the Inheritance of Democracy (2013), Haddad explores the political dimensions of Derrida's thought, especially the philosopher's concept of "inheritance." According to Haddad, inheritance in Derrida's philosophy refers to the ideas, values, and institutions passed down from generation to generation, requiring critical engagement rather than passive acceptance. Haddad argues that this inherited legacy of democracy is fragile and demands constant renewal through reflection and action, underscoring the ethical responsibility individuals bear toward democratic institutions. Haddad's philosophy is distinguished by its commitment to ethical responsibility, particularly regarding the legacies we inherit and pass on. He advocates for a kind of democratic citizenship that is active, questioning, and always in dialogue with others. His work on friendship and democracy speaks to the need for a society built on principles of respect, empathy, and shared responsibility, challenging us to rethink the ethical and political foundations of our lives.

Haddad's book Derrida and the Inheritance of Democracy investigates the relationship between friendship and democratic values, proposing that democracy itself can be seen as a form of ethical friendship. He suggests that democratic communities should embody the values of openness and mutual respect, where individuals engage with each other's perspectives in a manner that resists domination. This vision of democracy emphasizes that ethical and political bonds must be built on respect for diversity, allowing for a constantly evolving, inclusive political landscape.

In addition to his works on Derrida, Haddad has contributed extensively to the philosophy of education, emphasizing the role of teaching in fostering critical and independent thought. His essays discuss how educators can encourage students to question inherited norms and engage in philosophical

 | DOI:10.1163/9789004732902_008

inquiry that challenges societal assumptions. This aligns with his broader philosophical project, which calls for a reflective and self-critical stance toward established structures of knowledge and power.

Sema Cevirici Atilla* [*SCA*]: *In some of your works, you have drawn attention to the concepts of democracy and inheritance in Derrida. First, I would like to ask you what motivated you to work on the concept of inheritance.

Samir Haddad [SH]: My interest in inheritance began in my doctoral research. I had originally wanted to write a dissertation on the relationship between time and politics in Derrida's work. But this is a huge topic to take on – time and politics are each very broad categories – so by focusing on a particular temporal concept, namely inheritance, and a particular political concept, democracy, I was able to make my research more manageable. But as for why I chose those particular concepts and their relation, and not others, I was really led by the work itself. At the time I started my PhD studies, in 1999, three of Derrida's most prominent political texts were *Specters of Marx*, *Politics of Friendship*, and "Force of Law." Inheritance is subject to an explicit and lengthy theorization by Derrida in *Specters of Marx*, and it seemed to me that any substantial engagement with that book needed to take on the concept of inheritance to really understand the claims being made. In *Politics of Friendship* inheritance itself doesn't receive that kind of direct attention, but the book itself is an immense, complicated act of inheritance, at the same time as it traces the inheritance by others of its guiding phrase, attributed to Aristotle – "O my friends, there is no friend." And when I started to look more closely at "Force of Law," I saw that here too inheritance was doing important work, even though this wasn't immediately apparent.

So I started to investigate inheritance in Derrida's political writings, and in 2002 I was lucky to read a draft version of Derrida's essay "The Reason of the Strongest (Are there Rogue States)?" in Samuel Weber's seminar, before it was published in *Rogues* in 2003. I say I was lucky because I had by that time started working on my dissertation, and because I was already thinking along these lines, the connection in that text between inheritance and democracy to come seemed very clear, and worth exploring further. So this became the central focus of my dissertation, which also engaged Hannah Arendt's work on similar questions. Several years after defending my dissertation, after a lot of revisions (removing the engagement with Arendt's work, and greatly expanding the reading of Derrida), this work was published as *Derrida and the Inheritance of Democracy*.

But taking a step back, I'd also say that I've long been interested in questions of method in philosophy, and while there are reasons not to describe deconstruction as a method per se, it's certainly the case that inheritance is key in understanding how deconstruction takes place in Derrida's writings. So to understand Derrida we need to understand how inheritance works. Of course I'm not the first to note this – Geoffrey Bennington often foregrounds the notion of inheritance in his readings of Derrida, and Michael Naas's *Taking on the Tradition*, from 2003, also places this at the center of Derrida's work. Similarly with Matthias Fritsch's *The Promise of Memory* from 2005. So I've been able to benefit and learn from a lot of really fine work done by others on what inheritance means for Derrida, how it relates both to his work as a whole and his approach to doing philosophy, as well as its relation to political questions.

SCA: *There is an element in the nature of democracy that can put itself at risk which Derrida explains as the concept of autoimmunity. He emphasizes that the process of autoimmunity is not external to democracy and that there is nothing unfortunate that interrupts its development. What do you think about the autoimmune structure of democracy in this sense?*

SH: I think autoimmunity is a very helpful way to think about the self-undermining feature of democracy that you mention, which is central to Derrida's analysis. Broadly speaking, autoimmunity defines a process by which a body's defense systems misidentifies parts of itself as foreign, and attacks these parts. This is helpful because it reminds us that the threats to democracy are not always external – something that we do not always acknowledge when we champion democracy – and that the pursuit of democracy can have undesirable outcomes that damage it, because of features of democracy itself. On the other hand, I also think that autoimmunity poses a particular challenge to our ability to theorize democracy, since, when we start to think it through, autoimmunity also undermines a coherent understanding of the self. We presuppose that there is a kind of "self" to democracy, a coherent thing called "democracy" that we can talk about and examine in order to get our analysis underway. I presuppose this in my work and you've presupposed it in your question. But, as Derrida argues in "The Reason of the Strongest," autoimmunity also challenges the very idea of the self. So if the very notion of the self is challenged by autoimmunity, then making autoimmunity central to our analysis we seem to be calling into question the very presupposition that makes our analysis possible. I myself haven't quite worked out what to say in the face of this challenge. I don't think it means we should abandon talk of autoimmunity in democracy, but that we need to think further on this structure that has implications for the democratic theories we develop and promote.

SCA: *Do you think this autoimmune structure gives life to the democracy to come?*

SH: I wouldn't quite put it this way, since it implies that autoimmunity is somehow a cause of democracy to come. Autoimmunity is certainly a feature of democracy to come, and this is inescapable, for better or worse. I'm also not sure that democracy to come is something that "has life," or can be "given life." Is democracy to come something that could ever be "alive"? I have used the vocabulary of life in the past in this context, and the biological associations of autoimmunity encourage this. But at the same time, we can also recall that "immunity" was originally a political term, before it was transferred to biology in this way. And in English at least, the "auto" of "autoimmunity" carries connotations of the mechanical. If I was to pursue this analysis today I would be inclined to amplify these legacies that inform the autoimmune over the language of life (without dismissing this language of life entirely), since I've become more wary of invoking the latter in connection to democracy.

SCA: *As you mention in your work, Derrida's use of the term autoimmunity while analyzing the concept of democracy is too general and vague. What aspects of this argument do you think need further clarification and elaboration?*

SH: I made that charge quite a long time ago, and I'm not sure that I would express it in exactly these terms today. I now see Derrida's use of autoimmunity as a tool of analysis to be more experimental than definitive. It plays an important role in two texts, "Faith and Knowledge" and "The Reason of the Strongest," in Derrida's analyses of religion and democracy respectively, as well as in the interview "Autoimmunity: Real and Symbolic Suicides" (whose content overlaps with "The Reason of the Strongest"). But it also appears in passing in several other texts dating from the last decade or so of Derrida's life, where it is as if he drops it into a different discourse in order to see what might happen. It is true that in all of these appearances, both the more sustained and the more fleeting, autoimmunity is not always used in the same way. So if one tries to determine, as I have, what autoimmunity means for Derrida on the basis of its appearances in his texts, it does appear somewhat general and vague. But I would now read Derrida's varied invocations of the term as a strategic move (whether always intentional or not) that aims to generate new insights. Sometimes it works, and sometimes it doesn't, but the test of this is really left to us, as readers of Derrida – what do we do with these analyses? How do we respond to them? This is the measure of the strategy "working" or not.

Thus, to answer your question, I don't think there's a general answer to be given for what in autoimmunity needs further clarification and elaboration. Rather, each time we use the notion in a specific context, we should be clear about what we mean by it. Just invoking autoimmunity is not enough – each time, what matters is *how* a particular structure or phenomenon is autoimmune.

SCA: *Do you think that democracy to come is a political Khora?*

SH: That depends on what you mean by "a political Khora"! "Khora" is an enigmatic term in Derrida's work, and without a clear understanding of it we don't gain much from equating it to democracy to come. While I've discussed khora briefly in my work, I haven't had the occasion to engage with it at length, because I haven't pursued the kind of intervention I think it's most suited for, namely to challenge the standard readings of Plato. The power of the term is that Derrida uncovers it within Plato's corpus as an alternative to the good beyond being that has the potential to take Platonism in a different direction. Work in democratic theory that more directly engages Plato has interest in exploring this connection, but this is not something I've done myself.

SCA: *As Derrida argues, inheritance is never given; it is always a task before us. Even if we have inherited from the past, the legacy still stands before us as something to come. Similar to inheritance, deconstruction is a practice in which we relate to what has been given to us from the past, but is always in the future. Given this, how would you explain the relationship between deconstruction and inheritance? Is deconstruction the same as legacy?*

SH: Yes, deconstruction is a legacy, in the sense of something that we can inherit, and I would say that practices of deconstruction are practices of inheritance, if we follow Derrida's definition of inheritance. Derrida himself suggests in "As if it were Possible, 'Within Such Limits'" that we can define deconstruction as inheritance [p.81 of English edition *Paper Machine*], and I've tried to justify this claim by arguing that inheritance for Derrida involves a specific engagement with aporetic structures that come to us from the past, where we do not aim to do away with the aporias but instead seek to increase their tension and amplify those elements most open to change and transformation. This also strikes me as a good way to describe deconstruction – a deconstruction never aims or claims to overcome contradictory tensions, but rather seeks to keep these tensions in play through a certain kind of amplification. Given this, it makes sense that both deconstruction and inheritance have similar temporal structures, involving both past and future in a precise relation, as you've suggested.

SCA: *What is the relationship between inheritance and democracy?*

SH: One of the central theses of *Derrida and the Inheritance of Democracy* is that there is a tight relationship between these two notions. For Derrida, democracy not only involves acts of inheritance, but democracy requires us to inherit in the specific way that I've just suggested. This is because democracy carries with it the injunctions to self-criticism and to question its own history, as well as a demand to increase openness, and the history of democracy and our understanding of it contains aporetic structures. This means that one way of realizing these democratic injunctions is to inherit, as Derrida has defined it – namely to engage the aporetic structures in the way that Derrida advocates, through intensifying the aporias in the direction of greater openness.

***SCA:** Is democracy the only political system that includes the right to self-criticism and the right to question its own history, namely the right to inherit? Are there any other political systems that might be related to this interpretation of inheritance?*

SH: I think democracy is, if we understand inheritance in the way I've been describing. I can't think of other political systems that champion or promote such a right. Can you? If I'm wrong about this and there are such systems, then we would also have the option of labeling that aspect of them as "democratic." But in the end I think what we call such a political system (or aspect of a political system) is less important than the right itself. I agree with Derrida when he acknowledges on occasion that we might have strategic reasons to change the name. There would be consequences to such a change, because whatever other name we choose would have its own history that would call for its own inheritance, and such a choice should be taken with this in mind. But I don't think we should cling to the word democracy at all costs – there might arise contexts in the future where a different term better serves the kind of intervention we wish to make.

***SCA:** In your work, you express, "Inheritance involves an acceptance that not only seeks to take away the deadlocks from the past, but also to increase the tension of these deadlocks and open them to greater degrees of unconditionality." Following this model, legacy in democracy would require us to return to the deadlocks that live in our understanding of democracy and reshape them in a way that brings up levels of openness. Do you see a policy in line with the legacy of democracy in today's world?*

SH: One interesting contemporary example is a recent law passed by the New York City Council granting non-citizen residents the right to vote in local elections for mayor and other offices. This kind of law challenges our understanding of who counts in the demos – we usually take it for granted that citizenship is a necessary condition of voting within a nation-state, but why shouldn't all those living in an area, be it a city, state, or country, have a say in how they are governed? And as it turns out, there is a long history of such laws in the United States – for much of the 19th Century many U.S. states had similar policies. So this can be seen as a case of democratic inheritance, returning to a past tension in democratic thinking, in this case between the desire to expand democratic participation at the same time as recognizing the need for limits on this expansion, and opting for the former over the latter, without doing away with the tension altogether. Now after this law was passed a judge ruled that it violates the New York State constitution, so the law is not currently operative. But it may work its way further up the courts, or be revisited in a different manner in the future.

***SCA:** Democracy refers to a model of citizenship based on an understanding of both a nation and a universality aiming at more, and in this sense, it exists with its*

aporias. Can we say that an understanding of democracy that consists of aporias is closer to the notion of democracy to come?
SH: Yes, I think we can, insofar as democracy to come contains aporias, so an understanding of democracy that acknowledges its aporetic nature is closer to what is understood by democracy to come. But note that we are talking about understandings here, that is, about the way we conceive democracy and democracy to come. In this register it makes sense to speak of being closer, or on the other hand of being more distant – an understanding of democracy that does not take aporias into account would be more distant from the notion of democracy to come. This is different, however, from speaking of democracy "itself" and democracy to come "itself," – insofar as we can speak of "selves" here – for in a strong sense democracy is always democracy to come. "Democracy" and "democracy to come" are not two competing things between which can choose – democracy just is aporetic, or, to use the language we were discussing earlier, autoimmune, whether we understand it this way or not, and because of this it is already structured in the ways that Derrida describes "democracy to come." So here it wouldn't be appropriate to use the metaphors of being closer or more distant.
SCA: In Politics of Friendship, *Derrida argues that there is no deconstruction without democracy and no democracy without deconstruction. What kind of relationship is established between democracy and deconstruction in your opinion?*
SH: This is one of those somewhat enigmatic, charged statements about deconstruction that Derrida sometimes makes, whose interpretation is not obvious and thus calls for further thought. The interpretation I offer in my work puts together the two pieces we've already discussed – if deconstruction can be understood as an act of inheritance, and democracy requires acts of inheritance, then we can make sense of the claim that deconstruction and democracy go together as this phrase suggests. So it is inheritance that provides the link between the two.
SCA: Against the understanding of the concept of friendship on the basis of sameness and brotherhood, Derrida points out that it is necessary to think beyond this friendship. According to Derrida, the concept of friendship not only brings together philosophy and politics, but also plays a decisive role in understanding justice and democracy. How can Derrida's outlook on friendship be linked to justice to come and democracy to come?
SH: I'll start with democracy to come, since I have a clearer sense of this. I read Derrida's *Politics of Friendship* as an act of democratic inheritance precisely along the lines we've been discussing. In that book Derrida engages aporetic understandings of friendship in a tradition of Western thinking, specifically as they inform conceptions of political belonging, not to dissolve or resolve

the aporias, but to increase their tensions in a direction of more openness. So for me Derrida's treatment of friendship operates as an example of how to respond to the challenge his work on democracy leaves for us – this is one example of democratic inheritance that we can learn from. That said, one of the things I believe we learn from this treatment is that for Derrida friendship isn't a particularly promising concept to be pursued within democratic thinking. This is because of the persistent role that fraternity plays in the tradition that he investigates – time and again Derrida shows how the different thinkers he engages end up closing down the possibilities of their own thinking by reasserting a masculine ideal of friendship, to the exclusion of friendship involving women. So it's not surprising to me that friendship is not a prominent term in Derrida's work appearing after 1988–1989 (the date of the seminar on which *Politics of Friendship* is based), in connection to democracy or indeed to anything else.

However, this is not to say that we should give up on engaging friendship in our thinking of democracy, even if Derrida did. The tradition Derrida reads in *Politics of Friendship* is itself very specific, an idiosyncratic lineage constructed around the inheritance of the phrase I mentioned earlier attributed to Aristotle, "O my friends, there is no friend," which doesn't even come close to exhausting the tradition of political thinking (and it's also worth noting in this context that Derrida only reads men in this lineage). We ourselves might turn to other accounts of friendship in politics, not discussed by Derrida, and uncover more promising resources. In *Derrida and the Inheritance of Democracy* I pursue a path more internal to Derrida's work and examine the notion of "birth." There I argue that Derrida's diagnosis of the persistence of fraternity in accounts of friendship rests on a very traditional understanding of birth, and that we can find elsewhere in his work a more open and aporetic conception of the birth that could be the basis of a more open conception of political belonging. But we would need to explore this further to see if this is the case.

As for the link to justice, or what you've termed "justice to come," I don't see such a direct link as we see with democracy. It's true that there are elements of Derrida's treatment of friendship, such as the recurring motif of alterity and the idea he explores at one point of the other making the decision in me, that can be related to what he has to say about justice. But friendship itself doesn't seem to figure much in Derrida's work on justice. Which is not to say one couldn't make such a link, using *Politics of Friendship* as a starting point, it's just that I haven't done that work myself.

***SCA:** Can we argue that the deconstruction of democracy is a necessity for justice in the first place?*

SH: This seems to me to be too broad of a question to be answered. I would want to know what is the context for justice in this instance – justice where, in what situation, for whom? If we are speaking of justice in a political context then democracy to come might be relevant, but not necessarily in other contexts. As you might be able to tell from my answer here and to the last question, I have difficulty understanding and developing further the idea of justice as it emerges in Derrida's work. I personally find it one of the most enigmatic notions in Derrida's writings. It is treated at length in "Force of Law," and referred to elsewhere on a number of occasions, and while I've spent a lot of time studying these discussions, I've never felt like I've fully grasped what Derrida means by justice, and what we are supposed to take away from his work on the notion. Part of the problem might be that justice has multiple meanings in French and in English, and so translating the relevant texts is a perilous undertaking, with the consequence being that I get misled when reading these texts in English, or mislead myself when reading them in French. I generally feel I have a good understanding of what's going on in Derrida's texts, especially the later work engaging ethical and political concepts, but when it comes to justice I come up short. Which doesn't mean that I have nothing to say about it, but I do so more tentatively, with hesitation.

SCA: *As the classical understanding of friendship is based on sameness, indeed it has a structure that eliminates otherness and difference. This situation also manifests itself in homogeneous structures such as family, nation, and religion. What sort of a picture emerges when we reconsider the understanding of friendship beyond sameness within the framework of Derrida's ideas? Do you think it is possible to stop thinking about friendship and politics based on samenesses?*

SH: I read Derrida's analysis of friendship to demonstrate that the classical understanding, even though it privileges sameness and attempts to eliminate otherness and difference, never fully succeeds in this attempt. Like the other concepts we've already discussed, the classical vision of friendship is aporetic, caught between dual demands of sameness and difference, even as the first is privileged over the other. So while the classical understanding supports traditional structures such as family, nation, and religion, these structures are not fully homogeneous – traces of otherness and difference remain in them, because the aporia is inescapable. At the same time, Derrida also shows how an alternative tradition of thinking on friendship, pursued by thinkers such as Nietzsche and Blanchot and starting from otherness and difference, contains inescapable elements of sameness, so it too is aporetic. So we will never, according to his analysis, get beyond thinking friendship in connection to sameness. We can certainly shift the privilege granted to sameness, or, in the term you use, stop basing our thinking of friendship and politics on sameness.

Instead we can start from the aporetic concept of friendship and see where this will lead us in rethinking political belonging. But this is not to do away with sameness altogether, as it is still an element in the aporetic structure.

SCA: *Derrida states, "The concept of friendship must be deconstructed for the democracy to come." How should be the deconstruction of this concept? Where would you start if you were to deconstruct the concept of friendship?*

SH: As I've just suggested, Derrida himself seems to abandon a direct engagement with friendship, so I'm not sure that friendship as such needs to be a target in future deconstructions that are on the side of a democracy to come. In "The Reason of the Strongest," his most sustained work on democracy, more important is the notion of fraternity, in the reading of Jean-Luc Nancy, and while that concern comes out of the earlier deconstruction of friendship, friendship itself barely appears. I am inclined to follow Derrida here in not focusing on friendship, which is not to say that others shouldn't, since, to repeat, the tradition Derrida reads in *Politics of Friendship* is highly selective, and there are so many more theories of friendship and political belonging that would be worth exploring. But personally I find the "foreign" a much more fruitful and interesting notion to explore in connection to democracy. This is why Derrida's work on hospitality is so important to me, because it's there we get a thorough engagement with this term. And while Derrida does in some ways connect hospitality to democracy, there is a lot more work here to be done. Either literally such as in the discourses of white nationalism and nativism, or more subtly in discourses against groups in society such as sexual minorities, the category of the foreign is operative in so many contemporary political forces. And it's not just in discourses that I oppose, since it's also an inescapable category for democracy. One of the aporias of democracy involves an openness in its borders and categories of belonging, at the same time as it needs borders and boundaries in order to define itself. So if I were to work more on democracy, I would begin with the foreign, rather than friendship. Of course, these two notions are themselves not without relation, so it may be that if I pursued this work I would find myself needing to engage with friendship once again.

SCA: *According to Derrida, justice does not assume harmony, as Heidegger argues, but rather being out of joints and separation. Justice is in separation rather than in harmony, because every harmony actually has a dimension that distinguishes the other from its difference. For Derrida, justice is incalculable, immeasurable and incomprehensible in a certain harmony, as only in this way can we open up to otherness. In the frame of this comparison, do you think justice emerges in harmony or in separation?*

SH: I've already said that I'm not confident that I fully grasp Derrida's work on justice, but I'll hazard an answer nonetheless! Separation, disharmony, or being "out of joint" is certainly the contrast that Derrida draws in *Specters of Marx* between his understanding of justice and the view he attributes to Heidegger, but I would be careful of casting this as a strict opposition. Like all the other concepts we have been discussing, justice too is aporetic for Derrida, which means that it will involve both harmony and separation in a certain kind of necessary relation. Or, to use another term you invoke, as he states in "Force of Law," "justice is incalculable, it demands that one calculate with the incalculable" [Force of Law, p.244 of Acts of Religion]. Justice requires that we calculate with its incalculable dimension – transferring this back to the context of *Specters of Marx*, we might say that justice requires that we seek to "set right" what is out of joint, which is indeed how Hamlet receives the injunction from the appearance of father's ghost, without ever dispelling the disharmony altogether. So I would say that justice emerges in both harmony and separation, together.

SCA: *Derrida remarks, "Inheritance is a concept that is foreign to time, foreign to the idea of process, and it defies linear time. Like inheritance, justice is foreign to the idea of process." How do you conceive the relationship between inheritance and justice in this context?*

SH: As you might imagine, given what I've already said, I think that "foreign" is a good word to use here, because to be foreign *is* to be in some kind of relation – a relation of estrangement and difference, but a relation nonetheless. Now I wouldn't say that inheritance is totally divorced from linear time, but rather that the relation is one in which inheritance disrupts linear time, both through the particular scrambling of past and future (for Derrida we inherit from the past but this inheritance is always to come in the future) and because there is a spatial dimension introduced (Derrida will often speak of a legacy being "devant nous," "before us," where "before" primarily carries a spatial sense – in front of us). Similarly, justice is not totally divorced from process, but, as suggested in the dual necessity of calculation and incalculability that inhabits its aporia, justice must engage process in order to be just.

Now on its own I wouldn't say that this parallel of sorts between inheritance and justice is enough to establish their connection. Rather, I would argue (and indeed I have argued in *Derrida and the Inheritance of Democracy*) for a more direct relation, namely that justice requires inheritance. If justice is aporetic, then we need to grapple with this aporia, and one way to do this is inherit past conceptions of justice. Derrida himself suggests this in "Force of Law," writing that "One must be *juste* with justice, and its first justice to be done is to hear it, to try to understand where it comes from ... Consequently, never to yield on this point, constantly to maintain a questioning of the origin, grounds and limits of our conceptual, theoretical or normative apparatus surrounding justice".

[Force of Law, p.248 of Acts of Religion] This passage receives less attention than others in "Force of Law," since the first half of this text is primarily focused on a more abstract or logical analysis of the aporias of justice, but it justifies what Derrida does in the second half, when he reads Benjamin's "Critique of Violence" – Derrida's reading can be interpreted as an act of inheritance of a past discourse connected to justice.

SCA: *Do you think that saying that the concepts of justice are inadequate is a sign of indifference or an increased sensitivity to justice?*

SH: I think it is very much a sign of increased sensitivity, and to ignore it is a sign of indifference. Even if they do not agree with what Derrida has to say about justice, I'm not sure that many philosophers believe that our current concepts of justice are adequate (and note that by speaking here in the plural – concepts of justice – we are perhaps already admitting this inadequacy). This is why they are a matter of ongoing debate! And for many, I imagine, the desire to improve them, to make them adequate, comes from a sensitivity to justice. Now Derrida's claim is that the inadequacy is not something we will ever be able to overcome – we will never be able to set right what must be, to a certain extent, out of joint. Derrida may be right or wrong about this claim, but the only way to show him to be definitely wrong is to come up with a conception of justice that is adequate. If we arrive at that point, then there's no need for further debate, but we are not there yet.

SCA: *In your opinion, the statement that deconstruction is justice actually serves as a provocative call to further thinking rather than a statement of an established fact. Could you expand on this subject a little further? What kind of opportunities does this statement offer in terms of thinking differently rather than being a mere definition and description?*

SH: The statement "*Deconstruction is justice*" is one of the reasons I said earlier that I'm not confident I fully grasp Derrida's engagement with justice. To be honest, part of me would be happier if Derrida never wrote this sentence. But he did write it, and as someone who wants to interpret his work I have to try to come to terms with it. I've done so, as you state, by suggesting that we should read it less as a statement of fact and more as a provocation. Perhaps I can justify the first claim, why we shouldn't read it as a statement of fact, or (why don't I just come out and say it?), why I don't think it's true. The problem is that I can't reconcile this statement with what Derrida says about both deconstruction and justice elsewhere in his work, starting with the lines that immediately surround it. Let's place it in context: It appears relatively early on in "Force of Law," after Derrida has been discussing the phrases from Montaigne and Pascal that give him his subtitle ("On the Mystical Foundation of Authority") and the question of the legitimacy of the law's foundation. From this discussion he draws out the claim that the law is deconstructible, and that this is a good thing. He then claims that this makes deconstruction possible, and immediately draws a contrast between the deconstructibility of law with both justice and deconstruction, leading to the phrase in question: "But the paradox that I would like to submit for discussion is the following: it is this deconstructible structure of law or, if you prefer, of justice as law, that also ensures the possibility of deconstruction. Justice in itself, if such a thing exist, outside or beyond law, is not deconstructible. No more than deconstruction itself, if such a thing exist. *Deconstruction is justice*." [Force of Law, 242–3 of Acts of Religion]. I have a lot of trouble agreeing with these claims. I don't know what to make of the phrase "deconstruction itself" – so much of Derrida's work seems to justify a claim that such a thing does not exist. His work also demonstrates that anything that *exists* is open to deconstruction – in the face of this, at the very least, we need some justification for the claims that justice in itself, and deconstruction in itself – *if they exist* – are not deconstructible. And even if we accept these two statements, that doesn't warrant thereby identifying deconstruction with justice – both can be undeconstructible without thereby being the same thing. So I just don't see that the pronouncement "*Deconstruction is justice*" is warranted by the claims preceding it.

It's also worth keeping in mind that, as I've just quoted, Derrida presents these claims as a paradox submitted for discussion, and shortly after he speaks of "the hypothesis and propositions toward which I am tentatively moving here" [Force of Law p.243 of Acts of Religion]. So it's not clear to me that he himself sees this as a statement of fact either. Rather, I see it as more akin to similar statements that appear elsewhere in Derrida's writings, such as "Deconstruction *is* America" [Memoires for Paul de Man, English edition, p.18] (a statement he also describes as a hypothesis) – I don't take these to be a strict identifications, and if we do, we should then also agree with a statement such as "America is justice" which I do not want to endorse. They are rather, as you say, provocations for further thought.

SCA: *You have some doubts about the Derridean approach to the concepts of democracy and inheritance. First of all, you pose the following question: "Do we have any assurance that democracy will promote what is good? If not, why should we put democracy above all else?" Another question is that even if the link between democracy and heritage has been established, the details of how this legacy can be realized and how to justify defining it as democratic are still not determined. Have you found any answers to these questions so far? What would you like to say about this?*

SH: Overall I don't have doubts about the Derridean *approach* to democracy and inheritance, but it is the case that the results of this approach lead me to have doubts about democracy. As you suggest, one result of Derrida's analysis is that democracy is not guaranteed to coincide with the good. That kind of assurance just isn't available to us if we agree with Derrida's claims, because of the essential openness of democracy's future, and the processes of autoimmunity. If the "to-come" really is open in the way that Derrida insists it is, then it needs to be open to the good and the bad. Thus, we can get worse outcomes by being more democratic, and we can't always determine what these will be in advance. So why choose democracy? Well, we can make a decision which in a given context democracy appears to be our best option, better than the alternatives. And it's not as if the alternatives are free from an uncertain future themselves, so there isn't a choice we can make that will eradicate this uncertainty. But we make that choice for democracy knowing that it may turn out differently than we hope, so we must remain vigilant as the future unfolds. And one nice feature of democracy is that it also encourages this ongoing vigilance. Its fluid nature calls for continued action, continued decisions, allowing us to reassess where we are each time.

As for your second set of questions, I would say that there is some determination of how to realize the legacies appropriate to democracy, at least on Derrida's view. This is, as I said earlier, to intensify the aporias with a view of bringing about greater openness. But you're right that how precisely this is to be realized is not determined, and, given what we've just said about democracy not guaranteeing the good, whether we would want to bring about a greater openness in a given instance needs to be determined. Here the determination would depend again on context – not a very satisfying answer, I know, but I really think that general answers in this area are only useful up to a point, beyond which they tell us very little.

SCA: *What kind of a legacy is deconstruction with its advantages and disadvantages?*

SH: Following on from what we've just discussed, the first thing I'd say is that as a legacy, deconstruction also does not necessarily coincide with the good. I tend to find myself in favor of deconstructive strategies of reading, but I also need to acknowledge that they can be coopted by forces I don't agree with, and would want to oppose. But to address your question more directly, I think that one advantage of deconstruction is that it encourages attention to what's actually being claimed in a text. It's all too easy to move too quickly when we read, to simplify or assimilate what we are reading into ideas or structures that aren't in the text. This is a necessary dimension of reading – we can't help but do it – but it has its dangers, and deconstruction works to keep this tendency at bay. Of course, there is also a danger that we assimilate a text into a preconceived understanding of what deconstruction involves that would be inappropriate to it – this is perhaps one reason why Derrida would always push back against characterizing deconstruction as a method. But if we also keep this in mind, deconstruction teaches us that texts are always more surprising and strange than we assume. As for a disadvantage, its parasitic nature means that deconstructive readings will always be limited to some extent by the texts they engage. All texts have limitations, and every deconstructive reading, even as it challenges certain limitations, will keep others in place. Which serves as a good reminder to those of us reading a deconstructive reading, to look for the limits that are left unchallenged, and put pressure on them in turn. As I mentioned earlier, I have tried to do this in my own work with respect to the notion of birth in *Politics of Friendship*.

SCA: *Derrida says that the concept of unconditional hospitality cannot actually have a legal or political status and that unconditional hospitality exceeds the concepts of politics and law. In this sense, unconditional hospitality is something that the state cannot sustain and inscribe in the law. For the condition of unconditional hospitality is that you relinquish the sovereignty of your home and nation. I would like to ask you two questions. The first question is, is unconditional hospitality an unrealistic concept or an ideal that encourages us to do better towards the other? Secondly, how would you evaluate the current immigration policies in the context of unconditional hospitality?*

SH: I don't think we should think of unconditional hospitality as an ideal. An ideal is something that, if it were realized, would produce a better state of affairs, but this isn't the case with unconditional hospitality. You're right that it cannot have a legal or political status, because it's not a fully coherent concept – complete openness leads to the dissolution of the self or the home, which is a precondition of being hospitable in the first place (and a precondition of being written into law). And getting closer to realizing unconditional hospitality does not necessarily lead to desirable outcomes, as it really depends on the context. If we are speaking of an entity – a self, a community, a nation – that is in a position of superiority vis-à-vis certain others, then yes, more openness towards these others is something I would often endorse. But what about when an entity is in a position of weakness? Should we encourage poorer nations to open their borders to all comers, to companies, governments, and armies from elsewhere to come in and do as they please? This is often what happens – poorer nations are unable to prevent interference from other nations, forces, or multinational corporations, but it isn't a good thing, and yet it is what striving towards unconditional hospitality would require. I'm also wary of speaking of "the other" in the singular in this context. We are never in relation to just one other, there are always other others, and any relation of hospitality we have towards any specific other implicates them as well. If I welcome one other, they might come in and harm other others. How would I even begin to judge that I am doing better towards “the other” in such a situation?

So rather than think of it as a criterion by which to judge current immigration policies (which the status of ideal would suggest), unconditional hospitality is perhaps better conceived of a demand for more openness that imposes itself in certain contexts of conditional hospitality, but not others. As a citizen of the United States, I feel the force of the demand to be more open towards certain others when considering the immigration policies of this State. I'm also an Australian citizen, and the demand also imposes itself upon me there, perhaps even more so given that Australia's immigration policies are more restrictive than those of the U.S. in several key ways. But I also acknowledge that for other others with respect to these States, or for other States in certain conditions or towards certain others, the demand may not present itself – there are good reasons for restricting the welcome given to others who may harm other others. Of course, this is precisely what anti-immigrant rhetoric appeals to as well, for example with Trump's claims in 2015 about Mexican rapists crossing the border. But we aren't going to be able to eradicate the possibility of such statements, as they too are made possible by the structure of hospitality. So we are called to respond to them each time they are uttered.

SCA: *In an interview after the September 11 attacks, Derrida remarked that the concepts that name and categorize this event were the products of a dogmatic sleep, and that what would wake us up from this sleep was a reflection on philosophy, especially political philosophy and its legacy. What are your thoughts on this? Did the 9/11 attacks lead to a new reflection on philosophy and political philosophy in particular?*

SH: I certainly think that after September 11 there was a significant turn towards examining politics and political issues and concepts within the community of philosophers and theorists I count as mine, namely those working with the continental tradition, broadly conceived. One would need to do a systematic analysis of colloquia, conferences and publications to show this is the case, but my impression is that there was a rapid increase in the amount of political philosophy being done in the early 2000s by the “average” philosopher engaging in continental thought, with treatments of concepts like sovereignty, war, torture, and terrorism being most prominent. Although this was perhaps more in response to the U.S. response to September 11 than September 11 itself. And it seems to me that the focus on political issues has continued more or less uninterrupted since then, even as different questions have emerged, most notably in more recent years with topics related to racism and colonialism being addressed. Of course, there have long been some philosophers in this community treating such questions, and this time period also coincides more or less with my time in the profession. So it may be that my impression of the past is inaccurate – it's difficult not to privilege one's present as an advance over the past, even if one is theoretically suspicious of the concept of progress. It is no doubt too early to write the intellectual history of this community spanning the time before and after September 11, but I would love to read such an account.

SCA: *In the context of the September 11 attacks, Derrida makes the following remark: "The arrival of the other or the visit of the other can be very dangerous indeed, we must not deny this fact, but a hospitality without risk, a hospitality assured by certain guarantees, a hospitality protected by an immune system against what is entirely other, is not real hospitality." Do you think genuine hospitality should be considered as opening the door to the arrival of the other even if it leads to an outcome like 9/11?*

SH: Yes, absolutely, as I've already suggested. There is no hospitality without risk, and if we were somehow able to establish such guarantees against danger, then I agree with Derrida that we wouldn't call this hospitality. Another way to think of this, even though I don't think Derrida ever puts it this way (and might have had reason to be wary of such a formulation), is that hospitality requires some degree of freedom to be granted to the other, and as soon as we have freedom, we have risk. It's another question, as we've discussed, as to whether one thinks that hospitality is something we should strive for in a given situation. We might determine that the risks are too great, and so attempt to not be hospitable. But we can't decide to be hospitable without risk.

SCA: *Do you believe that the state of uncertainty or doubt is indispensable in politics? In other words, should we abandon the absolute foundations and turn to doubt and uncertainty so as to have real democracy, real politics, and real justice?*

SH: I think uncertainty or doubt is indispensable insofar as it is simply an ineradicable feature of politics. We can act as if we have an absolute foundation to our political action, but to me that is just denying the way things are – it's just true that any foundation for our politics that we posit is open to revision, whether we like it or not. This doesn't mean that we have to revise it – if a foundational principle is called into question, we may respond by reaffirming that principle again. And that act of reaffirmation is itself a political act. But I'm always puzzled by those who insist that a foundation is absolute – if it were absolute, presumably it wouldn't need anyone to come to its aid and insist on its status, it would just be there, regardless of any criticism, standing firm. That one has to insist is itself evidence that things are a little more shaky than one might hope.

SCA: *Do you think it is a paradox to build the concept of justice which was once seen as the supreme foundation on vague concepts such as uncertainty and undecidability?*

SH: I don't think there's anything paradoxical here, insofar as we can split the terms in question across time, as your question implies. Justice may once have been seen as the supreme foundation, but if it is now acknowledged to rest on concepts such as uncertainty and undecidability (concepts I would not describe as vague – the concepts can be clearly defined, even if they might lead to vagueness in our resulting idea of justice), then what we are witnessing is a change in our understanding. Justice was once seen as the supreme foundation, and now it is not. That's not a paradox – there's no contradiction here of conflicting terms or values being proposed *at the same time* – even if some find it undesirable.

SCA: *Derrida's deconstruction forces democratic struggle to remain alive, as it reveals the impossibility of forming a political consensus without exclusion. Since the condition for the existence of democratic politics is viewed as uncertainty, any consensus is risky, because it brings stability and order to what is essentially unstable and chaotic. In this context, can we say that permanent stability and reconciliation will be the end of politics and ethics, as Derrida argued? To what extent is the idea of stability and reconciliation necessary for democracy and how dangerous can it be?*

SH: I think *permanent* stability and reconciliation would bring about the end of politics and ethics, insofar as it seems to render these activities redundant. But the emphasis here really is on the "permanent," and this doesn't mean that stability and reconciliation are opposed to democratic politics. Perhaps it is better to speak of stabili*zation* and reconciliation, so as to underline the fact that we are talking here of tendencies and movements, not final states. Democratic politics will sometimes pursue stabilization, and sometimes seek to destabilize what has been stabilized. Similarly, there are times in a democracy when reconciliation is sought, but reconciliation in itself is not always in the service of democratic politics – as you suggest, citizens within a community can be reconciled with each other on the question of excluding foreigners, and this exclusion can also be challenged by appealing to democratic principles. This kind of movement between stabilization and destabilization seems to me to be the very movement of democracy, and it is when we have one or the other exclusively that democracy disappears.

SCA: *At this point in the debate on justice, it seems that justice is merely an ideal and injustice is a reality. For this reason, can we say that the best way to achieve justice is to define injustice and eliminate the cases of injustice instead of developing theories of justice?*

SH: I'm not sure this is an exclusive choice – we can both examine injustices and aim to eliminate them as well as work on constructing a positive theory of justice. Key here would be to emphasize the "we" that you invoke in your question – it is perhaps too much for one person to pursue both inquiries, but there's nothing preventing us, as a community of scholars, from doing so, and to share our results and learn from one another. Which is what I imagine has been done for most of the history of thinking about justice. While positive theories of justice often present themselves as standing in isolation or in conversation only with other such theories, I find it hard to believe that the work that goes into them is uninformed by analyses of injustice. And vice versa. So the best way forward would be for us to pursue both paths, together.

Suggested Readings

Samir Haddad, *Derrida and the Inheritance of Democracy*; USA: Indiana University Press, 2013.

Samir Haddad, *Foucalt /Derrida Fifty Years Later: Them, Future of Genealogy, Deconstruction and Politics* (Coedited with Olivia Custer and Penelope Deutscher), USA: Columbia University Press, 2016.

CHAPTER 7

Human Rights and Justice: Seyla Benhabib

Seyla Benhabib is a distinguished Turkish-American philosopher known for her work in political philosophy, ethics, and feminist theory. Her thought is grounded in a commitment to democracy, human rights, and the ethics of inclusion, with a particular focus on issues of multiculturalism, migration, and the rights of marginalized groups. Deeply influenced by the critical theory of Jürgen Habermas, as well as Hannah Arendt's reflections on public space and political action, Benhabib's philosophy emphasizes the importance of dialogue, inclusivity, and democratic engagement in achieving a just society.

One of Benhabib's most influential contributions is her theory of democratic iterations, developed in her book The Claims of Culture: Equality and Diversity in the Global Era. In this work, she argues that cultural and political identities are not static but are constantly reshaped through democratic processes and open dialogue. Democratic iterations, in Benhabib's view, refer to the continual reinterpretation and adaptation of cultural and legal norms through discourse, which enables societies to accommodate diversity while upholding fundamental principles of equality and justice. This framework offers a way for democratic societies to respect cultural diversity without falling into moral relativism or sacrificing universal rights.

Benhabib's work on immigration and cosmopolitanism is also a central theme in her philosophy. In The Rights of Others: Aliens, Residents, and Citizens, she explores the ethical and political challenges posed by migration, arguing for a cosmopolitan approach to human rights that goes beyond national borders. Benhabib criticizes the exclusionary practices of nation-states that restrict immigrants' rights, emphasizing the need for a global perspective on justice that recognizes the rights of all individuals, regardless of citizenship. She advocates for a model of "porous" borders that allows for a degree of political autonomy while respecting the rights of migrants and refugees, proposing policies that reflect the interconnected nature of today's world.

Benhabib has also made significant contributions to feminist theory, particularly in her book Situating the Self: Gender, Community, and Postmodernism in Contemporary Ethics. Here, she challenges the patriarchal and exclusionary structures that have traditionally shaped political and social theory, advocating for an ethics that recognizes the voices and experiences of women and

 | DOI:10.1163/9789004732902_009

marginalized communities. She argues for a "situated" approach to ethics that considers the lived experiences of individuals and their cultural contexts, fostering an inclusive and empathetic view of justice.

In addition, Benhabib's work emphasizes the importance of deliberative democracy, an approach that prioritizes public dialogue and consensus-building as essential to democratic legitimacy. She contends that true democracy can only be achieved through participatory engagement, where individuals and groups contribute to shaping the norms and policies that affect their lives. Her focus on deliberative democracy aligns with her broader vision of a pluralistic society that values dialogue, respects cultural differences, and upholds universal rights. Benhabib's philosophy is a call to action for democratic societies to embrace both individuality and cultural pluralism. Her approach to justice and equality insists on a democratic framework that allows all voices to participate, creating an environment where diverse perspectives can coexist.

***Sema Cevirici Atilla* [*SCA*]:** *According to you, there is a strong link between reason and the justification of human rights. In this context, if we accept that reason is contextual, historical and influenced by certain factors, what problems can we encounter in justifying human rights?*

Seyla Benhabib [SB]: I think the best way to start thinking about this connection is to ask what justification means in the first place. There is a strong version of contextualism that was represented in philosophy mainly by the work of Richard Rorty in the late 1990s and early 2000s according to which the justification of human rights amounted to nothing more than ethnocentric bourgeois liberalism. I reject this proposition and I agree with Jürgen Habermas that even though reason is situated, there is always a transcendent moment to it. Any appeal to reason or *Vernunft* offers to the other to engage in conversation with me and to say yes or no. There are serious cultural issues involved in the context of the justification of human rights, but the fundamental idea behind seeing the human person as a being entitled to legal and moral rights is human dignity and my respect of the other as a being to whom I can offer some kind of reasoned argument so that I do not treat the other as an object, as someone in submission or as a being I can manipulate. In that sense, reason as reason-giving already involves respect for the capacity of the other to enter into conversation with me. This is the dialogic structure of reason and it is a transcendent moment even though that dialogue is going to be surely contextually situated. The dialogic structure of reason is one the most fundamental insight of philosophy, articulated by none other than Socrates. In his dialogue, *Euthyphro*, Socrates asks: "Is something pious because it is loved by the gods or is it loved by the gods because it is pious?" Now substitute justice for piety: Is it justice because it is what our city does or does our city do it because it is justice? There is always a moment of tension between the contextual and transcendent, and here you can see the link to moral and legal rights.

SCA: *There has been significant criticism of the Enlightenment in contemporary thought, but you think that we can still find positive elements in the Enlightenment. By criticizing postmodernism, liberalism, and feminism; and as you say, our aim is not to reject the Enlightenment altogether, but to critically reconsider the principles that the Enlightenment has given us. What should we expect from the Enlightenment? Which elements of the Enlightenment do you think can play a crucial role in solving problems?*

SB: The Enlightenment is a complex tradition. There is the French Enlightenment, the German Enlightenment, and the British Enlightenment, among others. So, when we talk about the Enlightenment, usually what we are suggesting as a kind of compact formula is the relationship between reason and critique, reason and some drive towards emancipation. This is certainly the case in Kant's theory and Rousseau's work but the British Enlightenment is much more contextual and skeptical. Here, I would like to talk about Kant who is the thinker who has been of great significance for me, my work, and the tradition to which I belong. Kant's idea of *Aufklärung* is associated with using one's own reason and reaching *Mündigkeit.* It is often translated as 'maturity', but simply put, it is the idea that government and the public authorities ought not treat you as if you were an underage child. They must treat you with respect by letting you use your reason in public affairs. Nevertheless, we know that even Kant himself made political compromises with Frederick the Great. He wanted to be left to pursue his scholarly work, but he accepted that may be the scholar and the intellectual should not interfere too much when it came to political public affairs. Traditional Enlightenment thinkers compromised in one way or another with the political authorities of their times. Today the Enlightenment is criticized by feminist thinkers, postmodernists and others for being Eurocentric and colonialist. And some of this critique is quite just and we have to go beyond the prejudices of the Enlightenment.

I believe the Enlightenment contains two moments. It was an opening of Europe to the world in the 16th-17th centuries. Thinkers like Diderot and Rousseau, for instance, were extremely curious about the other parts of the world. This is also true for Kant, who on the hand criticized western imperialist ventures but who, on the other hand, developed an *The Anthropology* based upon a theory of the division of human beings into races. Many have worked to try to reconcile these aspects of his thinking with one another. I believe it is necessary to be honest about the two moments of the Enlightenment: the first being an attempt to develop a concept of universal humanity that extends beyond Europe and the second being the limits of knowledge at the time of the

Enlightenment as well as their prejudices. Though we should be careful how we use the word. Montesquieu, for example, is the first person to write about the women of the Orient sympathetically in his *Persian Letters*. It is an amazing feminist work though one may not think so at first glance. Montesquieu uses the whole status of women in the *harem* to criticize Western women for their liberties and libertinisms, but then he turns things around shows that the women of the harem who seem oppressed and confined are actually more free than western women who are dependent upon admiration and approval by men. In that sense, I believe in not giving up this ambivalent legacy of the Enlightenment but criticizing it honestly and reconstructing its insights here necessary.

***SCA:** When we look at the criticisms of the Enlightenment, it is mentioned that there is a close relationship between reason and violence. To what extent do you think these criticisms are justified? What could save reason from violence?*

SB: Here, I disagree with some of the postmodernist critics who claim this, because historically Diderot, Rousseau, and Kant were extremely critical of the European imperialist project. Despite his racist anthropology, Kant did not propose that the West should go out, transform and educate everyone. Rousseau famously thought that it would be better to let the other civilizations do their thing. So, this question of the relationship between reason and violence would be hard to prove historically. But what is the conceptual core of this charge? Reason or, in Habermas' words, the "force of the better argument," seems like an attempt not at convincing but rather, at coercing the other. Yet this is completely wrong, because the whole purpose is to convince the others, so the violence of reason seems to be that when the other is recalcitrant or resistant then the task of convincing them seems to become a task of coercion. However, I think that if we cannot hold on to some kind of distinction between coercion and justification, the whole enterprise of philosophy just dissolves. No matter how difficult the distinction, we have to hold on to it, so in that sense I would strongly reject the proposition that identifies reason with violence.

***SCA:** In contemporary debate, universalism is understood as a "strategy of justification." What do you think can prevent this justification strategy from producing violence against the Other?*

SB: It is a good question. We need to be a bit more concrete and, as Richard Bernstein would have said, we need to be more pragmatic when we talk about "the Other." Are we talking about the cultural other? Are we talking about the gender other? Which other are we talking about? When we talk about the other with capital O, we run into the danger of exoticizing the other. In my own work, very early on I used the phrase "The Generalized and the Concrete Other." For me, there is a dual aspect to every human being. I see every human being as a being capable of both reason and emotion, as an embodied being capable of rationality. As embodied beings, each of us is a concrete being with a concrete history and a concrete set of emotions, capabilities memories, and the like. Our concreteness is also our situatedness. That's why I called one of my early works *Situating the Self* (1992). We have to demystify the talk of the Other with capital O. If we analyze the generalized and the concrete other, the other is a being like us with whom we can enter into communication, who has dignity and to whom we owe respect, and at the same time, realizing that even though we are situated differently in history, in our bodies, and in our emotions, this is not a chasm and we can negotiate these perspectives in ourselves as well as between us. As we learn from Hegel, each one of us is always self and "other." I am an other to myself and I am also another to another. In other words, I have the perspective of the other in me; I see the gaze of the other who sees me and I may or I may not like that. Therefore, the other is not completely an exotic different object. Each of us are self and other. At the same time, the gaze of the other is also part of me and how I think of myself. In that sense, we need to approach the relationship of reason and the other in a much more interactive and intersectional language, though intersectionality is mostly used to talk about gender, race, culture, etc. But it need not be so limited. I would argue that we have to demystify and de-exoticize the other with capital O and recoup this multiplicity of perspectives that enables us to be both self and other to ourselves and self and other within the community.

SCA: *What problems can arise when we regard the ethics of communicative discourse as a criterion of legitimacy?*

SB: Maybe this is a convenient moment to distinguish between the moral and the legal dimensions and approach the problem first from the standpoint of the moral point of view. Discourse ethics involves respect for the other as a being capable of communication with whom I enter into a dialogue of justification. It does not mean that we have to reach agreement always, we can disagree with one another. There can be a reasoned disagreement. I think that in some of Habermas' early work, certain formulations were interpreted as if reaching agreement (*Einstimmung*) represented a kind of Rousseauean general will. Political and legal society consists of people with many different viewpoints and the question is: At what level do we deal with this kind of pluralism? How can we agree to disagree? In contemporary societies, the issue of reasoned disagreement runs along many lines, but in the first place it concerns matters of faith and religion. Secondly, we can see similar controversies about the status of science. Is science the only authoritative source of truth or are there others as well.

In this respect, the Habermasian program of discourse ethics has learned a great deal from Rawlsian liberalism. Let me expand on this matter, as there is a great deal of misunderstanding about what this means because 'political liberalism in the Rawlsian sense is often identified with market liberalism. As Rawls explains, however, political liberalism is a *constitutional doctrine*. It concerns the constitution and its essential principles. It is neutral about how the economy is arranged, how much private property or social distribution you have. There has been a persistent misunderstanding about this point both in Turkey and France. In my opinion, this goes back to an old-fashioned Marxist rejection of liberalism as a class ideology.

In *Between Facts and Norms*, Habermas has argued that first, in a democratic republic, we consider each other as citizens entitled to the same rights and liberties and we grant each other. At the same time, we accept as an enduring feature of liberal democracy that there will be differences of opinion, when we have to agree to disagree. How do we reconcile these enduring differences? Rawls's answer, which I would support in terms of the legitimation for a framework of discourse ethics, is that you hold on to these two premises: you provide a constitutional framework, but you also respect the inevitable multiplicity of worldviews. I think this is a lesson that is very important for the legacy of a liberal democratic republic.

As you know, Turkey has been going through such conflicts in the last decades with respect to *laïcité*. In 1923, the Turkish Constitution accepted a French model of the separation of church and state. That model comes out of the French Revolution when the church was the owner of land and the relationship between the two domains of authority was not clear. The church was the power together with the monarchy and had to be fought against. However, in Turkey, this model of *laïcité* has given rise to all sorts of issues which cannot be solved within this secularist framework. Rawls provides us with a *post-laic* model of coexistence which is not *anti-secular*. Sometimes the term *post-secularism* is used. For me, this is misleading, because in defending the rights of religiously observant citizens, I certainly do not want to go back to a theocracy, be it Jewish or Islamic. Instead of calling for a post-secular society, I think we should talk about it as a post-laic society where there is no a single model of the separation of religious power and secular power. There are successful examples of this. One of the good things you can say about the United States these days is its capacity to create a post-laic society which is not post-secular. Countries like Canada, Great Britain, and until very recently also India, were credible examples of this kind of discursive legitimation compatible with deep pluralism.

SCA: *How do you assess the discussion of justice in relation to the demand for recognition rather than the redistribution of properties?*

SB: I think that the concept of recognition opened up an important dimension in contemporary debates about justice. I have written extensively about this in *The Claims of Culture* (2002). I think the term recognition as it emerges out of Hegel's philosophy has its virtues as well as limits, because recognition is about the phenomenological relationship between self and other. Nevertheless, in contemporary politics, 'recognition,' as first used by Charles referred to multiculturalism and the *politics of recognition*. At stake here were issues about collective identity and language. Canada, for example, is a very multi-plural society. It encompasses the French, the British, as well as First Nations. So these claims to recognition, as they arose in the context of the Canadian political conversation, were related to politics in so-called "pluri-ethnic" societies with settled ethnic communities. Applied to Turkey, the Canadian case is definitely analogous to the predicament of Kurdish people in Turkey. Kurds are more predominantly settled in some parts of the country than in others regions; they are concentrated in the south-eastern regions of Turkey; they have their own language and culture. They are like the Basques people who straddle the borders between France and Spain. But if we go back to the philosophical question, recognition of what and as what, the answers are open. In that sense, the juxtaposition of recognition and redistribution is too general. In her response to Axel Honneth, Nancy Fraser said it can be recognition in terms of culture, but it can also be recognition in terms of other identity markers such as race, color, and gender.

I am conflicted about the politics of recognition because I think that redistributive policies must always also retain a certain level of universality and cannot just be about group rights and cultural identities. A pertinent example would be healthcare. I cannot think about healthcare as being group-based. Redistributive politics are politics that should reach the most needy in the best way to produce justice. Yes, we also need to take into consideration group-specific language rights in the schools and recognition of religious holidays. In American universities, for example, we get a circular at the beginning of each year. It lists about 20 holidays one should recognize and I have an obligation as an instructor to respect a student's wishes and accommodate their schedule. I think the redistribution and recognition debate polarized too much and left open questions about what exactly the political implications of recognition were. As I said, healthcare is the best example of a good that cannot be based on group recognition claims. Language rights, on the other hand, are about recognition and concern a good that cannot be simply identified with money, rights or entitlements.

SCA: *How would you evaluate the debate between justice and the problem of the good life? Should we make a sharp distinction between them or rather consider*

them together? In relation to this, is it possible to have a theory of justice that people with different understandings of the good can accept in common?
SB: I hope so. Part of what I said in response to the question about political liberalism presupposes that would be possible. The argument that every conception of justice also presupposes some understanding of the good life is certainly plausible. When we talk about a "post-laic liberal democratic understanding of justice," for example, I am assuming that we are not living in an aristocratic society of virtue or distinction as Nietzsche might have liked, that is, in a society in which the whole purpose of the good life would be to produce the aesthetic individual beyond the last man, a kind of Zarathustra. Somebody like Nietzsche would say our societies that aim only at justice and leave questions of the good life aside are mediocre in that sense. May be the commitment to justice alone is too deeply egalitarian and anti-aristocratic. But is this commitment to egalitarianism at the same time, as Nietzsche would say, a commitment to mediocrity? I would say not. This here about American philosophers such as Ralph Waldo Emerson who talked about democratic individualism, a concept different from Nietzsche's aristocratic great man Zarathustra. The democratic individual is committed to equality and respect, yet at the same time attempts to cultivate selfhood. Undoubtedly, this is also a conception of the good life. It is different from a communitarian understanding or *cemaatçilik* as it is called in Turkish. It is different from what an observant Jew, an observant Muslim or an observant Hindu may consider the good life for whom the good of the community and her place within that framework are more significant than the cultivation of democratic individualism. In that sense, the kind of conception of justice that I am proposing based on discourse presupposes a conception of the good life, that is egalitarian and democratic. However, I do not think democratic individualism is necessarily egotistical, so the question is: Can democratic individualism create its own forms of association and communities that are not necessarily communities of faith and ethnicity but communities of affiliation? For instance, university communities and professional life are also communities of affiliation. So you and I come together because of our dedication to knowledge as an affiliation, not because we are the same ethnicity.

It is important therefore not to identify liberal egalitarianism with an anti-associational egotistical point of view. I think this was a polemical critique that was made of Kant and of the Kantian tradition by the communitarian critique of liberalism. I do not see this as being necessary goes back to a very important point that we are talking about in terms of *post-laïcité*. In a liberal democratic society, what is paramount is respect for the capacity of individuals and the right of individuals to form different forms of association. Certainly there are all sorts of controversial issues in constitutional jurisprudence like how far associational liberties can go without violating shared conception of public life and the liberties of others etc. Where the discussion between communitarianism and liberalism got stuck was when communitarians criticized the liberals for having a much too individualistic and almost egotistical conception of the self, as in Michael Sandel's critique. I don't believe that this is the case but more work needs to be done to articular conceptions of democratic individualism.

SCA: *As you know, we have been facing a judicial crisis since Kant. The basis of our judgments and how we judge has been seriously debated. Lyotard emphasizes the idea of judgment without criteria. Do you think it is possible to judge without criteria? In addition, how can we establish a relationship between decision making and fairness in cases where there are no criteria?*

SB: I am familiar Lyotard's *Le Différend*. I have developed a model of judgment in my own work that comes from Arendt and Kant. It originates with Kant's concept of die *erweiterte Denkungsart* or enlarged mentality. The enlarged mentality presupposes the capacity to be able to take the standpoint of the other and is central to the themes of the concrete and generalized other in my work. What is valuable in Lyotard's *Le Différend* is that it cautions us not to assume that the standpoint of the other is a simple extension of my own. This is the problem of narcissism. On the other hand, if *le différend* is so completely different and so completely other, then we may be exoticizing the other and or making her so alien to ourselves that we may not even want to enter into communication. So, two warnings here. One difficulty with the ideal of the enlarged mentality is projection, simply seeing the other just lime yourself. Another is assuming that the other is so different that you cannot enter into communication in the first place. We need to go beyond these either/ors and understand that the otherness of the other is only possible when the other communicates with us. This is a treacherous and difficult process. Sometimes mother and child do not understand each other, lovers do not understand each other. I think we have to appreciate Lyotard's warning without assuming that this is all that needs to be said. In *The Postmodern Condition*, Lyotard identified the other with women, natives, children, and mad people in a rather essentializing way. This was was the essentialization or substantialization of the other which I call the 'exoticization' of the other. Who assumes that they are the 'other' of reason and hence incommunicable? Similarly, Levinas' concept of the 'face of the other, 'fantastically powerful as it is, privileges the eyes, the gaze. But we also share language, and often, we get lost in translation. I think that Levinas' idea of 'the face of the other' is a beautiful insight, but you have to add communication to it. When human beings face each other, they try to communicate, through language as well as gestures.

In certain circumstances the best that you can achieve is procedural fairness, not justice. I am thinking of extremely difficult decisions that people have to make, say in a hospital, or in a life-and-death situation. What criteria do you use? Do we always have available criteria? At times you have to respect that you have just obeyed the procedure and may have failed to achieve justice. Besides doctors, in extremely nasty situations in family court you may be struggling and know that it is tragic when the children are going to be separated. Of course such situation when we do not have ready-made criteria exist, The difficulty arises when one makes this kind of situation of indeterminacy into a theory of democracy and justice at large.

Procedural justice may lead to a form of legalism, as my colleague Judith Shklar called it. What is the difference between legalism and procedural justice? In legalism is one follows all the formal rules but does not engage with those about whom one is rendering a decision through any kind of dialogue, deliberation or communication. My idea of procedural justice is that all those affected by a decision, which is a very abstract philosophical criterion, must have a say in it in some way or another. This cannot just be top-down legalism. I can give you many concrete examples about this. Take a project of urbanization where they are trying to reconstruct some part of the city. The legalistic understanding would be: "The decision has been made by the acceptable authorities" and that is it. The procedure of all-affected interests perspective I am representing would be that the broadest possible conversation with the inhabitants of that district should take place: a conversation should consider the interest of children, of the elderly and those who go to work; all those who would have an interest must come together with the architects, the engineers, government planners, and so on. This is called participatory urban planning. I am thinking of this kind of example, because so much that happens these days in Turkey is authoritarian legalism.

***SCA:** How do you see the future of nation states? Do you think nation states are losing their importance? Is a cosmopolitan democracy possible as long as nation states exist?*

SB: I will be talking a little bit about this tomorrow in my lecture on the concept of sovereignty. Let us talk about the global environment in which nation states exist today. They are so much more complex and also governed by many other organizations – IMF, the World Bank, giant media companies such as Amazon and Google – that reduce the capacity of nation states to control their externalities. For instance, financial markets and those who can dictate them bring governments to their heels. It is to counter this loss of capacity to steer the external environment of nation-states that federative solutions, such as the European Union have emerged. The United States is also a federation.

Nevertheless, federations as well have their own difficulties. Russia was a federation, except when it decided that it could change the terms of the federation and attack a member like Ukraine that was seeking more independence. So, I do see a general trend towards more federalist structures, despite the fact that crises do not stop there.

Now this is not incompatible with the cosmopolitan project, since the cosmopolitan project does not presuppose a world-state. Even Kant said very clearly that a world-state would be a world despotism, because a democratic republic presupposes its own public space, deliberative capacities, and assembly. Cosmopolitanism is necessarily a project of federalism and federalization, so it presupposes the spread of a culture of universal human rights. No matter how incredible it may seem in our world, cosmopolitanism dictates that conflicts among nations are not to be settled by war but by law. In that sense, cosmopolitanism remains a kind of utopia but it does not presuppose the elimination of smaller units, whether these be the nation state or the growth of regionalisms. If we look at what happened within the European Union, we see a lot of independent regionalist movements such as the Catalan movement in Spain. When you are integrated into a larger unit, the smaller units can be more differentiated. I am afraid that the Middle East is much too far from this at the present, but it is something worth hoping for.

SCA: *How would you evaluate the refugee problem across the world?*

SB: There is so much to say about this. I think we have to begin with the anthropological proposition that human beings have always moved. Movement is part of the ontology of the human condition. It is not an exception; it is the rule. From the standpoint of the nation state, the refugee problem is an administrative, economic and political crisis at once. The Universal Declaration of Human Rights, especially in articles 13, 14, and 15, lays out the principles for human mobility in the world. Article 13 says that every individual has a right to leave their country and re-enter. Article 14 says every individual has the right to seek asylum in another country. Article 15 states that there is a right to citizenship and to reduce statelessness. The difficulty arises from the fact that these rights are aspirational in the sense that you have a right to leave your country, but not to enter any which one you choose. The world is territorialized. The minute you exit one piece of earth, you are on somebody else's land. That's why we have borders, passports, and soldiers guarding borders. That's why people die over a small piece of land or territory. Most of the time these territorially circumscribed nation-states work because there is reciprocity. For example, if Greece closes its border to Turkish citizens, Turkey will close its border to Greek citizens. In case of war and conflict, this has often happened, yet the system works with porous borders most of the time, because there exits reciprocity and good will or what in international law is called 'comity.' Without this, we would have perpetual border skirmishes, border crises, and so on. I think the most difficult question is to reconcile what I call anthropological cosmopolitanism with the rights of bounded communities. I have always struggled with this, because I do not represent a radical *open borders* perspective. From a moral point of view, I think that borders are irrelevant. From a political point of view, borders are part of self-definition and self-determination. Therefore, what I have always argued for is respect for the rights of others, porous borders, and recognition of human rights.

This is a big topic in Turkey in that there is a fear that every Syrian refugee may potentially be an immigrant and change the nation. The distinction between the refugee and the immigrant that is so much a part of international law is under incredible stress right now. It is under stress in the sense that political refugees, in particular, refugees coming out of war zones are not able to go back, so they become permanent migrants. The world is full of unresolved conflicts, and this is a very dangerous situation in the first place for refugees themselves. For example, we can think of the 50,000 Iraqi, Afghani, and African refugees stuck on the Greek islands who cannot move forward, because European states they want to move to will not accept them. We can look at what is happening in the southern border of the US. The US may be violating its own laws and the 1951 Geneva Conventions. When people come from Latin America, it says to them to go over the border and to wait in Mexico. They give them a piece of paper and tell them to come back for an interview. This is not the way it goes. According to the Geneva Conventions, when that refugee arrives, you have an obligation to grant them an asylum interview right there, and when this is not possible to have them wait until you can. Still, they send the refugees back to Mexico where they witness theft, physical attacks, rapes of women, and child prostitution. It is awful. It is both a moral and a legal catastrophe. Compared to this, Turkey is an interesting situation which I call "authoritarian hospitality." Actually, this topic came up in our discussion at Boğaziçi University two days ago, when I was visiting there. I think there is a special feature in Turkey that goes back to Ottoman imperialism. I learned a lot from Reşat Kasaba's book called *A Moveable Empire*. Kasaba talks about the tradition of the Ottoman Empire that the borders of the empire moves and incorporates communities, offers them protection, and they exercise self-governed; the empire is mobile, and like a lot of ancient empires, it does not have borders. They have boundaries which as far as their power reaches. To some extent, there are neo-imperial and neo-Ottoman practices, particularly in the Syrian border. Then, there is the geopolitical conflict with the Syrian Kurds in that region. On the other hand, Turkey now is the largest refugee receiving country in the world with 3.6 million of refugees. There is no other country that quite comes close to it. Pakistan, Uganda, and in Europe, only Germany, has about one million refugees. So, what Turkey has done with the Syrian refugees in that sense is quite remarkable. I think it is part of a neo-imperial mentality as well as part of the famous Turkish hospitality that there is a kind of openness. It surely makes a difference that in some cases, the Syrians are related ethnically to people in the south of Turkey and that they are Muslim. Being a Syrian in Gaziantep or Diyarbakir is not the same as being a Syrian in Gaziantep or Diyarbakir. I think difficulties are arising in two ways: This group of people are needy, a lot of whom have done battle and chemical weapons have been used against them. Their country has been destroyed. What is difficult for many Turks is to fear that Syrian refugees as group simply owe allegiance to one political party and that by speeding up the citizenship process AKP creates a permanent following among them. This is not unknown in the history of migration. In the 19th century when the Irish, the Italian, etc. arrived in New York, the politicians would go out to these communities, immediately naturalize them and try to get their vote. It is called "Tammany Hall tactics." These are tactics known in migration-receiving countries. Form a human rights perspective, it is right that Turkey grant these people citizenship. Nonetheless, I would say that it should not happen automatically. In my opinion, there has to be a period of residency in Turkey (3–5 years) and some kind of language and cultural acculturation courses. This is done in many countries all over the world, including the USA, Germany, the Netherlands, and so on. The idea is that you learn the language of the country, its history, its own principles and traditions; you learn the language of your host and enter into a dialogue with this other country and culture that is giving you refuge. I would suggest a six-month period of a language school as well as history and culture lessons. Absolutely, all children should be sent into the schools right away. In that sense, what Turkey is doing is both right and wrong. It is right to integrate Syrian refugees and set them on the path to citizenship; it is wrong to speed this process up in order to manipulate them and get votes for the AK Party. A lot of people and friends I have talked to are very confused and conflicted about this, because people do not want to be cruel and brutal. On the other hand, they are upset about the fact that all of a sudden these refugees are voting in Turkish elections.

***SCA:** At this point in the debate on justice, it seems that justice is merely an ideal and injustice is a reality. For this reason, can we say that the best way to achieve justice is to define injustice and eliminate the cases of injustice instead of developing theories of justice?*

SB: I think this is an excellent question and there is a great deal in it that I agree with. I think that Derrida's concept of justice as justice à-*venir* is an important proposition. It is a horizon.; and having talked about discursive theory of legitimacy, communicative ethics, and liberal democratic politics, I think it is good to see a theory of justice not as a cookbook recipe. When you are cooking something, you are following certain instructions. A theory of justice is not like that. A theory of justice can be a regulative and conceptual principle. In that sense, it is à-*venir*. For instance, I never considered Rawls's theory of justice, and I think he understood it this way as well, other than being the best clarification and the best elucidation of our intuitions and ideas about justice in terms of liberal democratic republic. In some ways, justice has to remain a utopian concept. On the other hand, we have to have some regulative principles to clarify our ideals and this is what philosophy does at its best. It clarifies our ideals and intuitions. I am not about to write a theory of justice, because I do not quite think that way. I like working more with the messiness of the phenomena. I am more Arendtian in that sense because I like going into history, culture, political conflict as well as cultural conflict and try to tease out philosophical principles and insights in that way. That has been my work and the orientation. Nevertheless, I find the philosophical task of clarification of our deepest principles as regulative ideas quite helpful together with the vision of a utopian aspiration that justice will always be justice à-*venir*. As I said at the very beginning, rationality always presupposes a transcendent dimension; it does not just completely disappear in the contextual.

Acknowledgement

This interview was conducted by Sema Cevirici Atilla in person with Seyla Benhabib on December 16, 2022 during her visit to Istanbul.

Suggested Readings

Seyla Benhabib, *The Rights of Others; Alies, Residents and Citizens*, UK: Cambridge University Press, 2004.

Seyla Benhabib, *Critique, Norm, and Utopia*, USA: Columbia University Press, 1987.

Seyla Benhabib, *Another Cosmopolitanism*, UK: Oxford University Press, 2008.

Seyla Benhabib, *Dignity in Adversity: Human Rights in Troubled Times*, USA: Polity Press, 2011.

Seyla Benhabib, *Situating the Self; Gender, Community and Postmodernism in Contemporary Ethics*, UK: Routledge, 1992.

Seyla Benhabib, *Exile, Statelessness and Migration*, USA: Princenton University Press, 2018.

Seyla Benhabib, *The Claims of Culture; Equality and Diversity in the Global Era*, USA: Princeton University Press, 2002.

CHAPTER 8

Pragmatism and Justice: Richard J. Bernstein

Richard J. Bernstein was a prominent American philosopher whose work spans pragmatism, critical theory, and hermeneutics, with a deep focus on ethics, democracy, and pluralism. Known for his integrative and dialogical approach, Bernstein dedicated his career to bridging gaps between various philosophical traditions, including American pragmatism, Continental philosophy, and analytic thought. His philosophy reflects a commitment to open dialogue, mutual understanding, and the importance of democratic practice in addressing social and ethical issues.

One of Bernstein's most influential contributions is his development of pragmatic pluralism, a perspective that advocates for a flexible, context-sensitive approach to knowledge and ethics. In his foundational book, Beyond Objectivism and Relativism: Science, Hermeneutics, and Praxis, Bernstein argues for a "third way" between rigid objectivism and extreme relativism. He contends that while no knowledge is absolute or context-free, this does not lead to a nihilistic or relativistic outlook. Instead, he posits that knowledge and truth emerge through ongoing dialogue and practical engagement with the world. This pragmatic pluralism is rooted in the belief that ethical and political problems are best addressed through open, inclusive conversation and by acknowledging the multiplicity of perspectives that contribute to a fuller understanding of complex issues.

In The New Constellation: The Ethical-Political Horizons of Modernity/Postmodernity, Bernstein explores the ethical and political implications of modernity and postmodernity, critically engaging with thinkers like Habermas, Derrida, and Foucault. He argues for a philosophy that can incorporate the critical insights of postmodernism – such as its skepticism of grand narratives and its sensitivity to power structures – while remaining committed to democratic ideals and human solidarity. Bernstein's vision of democracy is one that resists authoritarianism and encourages active, participatory engagement from citizens, fostering a society that values both critical self-reflection and collective responsibility.

Another significant aspect of Bernstein's work is his commitment to understanding violence and tolerance in modern society. In Violence: Thinking Without Banisters, he delves into the origins and manifestations of violence,

 | DOI:10.1163/9789004732902_010

investigating how modern societies can better address the conditions that lead to violent behavior. He examines the philosophical roots of violence and the ethical imperatives of resisting it, advocating for a more empathetic, dialogical approach to resolving conflicts and promoting peace.

Bernstein also made major contributions to pragmatism, particularly in Pragmatic Encounters, where he re-examines the work of classic pragmatists like John Dewey, William James, and Charles Sanders Peirce, and demonstrates their relevance to contemporary issues in ethics, politics, and epistemology. His work in pragmatism emphasizes the importance of experience, community, and practical reasoning in navigating moral and philosophical challenges.

Sema Cevirici Atilla **[*SCA*]*:*** *You are one of the leading figures of pragmatism. In one of your articles, you mention that Derrida is obsessed with the concept of decision, as every great philosopher focuses on a specific theme and develops their philosophy based on that. Which concept or theme has been the main focus in your own philosophical work apart from pragmatism when you look retrospectively?*

Richard J. Bernstein [RJB]: I think that I am particularly interested in the concept of pluralism and how pluralism relates to democracy. There was somebody who asked me the same question. That is what I would answer.

SCA: *Why did you specifically choose this theme?*

RJB: Because I do not believe there is any perspective or anything which has a single grasp on the truth. I think we have to be always open to different perspectives from individuals, from different peoples, etc. I believe the task is to try to creatively engage with them. There are a lot of things and traditions you have experienced in your life which I, as a person coming from New York, do not really understand. Nevertheless, we can really try and have a serious dialogue in which I try to come to understand where you have come from, what things are important for you, etc. I believe the theme of being openness to the other is a tremendously important theme both in pragmatism and in deconstruction.

SCA: *How do you evaluate the relationship between pragmatism and deconstruction? Can we argue that pragmatism is deconstructive or that deconstruction is pragmatist since both share a common ground as opposed to foundationalism? In this context, what would you say when you compare the similarities and the differences between pragmatism and deconstruction? In addition to this, Derrida draws a similarity between deconstruction and pragmatism in his article "Reflections on Deconstruction and Pragmatism." What kind of relationship do you see between justice and pragmatism considering that Derrida defines deconstruction as justice? Does pragmatism have concerns about justice?*

RJB: When you make comparisons, you have to be sensitive to similarities and differences. Deconstruction does not mean the same as pragmatism and the things that it emphasizes are not the same as pragmatism. However, we can see common themes. Both are very skeptical of any appeal to fixed foundations, and thus the anti-foundationalist theme can be seen in pragmatism as well as in deconstruction. There is a sense in which Derrida is very critical of the so-called metaphysical oppression. The same would be true in pragmatism. Although Derrida does not use the word, he is certainly committed to the theme of fallibilism. Therefore, my idea would be to emphasize what you see as interesting similarities while keeping in mind that there are also very significant differences. The emphasis on undecidability is distinctive in Derrida and it is not a theme that you see in pragmatism. In fact, I think that there can be an interesting dialogue here, because the pragmatists would always emphasize that there is openness and ambiguity, but they would also speak about judgment and making a judgment. In some ways, Derrida is more radical, as he thinks that no matter what you say, there is always going to be an element of undecidability. And I think that is a radical form of pragmatism. One always has to be careful when making a comparison and should examine which similarities they find interesting. I mentioned a few of them; fallibilism, openness, anti-foundationalism, and the critique of metaphysics. One should also consider what sort of differences exist, since different philosophies have very distinct emphasis. For instance, the things that Derrida frequently emphasizes are not the same things that pragmatism emphasizes.

SCA: *Levinas poses the following question: "Can we talk about morality after Auschwitz?" Adorno states that writing poetry after Auschwitz is barbaric. After this tragic event, it is only just that we need to reevaluate our basic concepts, ethics and aesthetics. Wars and violent conflicts keep happening in today's world, although not as brutal as Auschwitz. It seems that the problem of evil will not come to an end as long as humans exist, yet the end of evil would also depend on human existence. How hopeful are you for humanity, the future and the current world politics?*

RJB: I think you raise very good questions. Nevertheless, the ethics questions are hard to answer in a few words ways. I am very pessimistic about the future in some ways. I believe that what we see all over the world as well as in this country is a move towards forms of authoritarianism which are ultimately anti-democratic. My greatest apprehension is that Trump will be re-elected in 2024. If he is elected again, I suppose America will be moving toward a form of ashes. In other words, I think that democracy is extremely fragile in the United States right now. One might argue that steps are being taken ultimately to undermine elections, to undermine democratic procedures and to undermine the structures and institutions of democracy. As the academics and some of the comments about Trump point out, he did want to bring about a real coup and takeover in America when he was defeated in the election. I fear a similar incidence could too easily happen in the future and that worries me. I am not quite sure that there is enough resources. The hopeful side in me says a majority of Americans are still opposed this, but I do not know if they have the resources to really prevent that. It is an old theme that goes all the way back to the xxx thinkers. They say that fascism can come out of liberalism, yet it is not a theme I was particularly sympathetic with. For a long time in my life, I never believed that this could happen, but I do believe that the democracy could come to an end. I admit that it is a pessimistic viewpoint. My optimist feelings are against that, yet that could happen. It would be unrealistic not to think that the US is moving towards a form of fascism.

***SCA:** Peperzak says that Levinas gives man the role which metaphysics assigns to God. In the face of others, a person takes all responsibility as if there is no God. Levinas emphasizes this point when he argues that the idea of God comes to mind through ethics. It is the feeling of shame I experience when I observe the poverty and nakedness of the other. The "self" begins to feel uneasy in its state of freedom and well-being in the face of the other's misery. Then, the ego opens up itself to the infinity which appears on the face of the other after realizing its own injustice. This awareness causes a feeling of uneasiness. Do you think Levinas' placing great emphasis on human responsibility as if God does not exist is an attempt to deal with theodicy, namely the problem of evil?*

RJB: In some ways, I think so. I believe that if we deal with Levinas at a theoretical level, I think that he has read the history of western philosophy. That is to a great extent to undermine or not recognize the otherness of the other in some ways. If you read Levinas as a kind of protest or sensitivity, then I am very sympathetic. Sometimes he overstates the case, yet I understand what he means when he argues that we have to take responsibility and not get caught up in metaphysics or the theme of the sameness and the other. I have technical objections here. I think his reading of the history of philosophy where he sees the dominant tendency is a bit overdrawn. For example, I would appeal to pragmatism here, but I do not see the pragmatism is guilty of what he is always charging of the sameness. What I sometimes feel is lacking in Levinas is a sense of institutional structures that are needed to further the kind of dialogue and openness that he talks about. Therefore, the theme is fine if you look upon it as a statement against some of the successors of Western philosophy. However, I suppose that he sometimes overdraws the contrast between the openness to others and the tradition of philosophy. At one point, he claims that he sees a certain continuity from Parmenides and Hegel, which is far too simplistic for me.

***SCA:** With respect to the story of Cain and Abel, Levinas argues that immorality begins when we lose our sense of responsibility. When God asks Cain where*

Abel is, Cain responds, "Am I my brother's keeper?" According to Levinas, all types of immorality began with Cain's answer. Levinas continues telling the story, "Of course I am my brother's keeper. I am a moral person, as long as I do not look for a special reason to be a moral person, because my brother's responsibility is what makes me an ethical being." How would you evaluate the relationship between immorality and responsibility within the context of this example, especially considering the current immigration policies? "Who are our brothers" and what responsibilities do we have for them as their keepers?

RJB: We have to manage to balance two things. Solidarity with our fellow men, recognizing the human beings and what we share with them without in some ways of literating this distinctiveness. Still, I do not always find in Levinas that the importance of the theme of solidarity with others is sufficiently dominant. Levinas touches upon the theme, yet I do not think it always gets the emphasis. I believe he is so concerned with the obliteration of individual responsibility that sometimes he overstates his case. I hope you understand that I am sympathetic with Levinas. I have written about him as you well know. Nonetheless, I suppose sometimes philosophers or thinkers make their point by exaggerating and emphasizing something which I think is neglect. I think this is important, because otherwise you do not see it and thus you do not become aware of it. At the same time, I could take a more balanced pragmatic view.

I think I can do two things with you: I can recognize our common humanity and what we share in common. I could also try to be sensitive to what is distinctive about you as a person. From my point of view, this is very pragmatic. Living a good life is balance. I think there are times, for example where all of us tend to be indifferent or hostile about what is distinctive. Let's take a problem in our country. I suppose you have heard or read a lot about white supremacy. I think one of the terrible things in this country is that many white supremacists and millions of people in this country are not properly sensitive to the distinctiveness of African Americans. And then character or classified them, we could not make it on the lowest level. Too frequently in this country, when people who are more sympathetic with white mastery look at an African American, they do not see an individual, rather they see an African American, a black that is associated with the other. In that sense, it seems to me that Levinas has great political significance. If I stop looking at you, an African American or somebody who is illiterate as a human being who is different than me, then I classify these people as just a poor white or just a poor black. Then, it seems to me that you are in great danger of failing your responsibility. Actually, I think this is a very serious problem in America. I must confess that I am still a bit mystified why in this country, in particular, there is such an adherence and obsession among certain whites with white supremacy that they cannot tolerate the idea that African Americans can be their equal. That is a great danger. I think one of the sad things about American history is that there were various moves which we thought would change this. They changed certain things, yet they have not eliminated this kind of deep prejudice. I do not know about your own political views, but there is some analogue to this in the way which many Turks look at Kurds. They do not see an individual, rather they see a terrorist or a threat to them. Therefore, you may have that kind of prejudice when you are convinced that you understand what they are all about and you can classify them. In this case, you do not see individual people. It is a problem that, I think, is just as severe in Turkey with the Kurds as it is here with African Americans and white supremacists.

SCA: *In the context of radical evil, I would like to point out to weak theology now. Weak theology rejects the idea that God is an overwhelming physical or metaphysical force. Instead, God is an unconditional claim without any force whatsoever. Weak theology puts emphasis on humans taking responsibility for their actions in the present moment and in this world. Thus, God is actually a call and merely the name of an invitation. It is a non-coercive and non-forced call. It is the responsibility of the humans whether to take this call or not. Do you think weak theology can solve the problem of evil? If God does not intervene in the evils of the world and is just a weak call, should man stop relying on the justice of God and build justice himself in this world? Has God handed over this responsibility to human beings?*

RJB: There is something that you said that I am very skeptical of. If somebody says a position or a statement can solve the problem of evil, I do not believe it, for I think evil is like Proteus. It can take on ever new forms and you would not know before it happens or what new forms it is going to take on. Therefore, the very talk of "Can we solve the problem of evil" to me is a bad orientation. We can certainly alleviate evil. Nonetheless, the idea that there is a philosophical, theoretical or theological way of solving the problem of evil strikes me as something that I am very skeptical of. Nothing solves the problem of evil. We have to fight it in different forms that it takes. I think that is also very pragmatic.

SCA: *In your book* Radical Evil, *you define evil as the conscious rise of darkness over light. As Heidegger puts it, evil attains its original reality in the soul, which opposes itself to God and can claim the whole of being for itself. In the context of Heidegger's critique of the modern subject, can we say that epistemic evil and epistemic injustice manifest when people view the world as a representation and objectify it?*

RJB: I have to reveal some of my biases here. One of the things I tried to bring out in the book on *Radical Evil* is that I do not think there is any essence to radical. I believe the evil can take on ever new forms and you have to be open to them. It might be my blindness, yet I do not find what Heidegger has to say about evil is tremendously remarkable. I would be much more critical of Heidegger on this. Certainly, some of the themes that I am emphasizing in the *Radical Evil* book, particularly in the last section where I expand on the theme of evil, demonstrate that it takes on ever new forms and we have to be open and sensitive. I do not see that is a theme in Heidegger. Therefore, I would make a much sharper distinction between myself and Heidegger.

SCA: *What would you comment on the following statements by Levinas about Heidegger? "We can forgive most Germans, but it is difficult to forgive some Germans. It is difficult to forgive Heidegger."*

RJB: If you want to be hermeneutically generous, you can say that Heidegger made a mistake in 1933 when he became rector considering the German academics and the history. That is forgivable, yet I would agree with Levinas on this point. The failure of Heidegger, act of a war, to acknowledge that he made a mistake, his failure to recognize the significance of the Auschwitz is unforgivable. That is how I would interpret Heidegger. In other words, at this point, he knows what happened, he knows what he did and he knows what the Germans did. Why did he not make a public statement? This is a question that Marcuse asked to him in which he repudiated this, yet Heidegger never did that. Thus, Heideggerw, who was a leading philosopher, did not acknowledge the horrors of the Holocaust in his statement, which I think is also unforgivable. In that respect, I believe that you cannot forgive Heidegger but his failure not to acknowledge the horrors of the Holocaust. When you take into account the fact that he supported a Nazi regime and what the Nazis did, then you have a responsibility to give them.

SCA: *I would like to ask you some questions about Gadamer. My first question is about Aristotle's concept of phronesis and its reception by Gadamer. There is a tension between the generality of the rule and the particularity of the event and justice emerges in this tension. In this context, a just decision cannot be made with the existing answers of a predetermined system. Phronesis is a mediation between the universal and the particular, between the generality of the rule and the singularity of the event so as to make just decisions. In your book* New Constellation, *you state that the hermeneutic understanding is a form of phronesis for Gadamer. Can one argue that hermeneutics is a search for just decision?*

RJB: I do not know if we can particularly eliminate that idea which I am very skeptical of. I think it is not just a localized theme, but I believe that it points to an idea. We live in an age where everyone is talking about algorithms and decisions procedures. I think what tends to be eliminated is the kind of judgment which you can only have by phronesis. I have some criticisms of Gadamer though, which you probably read in my own book. He claims that under any political situation there is always a role that is played by phronesis. However, I think that can be corrupted. In fact, I see this happening all the time. I think that people believing in a post-Cartesian world, very frequently, talk about mediating between the general and the particular, yet that is nearly subjective. You have to have clear decisions. That's why, I am very sympathetic with Gadamer on this respect. I do not think Gadamer has a deep understanding of the corruption and power in the contemporary world.

SCA: *Do you think phronesis can be applied in the current law and in fair decision-making processes?*

RJB: I think it has to be constantly proven. I believe this is a very deep problem which I felt throughout my life in different ways. I think there is a deep tendency in human beings to look for clear decision procedures, clear foundations, and clear distinctions. Therefore, when they hear about phronesis, they think it is subjective. I think that is a very distorted point of view. I think there is no procedure. Say I would like to teach you how to practice phronesis. We can only do this by example, by witnessing, and by exposing people who do, in some ways, exemplify that particular virtue. I do think there is a lot politically in the world that is conspiring against some people like us. I believe it is even in our language. For instance, we are living in a technological world where there is a conviction that everything can be solved with an algorithm. The idea that everything can be solved with an algorithm or a decision procedure is antithetical to cultivating phronesis.

SCA: *At this point in the debate on justice, it seems that justice is merely an ideal and injustice is a reality. For this reason, can we say that the best way to achieve justice is to define injustice and eliminate the cases of injustice instead of describing justice?*

RJB: I think that it is very difficult and tends to be very abstract to try to define justice. However, I do believe that people can recognize injustice phenomenologically. That's why, a better way of dealing with the issue is not to begin with justice; is to begin with injustice.If you take some of the incidents you may have followed like the murder of George Floyd, nobody would doubt that this is a tremendous injustice. This man was murdered by the police, yet it means that your sense of its being wrong is where it is dominant and that begins to be the way.

There is a clear example of injustice here. When you say this is not just, in that context, you mean something very specific. You may find yourself asking the question why this policeman did not treat Floyd as a human being instead of sitting on his neck. Therefore, I believe that we get clearer about justice by being sensitive and open to injustice. I think injustice takes primacy over justice.

Suggested Readings

Richard J. Bernstein, *Beyond Objectivism and Relativism: Science, Hermeneutics, and Praxis*, USA: University of Pennsylvania Press, 1983.

Richard J. Bernstein, *Radical Evil; A Philosophical Interrogation*, UK: Polity Press, 2002.

Richard J. Bernstein, *The Pragmatic Turn*, UK: Polity Press, 2010.

Richard J. Bernstein, *The Abuse of Evil; The Corruption of Politics and Religion since 9/11*, UK: Polity Press, 2006.

Richard J. Bernstein, *The New Constellation; The Ethical-Political Horizons of Modernity/ Postmodernity*, USA: The MIT Press 1992.

CHAPTER 9

Post-Anarchism and Justice – I: Todd May

Todd May is an American political philosopher who writes on topics of anarchism, poststructuralism, and post-structuralist anarchism. Drawing inspiration from figures like Michel Foucault and Gilles Deleuze, as well as the anarchist tradition, May advocates for a philosophy that emphasizes personal freedom, responsibility, and resistance against oppressive systems. His work is characterized by an emphasis on vulnerability, empathy, and the ethical implications of human relationships. His philosophy centers on ideas of agency, solidarity, and the possibilities of ethical and meaningful living in a world often marked by inequality, suffering, and existential uncertainty. Influenced by French philosophers like Michel Foucault, Gilles Deleuze, and Jacques Rancière, as well as existentialist thinkers such as Jean-Paul Sartre, May explores how individuals can live ethically and resist oppressive structures, advocating for a way of life that emphasizes compassion, social justice, and personal integrity.

In The Political Philosophy of Poststructuralist Anarchism (1994), May explores the intersection between poststructuralist thought and anarchism, proposing that a decentralized approach to politics is necessary for true freedom. In this book, May argues that poststructuralism's skepticism of grand narratives and rigid ideologies aligns with anarchism's emphasis on decentralization and anti-authoritarianism. He suggests that, together, these philosophies offer a framework for social movements that prioritize autonomy, community, and equality without relying on rigid ideologies or centralized authority. May's political philosophy encourages a form of activism rooted in pluralism and flexibility, capable of adapting to complex, ever-evolving social realities.

May also addresses questions about the nature of suffering, mortality, and ethical living. His book A Significant Life: Human Meaning in a Silent Universe explores how people can find purpose and significance even if life itself may lack inherent meaning. Drawing on existentialist insights, May argues that meaning is not something discovered externally but is instead created through the actions, relationships, and commitments that people choose to pursue. This perspective resonates with those who seek to live a purposeful life in the face of uncertainty, suggesting that meaning is found in the engagement with life itself, rather than in any transcendent truth or predetermined

 | DOI:10.1163/9789004732902_011

purpose. May's exploration of ethics is also evident in The Moral Philosophy of Poststructuralism, where he examines how ethics can be grounded in a philosophy that questions objective values and universal norms. May advocates for an ethics of care, responsibility, and relationality, where the focus shifts from abstract principles to the concrete experiences and needs of others. This approach to ethics aligns with his broader political philosophy, emphasizing that ethical action must be flexible, responsive, and context-sensitive, adapting to the specificities of each situation.

In addition to his academic works, May's philosophy has gained a popular following, in part through his role as a consultant for the television show The Good Place, where he helped develop philosophical themes around morality and the afterlife. He wrote most recently Should We Go Extinct?: A Philosophical Dilemma for Our Unbearable Times. He focuses on meaningfulness in life, friendship, nonviolence, death, fragility, ethics, political philosophy. He gives talks for universities and public venues on above mentioned issues. Because of the climate crisis, he prefers most of talks online.

Sema Cevirici Atilla [*SCA*]*: How did you come up with the idea of connecting poststructuralist philosophy with classical anarchism? What questions or problems made you bring these two different periods and movements together?*

Todd May [**TM**]: So, here is the thing, it actually happened by accident. I was describing Foucault on a train that I was taking with a friend of mine to a conference. And he said that sounds like anarchism. I never thought about this before, so I started to read anarchism. And I realized although much of post structuralist philosophy defines itself against Marxism, and particularly against a certain reductionism of Marxism, that anarchism was a more wide-open field, and for most anarchists is to oppose domination wherever it happens. That seems to be very much keeping with Foucault. So, I start to follow that path and realize that particularly Foucault and a bit Deleuze and Lyotard could be seen as people who are taking up the anarchist tradition and moving it into a more contemporary way of thinking.

SCA: *In an interview, Deleuze and Foucault drew attention to the connection between power and desire with reference to Wilhelm Reich who said, "No, the masses were not deceived, they desired fascism and that is what has to be explained." How do you evaluate the relationship between power and desire in this regard? Do human beings desire power rather than opposing it?*

TM: I actually wrote an article about Deleuze and desire, and his claim that, people weren't fooled and that it is about desire. My argument was that was actually half right. Desire gets mobilized, but I think it would be too much to say people don't get fooled. I think contemporary politics has borne me out on this. People do actually, partly out of desire they will look at certain news outlets. But then they come to believe what those news outlets are saying. So, I think there is an interaction between desire and misinformation. They reinforce each other, rather than the idea being that it's ultimately all about desire. Now that's for Deleuze. Foucault approaches this differently because Deleuze is taking and utilizing the Lacanian framework, but then try and turn the Lacanian framework back against Lacan. The idea being that desire is not a lack of something, which is Lacan's argument, but instead that desire produces things. And in this case desires produces certain political fascism. Foucault rejects the entire psychoanalytic framework, so he is not going to find desire to be somewhere at the bottom. But what he is going to look at is the relationship of power to the formation of who we are. So, we might form our desires because we are created or molded in such a way to have those desires, but the ontological notion of desire that's informing both Deleuze and in different ways Lacan doesn't appear in Foucault. This is because Deleuze is an ontologist, and Foucault is a historian. So, for Foucault he would take ontological categories and try to show how they are actually historically, politically and socially constituted. Whereas Deleuze is looking for ontological grounding that will allow him for the kind of analysis that you want.

SCA: *Deleuze and Foucault argue that "it is not right to speak for others and that no one can represent anyone, because the desire to speak on behalf of another is actually the desire to establish power over that person by taking away the right of self-consciousness." You have explained their opposition to representation in terms of two reasons. First, the idea of representation is the oppressive aspect of the practice of telling people who they are and what they want, and secondly, representing others helps reinforce other oppressive social relations. Do you think it is possible to dodge the problem of representation? If so, how do you think it should be done? If we cannot avoid it, can we solve this problem by minimizing the oppressive aspect in the practice of representation?*

TM: This is where anarchism really comes in, because the resistance to representing others, speaking for others, goes to the anarchist idea of radical equality, that everyone is equal to one another. So, the question that comes, can we do away with representation, which would be in some sense, the question of, can we have a utopian anarchist society? I don't think we can answer that in theory, but I suspect that it is probably unlikely, that it would be very difficult to have the kind of radical egalitarian structures that would eliminate representation altogether. But the non-utopian anarchists, people like Colin Ward, argue that we should not see anarchism as a blueprint for a utopian society, but as trying to form egalitarian relationships from the bottom up. So, the idea is to create egalitarian structures, institutions, relationships and to see how far that would go. The further it goes the better, but I don't think we can answer theory whether it can ever lead to a utopian society. I'm doubtful that it could, but I don't have a particular argument for it, and I think Colin Ward was doubtful as well.

SCA: *In "The Political Philosophy of Poststructuralist Anarchism," you show that poststructuralist thinkers, especially Deleuze, Foucault, and Lyotard, wanted to move away from ethical principles, but still based their thoughts on some ethical principles. What are the reasons for this paradox in your opinion?*

TM: Actually, I think it is largely historical. From the end of World War Two, ethical philosophy in France is actually pretty thin. If you move away from Levinas and maybe some of the religious thinkers like Marcel, there isn't a lot of ethical reflection. There is a lot of political reflection, like Foucault, Deleuze, Derrida. There isn't a lot of ethical reflection, though, so historically there aren't a lot of resources to work with. Whereas in Anglo-American tradition, starting about 1970 or so, you see there is a much richer ethical tradition. That is why I try to borrow from Anglo American philosophers. If we were to look for a theoretical reason, I think it goes to this idea of not speaking for others, that to hold people to ethical standards is to tell them what they ought to do or to be. Now it seems to be inevitable that you do this. For instance, if you tell someone, you should not speak for others, you are making an ethical claim. So, there is a nascent set of ethical commitments that they all have. Foucault's ethical commitments involve resistance to conformism, resistance to capitalism, things like that. Deleuze's have to do with more Nietzschean views of self-over-coming, creativity, things like that. So, you can see the ethical principles there, but they don't get articulated. The reason they don't get articulated is partly because the sphere of representing others, and partly because of historical resources for over ethical reflection just haven't been in the atmosphere in that period of France thought.

SCA: *How would you make a connection between anarchism and justice? That is, considering all its forms from classical anarchism to poststructuralist anarchism, what does anarchism have in common with justice? Do they have a common ground that is based on a concern for justice?*

TM: Let me turn this back to you, when you're thinking of the term justice here, what are you trying to get at?

SCA: *What I mean by justice is an ethical responsibility or obligation to the infinite other that is irreducible to our epistemic limits and thus being fair to the other where there is no absolute truth.*

TM: You don't want to say there is no such thing as no absolute truth. Why you don't want to say this, because it is an absolute claim. What you can say is, I haven't found any reason to believe in absolute truth. That you could get away with. But the denial of the absolute truth is an absolute statement, so you don't want to go there. But one of the things that people get tripped up about is, there is a certain kind of modesty that sometimes we have to take philosophically. So, when I say I haven't found any reason to believe this, I'm not pronouncing, I'm just saying that in my investigation, maybe I am wrong, here is what I have and haven't found. And I think sometimes with philosophy, particularly with continental philosophy. There are absolute statements, you need to nuance that a little bit, sometimes to avoid paradox, sometimes just to indicate the limit of how far theory can go.

But in any event, what you are sort of getting at with justice has a lot to do with fairness in the treatment of others. That would correspond to a lot of traditional views of justice, which is not a problem, that is fine. In this way, if we take it that way, then the fairness involved in one's relationship to others, in anarchist thought, is going to be treating them as equals. To be fair to another is to treat them as an equal. Here again there are misunderstandings that also come up. Some people say, "if I treat them as an equal, that means I can't criticize them," and I say that doesn't mean that at all. I would say if you were saying I can't criticize this person, then you're being patronizing, you know looking down on them. And so, to say you treat one another as equal is to say you treating the other person as a conversational partner someone you can engage with, someone that might have something to say to you. Gandhi once said that no person has all the truth. And if we take that attitude, I may not have the truth, then we're open to others, being people who can be conversational partners with us. So, in that sense, if we think of justice as treating others fairly, the ethical obligation to be fair to others, anarchism would say that ethical obligation consists in treating them as equals. Even though a lot of anarchists don't understand this, even adversaries would be treated as equal. Again, it doesn't mean we can't confront them or coerce sometimes, but it does mean we recognize them as fellow potential conversation partners.

SCA: *In your book called "Nonviolent Resistance," you mention that philosophy neglects to think about nonviolence. For you, nonviolence is a type of struggle characterized by respecting the dignity of the other. Considering the structure of Western metaphysical and humanistic thought that reduces the difference to the logic of the sameness and suppresses the differences, do you think that this way of thinking produces an epistemic violence, and precisely for this reason, has brought about other types of violence?*

TM: Okay good. I worry about the word "violence" sometimes. And the reason I worry about it is, some people take it and run off the end of the earth with it. So, for instance, Zizek once said that when you categorize something, you're doing violence to it. I don't see how calling something a cow does violence to the cow. It doesn't seem to me that the mere categorization of something is violence. So that is why we have to be careful about this term, "violence". I think it can operate sometimes linguistically, to oppress people. When I talk about violence, what I mean is, denying people the ability to conduct their lives in a meaningful way. And there are no bright lines as to when it's not violent and when it is. So, you can sometimes have little microaggressions, that are not necessarily undercutting a person's ability to live meaningful life. I wouldn't necessarily call them violent. On the other hand, there are things that we shouldn't do, and we can't say that because it's not violent, it's therefore okay to do. There are lots of things that are not okay to do, even if they are not violent. Now all of that is backdrop to the question. So, the question is, is reducing the logic of the same something that is violent? I would put it this way, I think that it is something that can be violent, but we have to know what the circumstances are in order to ask whether this is undercutting people's ability to live a meaningful life. So, for instance, when Martin Luther King says that all people are human being and we should treat people right as fully human beings that is a sort of logic of the same, isn't it? But it's not the sort of logic of the same as violence, it's a logic of the same that is trying to counter violence. That's why I say, sometimes we have to, rather than floating above the historical phenomena and saying is there a logic of the same which is violence, we have to ask, well what context is the logic of the same operating in? Sometimes it operates in a context where it undercuts people's ability to live a meaningful life.

For instance, when Foucault describes in "Discipline and Punish" putting people under psychological categories, that's tied to the whole practice of what I would call violence, making it impossible for them to live meaningful lives. In that case the logic of the same does work violently, while in the King case it works against violence. So, it always seems to be a matter of what the historical conditions are. That goes back to what I was saying before about the idea that you make these absolute pronouncements and you're not seeing the nuance of the phenomena.

SCA: *Derrida argues that the history of logos is the history of oppression. In this respect, can we say that abandoning the notions of logos, knowledge, and truth would be the only way to develop a system of nonviolent thought?*

TM: Good, this is actually where I had my debate with Caputo years ago. He is a sweet guy. So, in my debate with him, well he presented a paper that I responded to. What he wanted to say was, follow Derrida, that there is no such thing as truth capital T. But that seems like a truth capital T kind of statement. Leaving that aside, there is this problem of seemingly wanting to leave out truth without a capital T. What I said was, when my oldest kid was small, I said you should write like the Big T and small t. And he said no, it's not big and small, its capital and lowercase. And I said, I don't see what you mean here. He said, well here and he then took a piece of paper and wrote a lowercase t on it that was really large, and he says that's a big t, but it's lowercase. So, it is not big and small, it's capital and lowercase. I said to Caputo the lesson here is even if there's no capital T truth there are some lowercase t truths which are really big and important. And we need to recognize that. And asking about truth, I think we shouldn't ask how to get away from truth, I think we should ask which lowercase truths are important and which ones are not important.

There is this tendency, in some corners of philosophy, to fail to distinguish between some absolute grounded truths, capital T, and the important lowercase truths that we need in order to confront the kinds of oppressions that we see. So, for instance, if it is the case that psychology, as Foucault argued, pervades society and helps create people to be certain ways, that seems to me an important lowercase t truth that we need to operate. So, like some of the other questions, I don't want to say that there is this history of logos that is something that is oppressive, but rather that there has been a historical tendency to try to ground philosophy in something absolute and if we move away from that we don't need to move away from the idea that there are significant truths, but just move away from the idea that we need to be grounding these truths in something that would gather them all together under a single umbrella.

SCA: *In his lectures on the* Will to Know, *Foucault remarks, "Freud followed in the footsteps of the relationship between desire and truth and believed that Oedipus was telling him about the universal forms of desire. Whereas Oedipus was telling him the historical constraints of our truth system. Freud thought he heard the voice of desire, whereas what he heard was the echo of his own true discourse." How would you interpret this statement? Is Oedipus an expression of repression rather than a universal expression of desire?*

TM: Oedipus is surely not universal, if for no other reason Oedipus has to do with boys and has nothing to do with girls. You know, for Freud, there was the Electra complex for girls, but since girls don't really matter for him, the only thing that really matters is the Oedipus complex. So first of its not even universal on Freud's telling. But the idea that we all have this, I think is so implausible, even to think its universal even among boys. But I don't think it's a structure for oppression, I think the way I would put it is, and that would be the Foucauldian idea, it's a structure of creation, that you actually introduced the idea to boys: "this is what you want." And then they're like, "oh is that what I want?" And so, what's happening is people being molded in certain ways. They're encouraged to look at their families and their internal anthropological structure as the entire way to account for who they are, rather than looking at the social political conditions that are forming them. It seems to me that Oedipus functions politically, to mold people in certain ways and to mold them to look inside themselves for what's going on, rather than to look at their relationship to their social and political conditions.

SCA: *You have pointed out that poststructuralist thinkers call us to rethink what we mean by politics and to think about epistemological and political commitments in a radical way. What is the importance of poststructuralists' call for concrete politics from your perspective?*

TM: Okay good, here Foucault is particularly important. In traditional political thought, there is a centering around the state. What does the state do, what social contract should people have, informing the state, things like that. And that tends to conceptualize power as repressive, negative, what can the state do to you, and what is it not okay for the state to do to you. But what Foucault did was turn it around. You can see this in Deleuze and Lyotard as well but more clearly in Foucault. Well instead of asking the top-down question of what the state can and can't do to us, why don't we ask the bottom-up question, of how we get formed in different ways in learning different practices. And if we're asking, how do we get formed in different ways in learning practices and looking at some of those formations and saying they're to use because Foucault's word, "intolerable."

Then our politics is going to be much more grounded in something that's not resisting always the state or the big institutions but the also practices that form us, the ways through which our everyday world creates us to be conformist and unquestioning of capitalism and things like that. So, politics that recognizes that power doesn't just stop from things happening but actually creates them to be certain ways, is going to direct our political energies in different directions. Now that is not to say we shouldn't do anything around the state, but what it says is that we should just open our political practices, to recognize different openings for intervention, different ways of being together, different ways of forming ourselves.

SCA: *Lyotard shows that it is necessary to respect the plurality of language games and that preserving this diversity is related to justice. But is it ever possible to respect every language game or thought form? As you said, if everything is to be respected, then does not that mean that the thought forms and language games these thinkers criticize should also be respected? How can we resolve this paradox?*

TM: I don't think that there is a paradox. I think the paradox is if you only take the position that we word should respect all language games. And again, this is one of those absolute statements that gets people in trouble. Because then you have to respect the language game that says we should not be respecting people's language games. So, I think what we want to say here is that we should respect a multiplicity of different language games or discourses, whichever term you like. We should respect a multiplicity of language games and not try to reduce one to another. But there are those who think that morality, the moral language game, is always overriding. And there is philosopher Susan Wolf who I think made a compelling case against that. She says imagine this, imagine a woman whose son has committed a crime and the son goes to her house for shelter. Is she going to protect the son or not? Well, morally, probably what she ought to do is give the son over. But her love for the son is such that she doesn't. So, what she says is this is a case in which morality may no longer matter to her, but that doesn't necessarily mean that she's criticizable. It may be that there's this other value, love, which can stand alongside morality, and can have its own integrity. Morality isn't necessarily overriding. So now we have two language games, the language game of morality and the language game of love.

And in that case, it isn't necessarily the case that one should be all overriding over the other. We can think of that with aesthetics as well. I discussed this in my Significant Life book, I talked about narrative values sometimes clashing with moral values. It isn't necessarily the case that one out of prevail. So, I think that idea of respecting the multiplicity of language games is important, without having one being overriding. And the idea that we should respect a multiplicity of language games is a moral claim. But that doesn't mean we should respect every language game that comes down the pike. What that means is that there are a number of them that are worth respecting. And if we're not going to respect one we probably ought to have good reasons for not respecting it. And so, they onus is on the person that is the favor of respecting language games to give a reason why particular language games ought not to be respected. But to say that the onus is on them to give a reason is very different from saying we want to respect all language games.

SCA: *As you have stated, there is a problem that haunts poststructuralist thoughts and thinkers which is the epistemological inconsistency of the poststructuralist claims. Is it not more appropriate to view poststructuralist claims in terms of ethical concern rather than epistemological coherence? Can we argue that what is central in this thought is ethical concern and the desire for justice for all differences rather than epistemological coherence?*

TM: I think the desire for justice is significant and central. But I don't think you can say that we will substitute that in and then we can leave the other out. Because, in acting ethically toward others, there are epistemic considerations that need to be taken into account. So, for instance, when Foucault analyzes epistemic structures, the question is going to come up, what's the epistemic status of his own discourse? And that always seems to me a legitimate question. In my first book I'm trying to answer that, to show how when he moves from archaeology to genealogy, this is a way to ground what he says epistemically. But if your defense is simply something like, well it's going to lead to better ethical consequences, then the question is, well is it true that this will lead to better ethical consequences? And now you're back to epistemology. So, it seems to me that on the one hand while it's right to say that the fundamental concerns are political, I don't think you can lay epistemology aside, because it will come back in one form or another.

***SCA:** At this point in the debate on justice, it seems that justice is merely an ideal and injustice is a reality. For this reason, can we say that the best way to achieve justice is to define injustice and eliminate the cases of injustice instead of developing theories of justice?*

TM: Good, I'm going to say no, and here is why. Saying what things are not doesn't give us direction. It doesn't give us a sense of where we might move. What I think we need is a vision. Now that vision may be broad and big and hard to articulate, but it is nevertheless a vision, and we can move toward that vision. If we define that vision negatively, we don't know where to go, we only know where not to go. And so, swing back to the discussion that we had before, when we were talking about anarchism and justice as fairness. If we say that justice has something to do with treating other people fairly, that can open the question up. Okay, what are ways we might think about treating people fairly? And those are all positive proposals. Even fairness is a positive proposal, as vague as it is. And so, if we opened things up that way then we have a path to move forward. So I would say that the important thing is to think about justice and contrast injustice with that. But sometimes, in thinking about justice, we might say well that thing is clearly unjust over here and that should inform our thinking about justice. But that doesn't mean that we should try a purely negative path.

Suggested Readings

Todd May, *The Political Philosophy of Poststructuralist Anarchism*, USA: Pennsylvania State University Press, 1994.

Todd May, *A Decent Life: Morality for the Rest of Us*, USA: University of Chicago Press, 2019.

Todd May, *A Significant Life; Human Meaning in a Silent Universe*, USA: University of Chicago Press, 2015.

Todd May, *Reconsidering Difference; Nancy, Derrida, Levinas, Deleuze*, USA: Pennsylvania State University Press, 1997.

Todd May, *Nonviolent Resistance: A Philosophical Introduction*, UK: Polity Press, 2015.

Todd May, *The Moral Theory of Poststructualism*, USA: Pennsylvania State University Press, 1995.

CHAPTER 10

Post-Anarchism and Justice – II: Saul Newman

Saul Newman is a prominent political theorist and philosopher known for his work on post-anarchism, a movement that combines anarchist thought with poststructuralist theory. His philosophy examines the nature of power, authority, and resistance, questioning traditional assumptions within both anarchist and Marxist frameworks. Inspired by thinkers such as Michel Foucault, Gilles Deleuze, and Max Stirner, Newman critiques the centralized, hierarchical structures found in traditional political theory and advocates for a radical form of politics that resists all forms of domination and embraces individual autonomy and fluid identities.

One of Newman's foundational works, From Bakunin to Lacan: Anti-Authoritarianism and the Dislocation of Power, introduces the concept of post-anarchism, which merges classical anarchist ideals with insights from poststructuralism. He argues that traditional anarchism, with its fixed ideals and essentialist views, limits the potential for genuine resistance by imposing rigid categories and binaries. Post-anarchism, as Newman sees it, questions the foundational assumptions of authority, identity, and power, suggesting that power exists in more diffuse and complex forms than traditional anarchism assumes. This shift encourages a politics that resists all forms of authority and domination, not just those imposed by the state or capitalism, but also those inherent in cultural and ideological systems.

In The Politics of Postanarchism, Newman further develops his critique of modern political ideologies and expands on his vision of a decentralized, anti-authoritarian political practice. Here, he argues for a form of politics that is adaptive, flexible, and responsive to the specificities of each context. Instead of prescribing universal principles or ideological positions, Newman advocates for a "micropolitics" that operates at the level of everyday life, emphasizing personal autonomy, direct action, and local forms of organization. His vision of post-anarchism rejects the rigid structures often associated with both anarchist and Marxist movements, proposing a fluid approach that is constantly renegotiated in response to changing power dynamics.

Another important aspect of Newman's philosophy is his analysis of subjectivity and identity in a postmodern context. In Political Theology: A Critical Introduction, Newman explores the intersections between politics, religion,

 | DOI:10.1163/9789004732902_012

and identity, questioning the authority of established narratives and ideologies in shaping political and individual identities. He examines how political ideologies often take on quasi-religious qualities, compelling individuals to adhere to dogmatic beliefs and submit to authority. Newman encourages a break from such totalizing narratives, advocating for a form of subjectivity that is open, questioning, and resistant to fixed identities and allegiances.

Sema Cevirici Atilla* [*SCT*]*: You are one of those thinkers who try to find a common ground between classical anarchism and poststructuralist thought. Do you think that it is a necessary relationship or a bad partnership? Do we have an adequate and consistent basis for establishing a relationship between two different movements and periods? Is there any criticism that you find significant in this respect?

Saul Newman [SN]: What I would try to do is synthesize elements of classical anarchism with poststructuralist thought. So, I try to adopt both elements of classical anarchism and try to make it more relevant to contemporary struggles – over a whole range of different issues and problems and forms of domination and so on. The elements of classical anarchism that I think are still relevant would be its ethos of anti-authoritarianism, it's politics and ethics belief equality, freedom and non-domination, of being opposed to domination and all of its forms. Whether it's the domination of the state or the capitalism, or the domination and destruction of the natural environment. So, I think all of these elements of anarchism are still vital to contemporary struggles. What I tried to do with my theory of post anarchism was to develop an understanding of anarchism which is no longer based on kind of essentialist conceptions of human nature on some notion that there kind of an imminent rationality at the basis of all social relations. So, I am thinking about Kropotkin idea of mutual aid, for instance, which he saw as a natural, biological principle that was latent within all social relations. There are certain elements of classical anarchism, which I think are somewhat, and part of an Enlightenment humanist paradigm of thinking which is somewhat questionable today.

***SCA:** The survival of anarchism actually means the survival of the state or authority. There will be no anarchism given that there is no state or authority. Therefore, what anarchism rejects is what keeps it alive. Can we say that the destruction of authority or the state is the last thing anarchism wants? If the state disappeared, anarchism would disappear as well. As you state, if getting rid of power or authority is a dream, then can we argue that anarchism will always remain an utopia?*

SN: I think this is kind of based on a misconception. I don't think anarchism is simply about destruction of the state, I think it's an illusion to imagine that once the state is overthrown, that freedom will prevail, that we will be completely liberated. Firstly, it's quite hard to think about overthrowing the state would actually mean today. What call the state today is much more difficult to define, in the era in which power takes the form of decentralized networks of control. My point is that there will always power and there will be potential for domination in every type of society, even in a post-state society. So, I think some sort of anarchism will always be relevant because there is always going to be the risk of new relations of power emerging in the place of state. So, I take the Foucauldian idea of power as coextensive with any kind of society. That doesn't mean of course we can't have a less hierarchical forms of power. It doesn't mean power can't be made more reciprocal, more fluid or egalitarian. But I think there is always risk of new forms of domination emerging, so it seems to me anarchism will always be relevant.

SCA: While Kropotkin says that internal contradiction is the death of ethics, you argue against this that internal contradiction is the very condition of ethics. According to you, a thing must never be absolute in order to be ethical. Do you think it is an inevitable paradox that values such as ethics and justice which were once seen as absolute and the highest foundation are explained without any basis?

SN: What I've tried to suggest is, in a way that ethics and morality refer to different orders of being. In contrast to morality, ethics cannot be based on some universal abstract moral law, but is defined by contingent practices. Ethics can thus involve a challenge to existing forms of morality – or at least it kind of opens the space in which moral notions can be contested and modified. So, to me ethics is always based open a certain kind of contingency and it can never be fixed or absolute. Ethics also involves form of subjectification, by which the individual redefines him or herself in different contexts and through one's relations and interactions with others.

SCA: In The Politics of Postanarchism, *you state that "Let us understand postanarchism as a kind of deconstruction." How would you develop a relationship between postanarchism and justice considering Derrida's definition of deconstruction as justice? Can we argue that postanarchism is a search for justice or for a philosophy of justice?*

SN: Justice is something that cannot be absolutely defined. It certainly can't be wholly defined in a form of law or state institutions. Here I would agree with Derrida that while justice needs to take some sort of institutional legal form in order for it to be applied, at the same time it always exceeds its legal expression and deconstructs legal authority. Justice is that which often challenges the authority of the law, exposing it to its own indeterminacy, to a moment of ethical rupture. This point is obvious, because how else could laws and legal systems change, be reformed, at times be overthrown and replaced with something else? Justice is something that cannot be absolutely fixed or frozen in time or universalized. So there is an important ethical gap between justice, which is open ended, and law.

SCA: *With reference to John D. Caputo, you interpret Derrida's philosophy as a strategy of responsibility towards the excluded other and a "responsible anarchy." This anarchy is actually a search for justice that begins with ethical concerns. In this context, what does responsible anarchy mean when compared to other kinds of anarchism? Do they have any negative or positive implications?*

SN: As you know there are two different ways in which the notion of anarchy resonates. One is to think of anarchy in terms of chaos, disorder, violence, state of nature, anomie, the complete absence of any kind of ethical or moral standards whatsoever. For instance, that's often the association most people have in their minds when they hear the word anarchy. But of course, there is another notion of anarchy, which is in some ways related but also quite different, which is simply the absence of principle of authority or command. Anarchy quite literally means the absence of rule or the absence of rulership, the absence of sovereignty. Many people would suggest if you take away commanding principles, you end up with the anarchy of the state of nature or you end up with the kind of situation which there are no possible ethical values or standards of behavior. My point would be that anarchism has to try to kind of construct some sort of ethical and political action on the basis of ontological anarchy, on the absence of absolute principles and foundations. So, anarchism is the process of political innovation which isn't fixed or guided by sort of a rational telos or firm ontological principles. I suppose to put things quite simply, we could never say what a perfect anarchist society would look like, I think to do that is to already limit the practice of anarchism to a particular vision of the perfect society. In one of Foucault's lectures where he talks in the late 1970s (*The Government of the Living*) he outlines what he calls 'anarchaeology', an anarchistic method that starts rather than finishes with anarchy. In other words, we start with the basic principle that authority cannot justify itself on its terms, that it cannot command our obedience simply for its own sake, and this leads to its ongoing interrogation. And we proceed from there. It's not so much about reaching the goal of a perfect anarchist society of the future, but rather starting with this fundamental questioning of authority. We don't know where this will end up, or which direction it will necessarily take us in. So, I have always insisted that anarchism is about innovation, experimentation, and refers to a whole range of different struggles that are not defined by some ultimate goal or vision of a perfect society. To do would be to close down and totalize anarchism. So, anarchism is not just one political project, but many political projects, which cannot be predefined or predestined.

SCA: *Deleuze claims, "We are all little colonizers and it is Oedipus who colonized us." Do you think that psychoanalysis is a tool controlled by the state that curbs desires, as Deleuze said? Is the Oedipus complex a discourse that colonizes us rather than revealing our desires?*

SN: Deleuze and Guattari are quite famous on their attack on certain aspects of Freudian psychoanalysis which they argued was a way of colonizing our desires through the figure Oedipus, which is the construction of desire around repression basically. My view of psychoanalysis is a bit different from this. I think that, I mean yes, you can say that certain aspect of the classical Freudian psychoanalysis were in some ways quite conservative in the sense that they sought to adjust the desires of the individual to the constraints of the society and the constraints of civilization or at least make the tension between the individual desires and civilization more tolerable. I would say that psychoanalysis, importantly, reminds us of our limitations, it reminds us of some of the utopian illusions behind revolutionary desire. Lacan quite famously said to his rebellious students in the aftermath of May '68, "what you desire is another master" and I think this is very interesting. So perhaps psychoanalysis reminds us that hidden behind any revolutionary impulse is another kind of hidden authoritarianism, a desire for a new state or new master, a new form of authority. I think Lacanian psychoanalysis is quite important in, if you like, cautioning us against investing all our desires in this notion of revolution or in this idea of getting rid of the state. Because once you get rid of the state what happens then? Maybe we will simply invent a new kind of order, another Master to fill this empty place of power. Maybe we need to come to terms with the fact that the human subject always necessarily desire freedom, maybe in certain instances we desire our own repression, or own domination. We get back to the problem of voluntary servitude which I think reflects one of your other questions, this idea that we actually want to be dominated and maybe this kind of desire underpins the certain kind of revolutionary projects. So, to me that what's quite interesting about psychoanalysis. It makes us critically reflect on the fundamental fantasy of revolution, and on the way that we need to state to define ourselves against.

SCA: *Do you agree with Deleuze who said that to understand how power works and to see political power, we must turn to the little things, and therefore, politics must begin with micropolitics? Do you think politics is macro-politics or micro-politics?*

SN: It is both. Deleuze would say that to do micro-politics can also have transformative macro-political consequences. It's just that we need to start with micro politics. If you simply think about politics, and particularly radical politics in macro political terms, in terms of the great revolutionary event that will transform the entirety of social relations, then you will simply fall into a trap which is to kind of reinvent new forms of domination, new forms of exploitation, new structures or authority. So, what we need to focus on is kind of the micropolitical transformation which takes place within the self and the self's relation with others. The anarchist Gustav Landauer said the state itself is essentially a series of interpersonal relations, relations between the individuals and we destroy the state by transforming ourselves. As Max Stirner would say it begins with an insurrection against the self, which involves a working of the self out of power, something which can lead to a revolution on a broader society-wide scale, but which was fundamentally distinct from it.

SCA: In one of your interviews, based on the criticism of Lacan's giving a seminar at the time of the Paris riots of 1968, you remarked, "Making politics is also making theory and making theory is doing politics." Was Marx wrong when he said that "philosophers have only interpreted the world, but the point is to change it?" Do philosophers actually do politics while developing theories?

SN: I think my point is that we should not necessarily erect this artificial distinction between theory and practice. The invention of ideas and creation of new ways of thinking is also a practical political act. If I understand you correctly that, obviously Marx is saying that we need to move from theory to practice or what he calls praxis. I think Marx himself was a theoretician, Marx obviously believes that his theories about – historical materialism would obviously have that revolutionary impact. All I would say is that theoretical work is important, which doesn't mean that we can't just sit back and do nothing, we have to try to kind of implement them and live them. And nevertheless, I think the creation of new concepts, new ways of thinking can have potential consequences in the world of politics.

SCA: As you have shown in your work, the connection between Max Stirner and poststructuralist thinkers is very clear. Stirner is a forgotten link between the politics of classical anarchism and the politics of poststructuralism, as you said. However, how do you explain the lack of references to Stirner among poststructuralist thinkers?

SN: That is a very interesting question. Actually Stirner has been largely ignored in academia. I put this down to the influence of Marxism, and particularly to Marx and Engels' dismissal of Stirner as an idealist and bourgeois ideologist – which is a complete misreading. It's very interesting that Stirner has been so marginalized. I've always been fascinated by Stirner. I think the connection to post structuralist thought is really quite evident. But I'm not entirely sure why he is being pushed in the margins, but there is very little scholarship on Stirner, he turns up from time to time, and is then forgotten about again. Derrida discussed him in Spectres of Marx, Deleuze mentions him in his book on

Nietzsche. But from my perspective Stirner hasn't really been taken seriously philosophy and social and political theory, and I think it's about time that he was.

SCA: *There is a close relationship established between the state and the subject.* Accordingly, in representative epistemology, the subject represents the multiplicity and diversity in existence as an object immanent to his consciousness and represents them under a single concept. In a similar vein, the state is based on representational and conceptual thinking by gathering individual wills under unity and integrity, and thus establishes itself in this way. For this reason, Deleuze sees the philosophy of the state as an equivalent of the representative thought that guides Western metaphysics. How would you evaluate this relationship? Have radical critiques of the subject, along with poststructuralist thought, brought about critiques of the state and power or vice versa? In this regard, can we say that poststructuralist thought has done both a rational and a normative deconstruction of the critique of the state?

SN: Let's say that the liberal or the neoliberal notion of 'the individual' is a concept which is tied to representative structure of the state, through categories of citizenship, through ideas of rights, through forms of legal recognition. This is a limited idea of the individual as kind of the member of the state community. So, it seems to me that to question the idea of the state we also need to question this liberal idea of the individual, perhaps we need to have a different notion of the subject which is no longer seeks its validity or its recognition or identity within the state. A good example of this is temporary forms of identity politics. Whether it's about the left or the right, whether its questions about gender identity, cultural identity, religious identity, ethnic identity and so on. All of these claims have been made on the basis of identity and the claim for recognition – belonging to a certain group seen to be somehow oppressed, excluded or marginalised. At the same time this sort of politics inscribing the individual within the order of the state, through the granting of rights. This sort of identity politics for instance, doesn't in any sense challenge the structures of state domination or global capitalism in any sort of significant sense, all it does is simply inscribe the individual within certain kinds of groups, collectivities, which are kind of recognized by the state and given certain kinds of institutional rights and forms of legal recognition. I guess my point is to answer your question, that we need to fundamentally rethink the idea of the individual subject, in different kinds of ways, ways in which kind of allows a greater degree of autonomy, to kind of break this link, this discourse that is the heart of liberalism. This link between the individual on the one hand and the state on the other. And the fundamental misconception of libertarianism is to see the individual and the state as being opposed. But it seems to me that the relationship with the individual is more complicated because it isn't simply one of the opposition. It's rather actually, the individual is kind of constructed by the state and therefore to kind of insist upon, you know things like individual riots, right to recognition, it kind of bolsters the state or gives the state a greater legitimacy cause it's the state which kind of grants rights, it's the state which kind of grants recognition.

SCA: *In their book* Critical Jurisprudence: The Political Philosophy of Justice, *Costas Douzinas and Adam Gearey say that "justice is what society lacks and desires; it has no other definition." They both claim that justice cannot be completed in this world and that psychoanalysis constantly reminds us of this gap. As the attempt to reach justice actually originates from the gap which was opened in the primordial separation in the subject and from the symbolic castration, justice remains unreachable, because the concept of the good and justice as its political expression is identified with the Mother. Do you think the desire for justice should be based on an object of desire that can never be attained as it is expressed in psychoanalysis? How would you evaluate this relationship?*

SN: The whole point about psychoanalysis is that the object of desire can never be reached or attained, and this unattainability is something which maintains desire. We can only desire something which we cannot obtain, once you attain it that's the end of desire isn't it? So, perhaps we can think about justice in the same way. The promise of justice as the goal we are striving to attain is what keeps us moving forward, allowing us to develop different articulations of justice, knowing at the same time that the idea of a perfect, complete justice is impossible. As Derrida would say, justice is infinitely perfectible. We never reach a state of perfect justice, every time we try to institutionalize a perfect form of justice, once and for all, we end up in some sort of totalitarian disaster, and that's always the risk, as we've seen with many thinkers, from Plato and onwards. So, once again, the relationship to the psychoanalytic notion of desire implies that justice is kind of an open-ended goal. It's something which once again kind of opens up all existing legal and political institutions to kind of ongoing ethical interrogation.

SCA: *At this point in the debate on justice, it seems that justice is merely an ideal and injustice is a reality. For this reason, can we say that the best way to achieve justice is to define injustice and eliminate the cases of injustice instead of developing theories of justice?*

SN: I see the two things as inseparable in a sense because if you're fighting particular forms of injustice, whether its environmental injustice or economic injustice, racial injustice, gender injustice, you're working on the horizon of justice. You're fighting in the name of justice, a greater form of justice, whatever it is, equality or whatever. At the same time we need to be careful, (this is related to what we talked about before) about defining exactly what justice would look like, or what a just society would look like. Because I don't think you can ever eliminate injustice entirely, there is always new forms of injustice, new forms of exploitation, domination, violence or whatever, which emerge. Justice is therefore a kind of ongoing open-ended project which cannot be absolutely defined. Because when you try to define it institutionalize it it can potentially involve new forms of injustice. So, we have to kind of keep on fighting injustices at a kind of local level, being engaged with particular struggles. There is always a danger of trying to define concepts absolutely because that can kind of limit one's political scope and can potentially involve imposing a certain particular vision of justice from everyone else. It's sort of a convoluted answer to the question but I don't think you can kind of necessarily separate, particular struggles against injustice from some great notion of justice. I'm just saying that there is always a danger in trying to define absolutely what this greater notion justice is.

Suggested Readings

Saul Newman, *From Bakunin to Lacan: Anti-Authoritarianism and the Dislocation of Power*, UK: Lexington Books, 2007.

Saul Newman, *The Politics of Post-anarchism*, UK: Edinburgh University Press, 2011.

Saul Newman, *Political Theology: A Critical Introduction*, UK: Polity Press, 2018.

Saul Newman, *Power and Politics in Poststructuralist Thought: New Theories of the Political*, UK: Routledge, 2009.

Saul Newman, *Post-anarchism*, UK: Polity Press, 2015.

CHAPTER 11

Post-Anarchism and Justice III: Lewis Call

Lewis Call is a contemporary philosopher known for his influential work in post-anarchism and cyberpunk studies. His contributions primarily revolve around reinterpreting classical anarchist theories through post-structuralist lenses, drawing heavily on the works of philosophers like Friedrich Nietzsche, Michel Foucault, and Gilles Deleuze. This approach challenges traditional structures of power and authority, encouraging a more nuanced and flexible perspective on personal freedom, identity, and society. Call's work explores how these ideas intersect with the digital age, particularly within the context of cyberpunk literature, which he sees as a rich ground for anarchistic ideas to evolve and adapt to modern technological realities.

A cornerstone of Call's philosophy is his rejection of the Enlightenment ideals of universal truths and essentialist views on human nature, which many classical anarchist theories are rooted in. Instead, Call advocates for a form of anarchism that is decentralized, fluid, and adaptable, aligned with post-structuralist principles. He argues that concepts like freedom and identity are not fixed entities but are socially constructed and subject to change. His work suggests that power does not solely operate through state structures but exists in everyday interactions, language, and cultural norms, thus requiring a more holistic approach to resisting authoritarian influences.

In his seminal book, Postmodern Anarchism (2002), Call articulates this philosophy in depth. Here, he proposes that traditional anarchism's focus on direct opposition to the state overlooks other, less visible forms of authority and control that permeate society. He suggests that contemporary anarchism must evolve to address these more subtle, pervasive forces by embracing post-structuralist concepts, particularly those of Michel Foucault's theories on power and knowledge. Call's approach is not about dismantling all structures but understanding the complex ways they function and influence individual behavior. This perspective encourages a kind of "everyday resistance" where individuals critically examine their own lives and challenge social norms, fostering a more personal, internalized form of rebellion.

Sema Cevirici Atilla [*SCA*]*: How did you come up with the idea of connecting poststructuralist philosophy with classical anarchism? What questions or problems made you bring these two different periods and movements together?*

 | DOI:10.1163/9789004732902_013

Lewis Call [LC]: I remember reading Michael Ryan's *Marxism and Deconstruction*, and thinking that I'd like to do something a little bit like what Ryan had done, except that I wanted to focus on classical anarchism rather than classical Marxism, and I wanted to use twentieth century poststructuralist and postmodern philosophy more broadly, rather than specifically focusing on deconstruction. This was in the late 1990s, when the then-recent failure of Soviet state communism had made many Western intellectuals skeptical about the contemporary relevance of Marxism, and anarchism seemed like a more viable political philosophy. I thought that a poststructuralist or postmodern form of anarchist theory might give me a way to talk about some of the factors that seemed to be limiting the possibility of radical or revolutionary politics, such as the impact of mass media and the psychological factors identified by psychoanalysis.

SCA: *In your book* Postmodern Anarchism, *you first call attention to an anarchism of the subject. Do you think the anarchism of the subject that began with Nietzsche is solely an epistemological issue or a political issue beyond that?*

LC: I think that it starts out as an epistemological issue, but then it very quickly becomes a political issue. It's like that slogan from the American counterculture of the 1960s, "the personal is political." In my view, any serious discussion of revolutionary political theory or practice in the contemporary period has to include a critical discussion of the political subject who is meant to develop that theory or engage in that practice. It's become pretty clear by now that the stable, rational, autonomous individual subject handed down to us by the Enlightenment cannot serve as the basis for a viable radical politics in the contemporary period. So I believe that we have to reimagine political subjectivity in a pretty creative way if we hope to develop a radical praxis that might be suitable for contemporary conditions.

SCA: *You state that anarchism is a political philosophy which seems perfectly well suited to the postmodern world. What is the strongest link between postmodernism and anarchism in your opinion?*

LC: I think that anarchism shares with postmodernism what Lyotard regards as the defining feature of the postmodern, the incredulity towards metanarratives. Consider the anarchist slogan, "No gods, no masters." With this succinct four-word slogan, anarchists reject the Manichean and eschatological metanarratives of religion, and the political metanarratives that try to explain and justify state power (such as the Hegelian and Marxist dialectics).

SCA: *In* Postmodern Anarchism, *you draw attention to the dominance of the logos over the nomos. From your point of view, the task of the postmodern anarchist is to reverse the triumph of the logos. Can you expand on this subject a little further? What is the relationship between Logos and Nomos? How would you describe the role of the postmodern anarchist here?*

LC: In my book, I describe the relationship between logos and nomos as "complex and agonistic." I see logos and nomos as two principles that perpetually struggle against one another, but that struggle can never really be resolved. As I point out, a final victory for either logos or nomos would be a victory for binary thinking (and thus, ironically, a victory for logos, even if nomos was the nominal victor). Therefore the task of the postmodern anarchist, I argue, becomes more modest: their job is simply to render the nomos visible, to remind us that nomos is a possibility inherent in human thinking, to return nomos to discourse.

SCA: *In the same book, you say that postmodern anarchist thought opposes scientific thought forms that can actually contribute to political oppression, rather than abandoning scientific thought altogether. You cite Deleuze's royal science and nomad science as an example. What do you think will keep new forms of scientific thought free from domination and oppression? In other words, is there a way that can prevent the new forms of science from turning into a tool of oppression?*

LC: Unfortunately, I think that oppression is always a risk that exists within the scientific enterprise. As long as science continues to make truth claims, as long as it purports to create usable knowledge about the natural world, oppression will be a possibility. But I am encouraged by the turn that science has taken in the last hundred years or so, towards more modest claims. So much of twentieth and early twenty-first century science concerns the limitations of human knowledge, the things that can't be known. So we have ideas like Heisenberg's uncertainty principle, Gödel's incompleteness theorem, or Schrödinger's cat. I think quantum theory opens up some particularly interesting possibilities. In a quantum world, there is never any certainty, only waves of probability. Within those wave forms, anything is possible, and there is an infinite variety of possible meanings. It's only when the wave function collapses into a single meaning that oppression becomes possible. I use that idea quite a lot.

SCA: *There is a problem that haunts poststructuralist thoughts and thinkers which is the epistemological inconsistency of the poststructuralist claims. Is it not more appropriate to view poststructuralist claims in terms of ethical concern rather than epistemological coherence? Can we argue that what is central in this thought is ethical concern and the desire for justice for all differences rather than epistemological coherence?*

LC: Yes, I would agree with that. We are in the midst of an ethical emergency, especially in my country, the United States. Here in the U.S., the right wing is waging all-out war against difference. We're seeing a sustained assault on reproductive freedom, LGBTQ+ rights, the civil rights of people of color, the rights of the working class. In this political climate, we do not have the luxury of spending our time on obscure debates about epistemology, debates that never leave the ivory tower of the Academy. Our focus must be on ethics and justice. And that is related to the quest for new forms of subjectivity. In his preface to Deleuze and Guattari's *Anti-Oedipus*, Foucault described it as a book of ethics. He identified the book's strategic adversary as fascism, but not just the fascism of governments (which today would include Trump and the U.S. Supreme Court). He was concerned about the fascism "in our heads and in our everyday behavior."

SCA: *You state, "Postmodern anarchism asserts that the problems we face today are not the result of flaws in our political structures which can be alleviated through reform or through the seizure of state power. Rather the problem lies in the structures themselves and in the epistemologies which sustain those structures." In this respect, can we say that the main task of postmodern anarchism is to rethink epistemology?*

LC: My answer to this question may contradict my answer to the previous question, so I think I will invoke Foucault once again: don't ask who I am and don't ask me to remain the same; leave it to our police and our bureaucrats to see that our papers are in order! Yes, I do think it's crucial for postmodern anarchists to rethink epistemology. Specifically, I think we need to find more effective ways to connect epistemology with ethics. Any theory of knowledge that does not provide for ethical decision-making and effective, ethically informed political action is useless to us. In fact, I'll go further, and say that I think the barriers between the three main branches of Western philosophy – logic, ethics, and epistemology – have to come down. We need an ethically informed epistemology, and a form of reason that will truly allow us to think ethically.

SCA: *When you compare classical anarchism and poststructuralist anarchism, would you say the main claim of anarchism is freedom or responsibility towards difference and ethical sensitivity?*

LC: I think it must be the latter. When I was younger, I was enamored with anarchism's valorization of freedom, as young people often are. Now that I'm older, I see that freedom is such a broad category that it has limited usefulness, and it's too easy for political positions that claim the mantle of "freedom" to slide towards fascism. Take the American libertarian movement, for example. American libertarianism has degenerated into a kind of crypto-fascism, where "freedom" has come to mean that a 16 year old White nationalist boy can buy all the assault rifles he wants, while a 16 year old Black girl who is pregnant by her rapist can't get an abortion. To me, this calls for a bold ethical and political response. It is no longer enough merely to tolerate difference. To live in this bleak modern world as an ethical person, one must actively embrace and celebrate difference. I see this happening among young people today, particularly with respect to gender. So many young people are transgender, non-binary, gender queer, etc. I really think that the old binary concept of gender may die out in a generation or two. It's about time!

SCA: *In an interview, Deleuze and Foucault drew attention to the connection between power and desire with reference to Wilhelm Reich who said, "No, the masses were not deceived, they desired fascism and that is what has to be explained." How do you evaluate the relationship between power and desire in this regard? Do human beings desire power rather than opposing it?*

LC: Yes, I do think that human beings desire power. Power is seductive. I think there is something fundamental about human psychology that makes us want power – or more specifically, makes us desire a relationship with power, which is not the same thing. This is what fascinates me about BDSM, which was the subject of my second book and much of my third. I'm particularly interested in the dominance/submission aspect (DS). DS gives people a safe, consensual, ethical way to embrace power. The dominant can fulfill their desire to exercise power over another person responsibly. The submissive can fulfill their desire to give power over themself to another safely. Everybody wins! I think that in this way, DS provides a crucial alternative to fascism. It provides a safe outlet for the desires which, as Reich pointed out, can easily lead to fascism if no such outlet is available.

SCA: *Foucault commented in an interview that he did not believe in a pure idea of justice and that justice was a weapon in the power game. Do you think that a pure idea of justice independent of power relations is possible?*

LC: No, I agree with Foucault on this one. I find Foucault's concept of power very compelling. If power flows through every social relationship at all times and in multiple directions, as Foucault argues, and if justice is an aspect of the social, then I don't see how justice can exist independently of power.

SCA: *Foucault does not define himself as a postmodern-poststructuralist. In this context, how should we understand Foucault's inclusion in the thought of postmodern or poststructuralist anarchism?*

LC: I think Foucault himself gave us a way to deal with this in his famous essay "What is an Author?" Foucault is an author-effect. His name is a signifier that points to a certain body of texts. But since he has become so influential, his name has become more than that. Foucault is one of those "super-authors" (as he argues Marx and Freud are), so the name "Foucault" is now a signifier that initiates a specific type of discourse. In that sense, it doesn't really matter if Foucault defines himself as a postmodernist or poststructuralist. He would probably reject the label poststructuralist, and he would almost certainly reject postmodernist. But he's just the author, so what it does it matter what he thinks?

SCA: *How would you make a connection between anarchism and justice? That is, considering all its forms from classical anarchism to poststructuralist anarchism,* *what does anarchism have in common with justice? Do they have a common ground that is based on a concern for justice?*

LC: Yes, I would say so. Classical anarchism was certainly driven by a concern for justice. Initially, that took the form of a desire for justice for the working class and the peasants. In the hands of feminist anarchists like Emma Goldman, it extended to a desire for justice for women. The major blind spot of classical anarchism, in my view, was race and ethnicity. The anti-semitism of Bakunin, for example, was completely unsupportable. Like any political philosophy, anarchism had to evolve in order to remain relevant. I think that the poststructuralist form of anarchism has a broader and more inclusive concept of justice. This is one of the benefits of the anarchy of subjectivity we discussed above. The rational, autonomous subject that poststructuralist anarchism critiques was always, implicitly, a straight White male subject. So decentering that subject via poststructuralist critique opens up a political and ethical space in which we can seek justice for everyone, including people of color and LGBTQ+ folks.

***SCA:** Considering the structure of Western metaphysical and humanistic thought that reduces the difference to the logic of the sameness and suppresses the differences, do you think that this way of thinking produces an epistemic violence, and precisely for this reason, has brought about other types of violence?*

LC: Yes to both. I don't think it's going too far to describe the suppression of difference as an epistemic violence. The restriction of metaphysics to a narrow range of possibilities in the name of "humanism" is violent. And this certainly enables and produces other types of violence, including very real physical violence. I'm most worried about the violent suppression of minority subjectivities. I'm sorry that I keep going on and on about the U.S., but I can't really help it, because I am so disturbed by what's happening here now. We're seeing an epistemic violence which says you can't be gay, you can't control your own body if you happen to have a uterus, you can't walk down the street without being shot by police if you're a person of color. Recently, this epistemic violence has taken a potent legalistic form, thanks to the decisions of the most reactionary Supreme Court we've had in a hundred years. Right-wing "justices" are no longer even trying to conceal this violence. They blatantly violate American political and legal epistemology by saying that they are defending the original meaning of the Constitution – on the basis of legal texts written by misogynistic witch burners who lived a century before the Constitution was even written. Then fascist elements in U.S. society use this epistemic violence to justify real violence against women, as well as homophobic and transphobic violence, and racist and ethnic violence.

***SCA:** Deleuze claims that authoritarianism is not only found in the state, but also in the concept of human subjectivity which is a product of state coding. He relates* *this to the concept of Oedipus in psychoanalysis. While the father figure in Oedipus is the obstacle where we suppress our desires, the state has become the place where we suppress our desires and want the state-father to dominate us, which replaces the father figure in the Oedipal representation. In this respect, Deleuze embarks on a search for an illegitimate thought that has no ties to the state or to the father. How successful was Deleuze in putting forward such an idea? Do you think that it is possible to get rid of authoritarianism completely?*

LC: I agree with much of Deleuze's analysis. Structurally, it seems clear that the state can and does take the place of the father in the Oedipal dynamic, especially in a patriarchal culture. Thus the law of the Father can easily become the law of the state. Although psychohistory has fallen out of favor among historians in recent decades, I still believe that psychoanalysis has much to teach us about history, and especially the history of authoritarianism. I'm thinking of Erik Erikson's analysis of Hitler and the appeal of Nazism to the German people, for example. But I think that there were limits to how far Deleuze could go, writing in the 1970s. One significant and substantial change that has occured since then is the development of widespread information technologies in the Western world. By the mid-1980s, Donna Haraway was able to imagine the figure of the cyborg as an entity that might challenge authoritarianism. She understood that the cyborg was "the illegitimate offspring of militarism and patriarchal capitalism." So at first glance, it would appear that the cyborg might just become another oppressive father-figure. But Haraway emphasizes that illegitimate offspring are unfaithful to their origins, because their fathers are inessential. So while it may not be possible to eliminate authoritarianism completely, the cyborg can at least challenge it, and put forth a credible alternative.

***SCA:** Relatedly, in his lectures on the* Will to Know, *Foucault remarks, "Freud followed in the footsteps of the relationship between desire and truth and believed that Oedipus was telling him about the universal forms of desire. Whereas Oedipus was telling him the historical constraints of our truth system. Freud thought he heard the voice of desire, whereas what he heard was the echo of his own true discourse." How would you interpret this statement? Is Oedipus an expression of repression rather than a universal expression of desire?*

LC: One of the greatest weaknesses of Freudian psychoanalysis is its universalizing claims. Freud presented many of his theories as universally true and valid, and that made traditional psychoanalysis dangerously ahistorical and Eurocentric. Realistically, many of the psychic structures which Freud took to be universal may only be characteristic of the early twentieth century European bourgeoisie to which Freud and his patients belonged. The Oedipal theory is a good example of this. It may well be that the theory of Oedipal desire only makes sense given the structures and constraints of modern Western bourgeois families, including the patriarchal power dynamics and property regimes that shape those families. Desire itself is surely far broader, more diverse, and frankly more interesting than the Oedipal model allows.

SCA: *Deleuze states, "It is always a multiplicity that speaks and acts, even within oneself. We are all groups, and there is no representation anymore, there is only action." If representation is not possible any longer, what would we be facing? What are the advantages and the disadvantages of post-representation in your opinion?*

LC: I love that quote from Deleuze. I use it all the time. I think that what Deleuze highlights here is one of the major advantages the postmodernism offers over modern theories of representation. The concept of the self as multiplicity actually agrees with people's day to day experience living in the postmodern condition. My students grasp this intuitively. I say to them, look, you're one person here in class, you're a different person when you're at work, you're another person when you're with your family, you're another person when you're with your lover. People today seem to understand that this subjective multiplicity is a potential source of strength. It makes possible an exciting kind of intrasubjective diversity, which goes nicely with the intersubjective diversity that has clearly become a necessary condition for society to flourish.

SCA: *Poststructuralist thinkers call us to rethink what we mean by politics and to think about epistemological and political commitments in a radical way. What is the importance of poststructuralists' call for concrete politics from your perspective?*

LC: I have in mind what Laclau and Mouffe call "articulation." If we live in a world of floating signifiers and flexible, fluid meanings – and it seems increasingly clear that we do – then I believe that it makes sense to develop practical political tactics that partially fix meaning, and to explore the possibility of political actions based on these contingent, transitory meanings.

SCA: *It is clear that classical anarchism should transform itself drawing upon poststructuralist theory. When we imagine the opposite case, do you think that poststructuralist anarchism can benefit from classical anarchism? If so, how?*

LC: I think that poststructuralist anarchism could benefit from an engagement with anarcho-syndicalism and radical labor politics. One of the limitations of poststructuralist anarchism in its early manifestation was that it provided an insufficient account of the possibilities of collective action. This may be partly due to the fact that the theory was initially developed in the decade following the collapse of the Soviet Union. But we are now seeing a resurgence of labor activism, and a revitalized labor movement, even in the United States! I see Amazon workers organizing and fighting for their right to unionize. Meanwhile their boss, already one of the world's richest men, imposes viscious

Taylorist working conditions on them and refuses to recognize the union. He'd rather spend his billions on union-busting consultants and spaceships, when it would actually be cheaper for him to provide his workers with decent wages and working conditions. Amazon is churning through workers so fast that in a couple of years they are going to run out of wage slaves, and they know it. But they still won't recognize the union. The example of Amazon shows that in a way, we've gone back in time to a kind of nineteenth century, Dickensian capitalist hyper-exploitation. And a classical anarchist analysis can help us understand how that works and how to fight it.

***SCA:** If we are to consider the rejection of metaphysical thought as an ontological anarchism, do you regard Heidegger as an anarchist in this sense?*

LC: I don't see Heidegger as an anarchist, because I could never consider anyone who openly supported fascism to be an anarchist. Heidegger was a card-carrying member of the German Nazi party. He remained a Nazi even after the failure of his rectorship at the University of Freiberg. And he never really repudiated Nazism, even after the war. I'm not saying that we should dismiss his thought. He remains one of the twentieth century's most important philosophers. I myself have made extensive use of his philosophy of death. But I don't believe that a philosopher can be completely separated from his politics.

***SCA:** At this point in the debate on justice, it seems that justice is merely an ideal and injustice is a reality. For this reason, can we say that the best way to achieve justice is to define injustice and eliminate the cases of injustice instead of developing theories of justice?*

LC: To me justice is something that we approach asymptotically. We may never get there, but the journey is still important. I don't think we need to define justice. We know it when we see it. And we certainly know what injustice looks like. The main thing is to keep fighting specific injustices. In this way we can make the world a more just place, if not a perfectly just place.

Suggested Readings

Lewis Call, *Postmodern Anarchism*, UK: Lexington Books, 2003.

Lewis Call, *Sexualities in the Works of Joss Whedon*, USA: McFarland Press, 2020.

Lewis Call, *BDSM in American Science Fiction and Fantasy*, UK: Palgrave Macmillan, 2013.

CHAPTER 12

Human Nature and Justice: Noam Chomsky

Noam Chomsky, often regarded as one of the most influential intellectuals of the 20th and 21st centuries, is known for his contributions to linguistics, philosophy, cognitive science, political commentary, and social justice advocacy. Chomsky revolutionized linguistics with his theory of generative grammar, proposing that all humans possess an innate linguistic ability – a concept that challenged behaviorist theories dominant at the time. This theory is foundational in Chomsky's philosophy, reflecting his belief that human beings have inherent capacities and rights that must be recognized and preserved. His work extends beyond linguistics into ethics, social justice, and a critical examination of power structures, making him a prominent figure in discussions around justice, equality, and freedom.

Chomsky's approach to justice is deeply influenced by his anarcho-syndicalist and libertarian socialist perspectives, which emphasize individual autonomy, cooperative community organization, and skepticism of centralized authority. He advocates for a society structured around voluntary, decentralized associations, where power is not concentrated but instead dispersed among communities and individuals. For Chomsky, justice cannot be achieved through rigid structures of control or authoritarian governance; rather, it must arise from the freedom and empowerment of individuals within a community. This perspective is reflected in his critiques of political and corporate power, especially in works like Manufacturing Consent: The Political Economy of the Mass Media (co-authored with Edward S. Herman), where he explores how media serves to reinforce dominant power structures by manipulating information and restricting dissenting voices.

In addition to Manufacturing Consent, Chomsky's major works include Syntactic Structures, which laid the foundation for modern linguistics by introducing the concept of generative grammar, and Hegemony or Survival: America's Quest for Global Dominance, which critiques American foreign policy as an imperial project that threatens global peace and security. Another key work, On Anarchism, delves into his views on a just society structured around cooperative ownership, direct democracy, and a commitment to individual freedom. Chomsky is also known for Who Rules the World?, where he analyzes how elite interests shape global policies that often conflict with the broader

 | DOI:10.1163/9789004732902_014

public's needs, reinforcing inequalities and inhibiting justice on an international scale.

At the core of Chomsky's justice philosophy is a belief in intellectual freedom and the responsibility of individuals to question and resist authority when it acts unjustly. His concept of "intellectual self-defense" encourages people to educate themselves and challenge propaganda, a task he considers essential for a democratic society. Chomsky sees true justice as attainable only when individuals are empowered to make informed decisions free from coercion and misinformation, advocating for systems that promote equality and freedom.

***Sema Cevirici Atilla* [*SCA*]*: On 22 October 1971, Foucault and you held a significant debate on human nature at the Eindhoven University of Technology in the Netherlands. If you were to reconsider your discussion with Foucault today, especially your understanding of justice back then, what else would you like to say? Has there been a difference in your understanding of justice since then?*

Noam Chomsky [NC]: I have refined and changed my views over time, but not in any ways that bear on that discussion.

SCA: *In his discussion with you, Foucault remarks, "We must deal with politics." According to him, the reason for that is that the essence of our life consists of the political functioning of the society in which we find ourselves. Do you believe that politics is what makes us who we are? In what context should we deal with politics?*

NC: If by "politics" we mean the socio-economic/political system in which we live, then of course it's important to deal with it – even though it is not "what makes us who we are" (though it contributes to it)

SCA: *My next question is about post-anarchism. As you know, this concept is discussed based on the common aspects of classical anarchism and poststructuralist philosophy. How do you evaluate the relationship between anarchism and poststructuralism? Do you think that it is a must-have relationship or a bad partnership?*

NC: I don't see any relationship, but that is because I do not find much of substance in "poststructuralism". What I understand – which is limited – seems to me mostly either wrong or else complex and intricate ways of reformulating what we already know, often what is virtual truism. I should make clear however that this may well reduce to my failure to understand, and the inability of those who say they do understand to explain to me what I am missing.

SCA: *In this respect, are there any key features of poststructuralist anarchism which opposes power and authority that you find significant? If so, can you elaborate on that?*

NC: I cannot answer, for the same reason.

SCA: *You attach great importance to the concept of human nature that embraces freedom and human dignity in their full scope. In poststructuralist anarchism, human nature is presented as a repressive "place" that will dominate us with power rather than a liberating "place." The first person to place emphasis on this notion of human nature was Max Stirner and later it was radically highlighted in poststructuralist anarchism. How would you evaluate these criticisms taking into account your emphasis on the concept of human nature and its liberating potential? Is human nature liberating or repressive? How do you envision a just and free society based on your understanding of human nature?*

NC: On the criticisms, I have nothing to say. They seem to me assertions with no argument or evidence to support them. On how I envision a more just and free society (NB: *more*), I can only refer you to what I've written about this over many years, and to what I've done to try to advance the prospects.

SCA: *What is the underlying reason for your opposition to poststructuralist-postmodern theories and thinkers? Is it their political stance, their skepticism towards agreeable values, or is it because they argue that your interpretation of human nature is actually repressive? What do you oppose about this philosophy fundamentally?*

NC: I have no general opposition. As I mentioned, some seems to me wrong, so I oppose it; some seems to me right, but of little interest; and most I don't understand so neither accept or reject.

SCA: *Do you think that the poststructuralist and postmodern thinking is apolitical? Contrarily, can we argue that it is deeply political, since it politicizes so many things that we too often take for granted?*

NC: I can only repeat the same answers.

SCA: *You make a distinction between legality and better justice, instead of legality and ideal justice. You state that "we cannot create an ideal society in our minds, neither can we create an ideal justice system. Because we do not know much, we are very limited, we are very prejudiced, etc. But we are in a position to imagine a better society and also a better justice system and take action to create it. We need to act as responsible people in this position." As you say, a better system may also have certain flaws. It is clear that a system with flaws is actually not entirely fair and will be incomplete and unfair when it comes to decisions and policies. If the system we define as fairer is eliminated by another system that corrects its flaws and is more just than the previous one, our just judgment about the first system will suddenly become unjust. In this case, can we say that justice is like a horizon that can never be reached, but at the same time, it constantly encourages us to do our best? If so, is it justified that poststructuralist thinkers say that justice cannot be reduced to an existing definition, rule or system? How would you evaluate the resistance of justice to a definition in terms* *of your own understanding of justice? Can we argue that the beginning of justice is knowing that we are not completely just?*

NC: I generally agree with the passage up to "encourages us to do our best." I don't really follow the rest. If our understanding of justice is evolving, then by definition, it cannot be reduced to an existing definition; and we "evaluate" this limited understanding by recognizing it and seeking to do better.

SCA: *You have pointed out that we should be aware that our better system is not the ideal system. In this context, you also say that the concept of legality and the concept of justice are not identical, but not completely separate from each other. Your statement reminded me of the relationship Derrida established between justice and law. As Derrida argues, law is not justice, yet the realization of justice depends on the law. In this regard, do you see any similarity between Derrida's understanding of justice and yours?*

NC: The two views you mention seem similar.

SCA: *You are a famous linguist and called as the father of modern language. We know that you have criticisms of Derrida. What are your thoughts about Derrida's ideas on language?*

NC: I've tried to understand Derrida's opinions about language, with little success.

SCA: *In an interview, you remarked that Derrida had an incomprehensible language and continued: "Ask someone to tell you about Derrida's latest article in terms you can understand. They can't do that. At least they can't do it to me; I don't understand. I think you have to ask yourself if there was a great evolutionary leap that allowed humans to have this fantastic view that they couldn't convey to ordinary people about topics that nobody understands very much. One must be very skeptical of this, in my view it is another technique by which intellectuals dominate people. ... Usually a person who teaches learns more than a student. So whether you use knowledge, resources, or privileges, you must help and learn from other people. That's what respectable intellectual work is. In fact, the intellectual is a slave trying to understand better with other people." I would like to ask you two questions here. First, do you think that philosophy should be understandable and accessible to the general public? If people cannot understand what philosophers or intellectuals say, should it be regarded as epistemic domination? My second question is, in what context do you interpret Derrida's complex discourse as a form of intellectual domination?*

NC: There are many levels of understanding: it's not a Yes-or-No affair. Richard Feynman once commented that no one understands quantum mechanics. Really understands, that is. And few understand it at his level. But there are lesser levels. Popular work by outstanding scientists provides a general idea of the principles, achievements, quandaries, even at the level of excellent books for children.

Turning to philosophy, the great work from Plato to Descartes to Russell and on can be grasped by a diligent reader, with its contributions and flaws. And can be explained to those less engaged at various levels, and has been. It may be that some new forms of philosophy have been created that are so profound that people like me just can't hope to understand them at any level, and that unlike, say, quantum physics, it is even impossible to explain the general ideas and results in a manner that people like me can appreciate. In short, it may be that some extraordinary intellectual leap has been taken to levels of profundity that are, for the first time in history, utterly beyond the grasp of ordinary mortals. It would entail no domination, epistemic or otherwise. Just a new phase of intellectual history. It might be fair to entertain some skepticism about that possibility.

SCA: *You argue that although using violence is in a sense unfair, it is not wrong to use it in certain circumstances, because there are relative justices and it is necessary to strive for the better and using violence and creating a certain degree of injustice may be justified on the basis of achieving a fairer outcome. You describe violence as utterly immoral unless there is such a justification. How can we consider the terms violence and justice together? Do you think that it is possible to establish a consistent relationship between justifying violence and justice? Would you say justice that brings about violence is really justice? Could we possibly have a system which controls that violence is used only when absolutely necessary?*

NC: Sometimes it may be necessary to resort to violence to reduce injustice, though resort to violence carries a heavy burden of justification. Controlling that violence is justified and possible. I don't see any inconsistency in this position.

SCA: *In* Debate: On Human Nature, *you did not agree with Foucault when he stated, "justice has no objective definition and it is nothing but a power struggle." Related to this, you also expressed your disagreement when Foucault said that we did not need to use the concept of justice in a classless society. In your view, it is not correct to characterize our current justice systems as merely systems of class oppression and we will have such concepts in any future society. Do you still have the same hope and believe in a pure concept of justice? Have you agreed with Foucault's opinion at some point up until now?*

NC: I don't know whether we can reach a "pure concept of justice," or whether such a concept exists. The concept of justice would be relevant in a classless society because many forms of injustice are not based on class. I have never seen any reason to entertain the belief that justice "is nothing but a power struggle." Frankly, it seems to me what Jeremy Bentham called "nonsense on stilts."

SCA: *In your view, any form of authority, domination, and hierarchy must justify itself, as there is no a priori justification. For this reason, the burden of proof rests* *with the person who says that authority can be justified, which you consider as a fundamental moral principle. That is, if the authority can justify its claims and acts, it is just and if not, it is not justice but authoritarianism. In this regard, do you think the discourse of justice is a question of justification?*

NC: How could it be otherwise?

SCA: *Is the authority justifying itself the proof that its claim or action was right? If an authority justifying itself with persuasive rhetoric dictates wrong things rather than right ones, how can we distinguish them and eliminate injustice?*

NC: We can evaluate the justification by rational inquiry. We can eliminate the unjust situation by our actions, as has been done throughout history.

SCA: *I would like to ask you a question about the relationship between justification and justice in the context of your statement that authority should justify itself. Heidegger uses the two concepts while criticizing metaphysical thought. According to Heidegger, a human has the desire to control and manipulate reality by representing it. Thus, he emerges as the "master and measure of being." He claims that the subject's justification of his confidence in his representations emerged as justice and defined justice as the name of the subject's sovereignty. If we consider the problem of the sovereignty of the subject in a broader framework, the emergence and self-justification of the subject, whether on the basis of an individual, family, state or institutions, will actually lead him to justify his sovereignty or authority and call it justice. However, can we say that such justification is justice itself? How would you evaluate the self-justification of authority and your conception of justice in the context of the Heideggerian reading?*

NC: Efforts at self-justification have to be evaluated like all others. I see no merit in the "Heideggerian reading" proposed here.

SCA: *In one of your works, you state that "the human mind is a mistake that brings its own end." The domination we exert on nature is the clearest example of this. It seems that such problems will not end as long as human beings exist. However, the end of these problems would also depend on human beings. Do you believe that the human mind which brings about its own demise can achieve justice in the world?*

NC: Not a matter for idle speculation, but for action.

SCA: *You define intellectuals as people who tell the truth and expose lies. According to you, intellectuals are defenders of the truth who uphold the highest values and stand up to power and evil with courage and integrity. Yet what can save intellectuals from being part of power? In addition to this, can we regard intellectuals as pioneers of justice?*

NC: That's not how I "define intellectuals." It is their responsibility. As I discuss at length, meeting that responsibility is a rarity in intellectual history. What can save intellectuals "from being part of power" is not succumbing to the temptations of "being part of power."

***SCA:** In an interview, Deleuze and Foucault called attention to the close relationship between power and desire with reference to Wilhelm Reich who said, "No, the masses were not deceived, they desired fascism and that is what has to be explained." In this context, they raised the following questions: "What should one do not to be a fascist while believing that he is a revolutionary militant? How can we free our words and actions, our hearts and our tastes from fascism? How to expel the fascism that has permeated our behavior?" In this sense, do you see a relationship between power and desire? Do human beings desire power rather than opposing it?*

NC: Our choice.

***SCA:** Relatedly, they also emphasize the significance of opposing the decentralized power which is primarily within us rather than an external and centralized power. In their opinion, first, it is necessary to seek a way to escape from the power and state coding within us and start with an internal anarchism. Do you agree with the idea of anarchism as an internal opposition to power in this respect?*

NC: It seems close to truism that we should try to free ourselves from prejudice and bias, often reflecting external power systems.

***SCA:** Are you more hopeful for the current policies of justice in comparison to those in the past?*

NC: The most appropriate comment I can think of is the one that Gramsci made famous: pessimism of the intellect, optimism of the will.

***SCA:** At this point in the debate on justice, it seems that justice is merely an ideal and injustice is a reality. For this reason, can we say that the best way to achieve justice is to define injustice and eliminate the cases of injustice instead of developing theories of justice?*

NC: If someone can establish "a perfect idea of justice," we will be in their debt. Lacking that achievement, we seek to eliminate injustice and improve our understanding of justice.

Suggested Readings

Noam Chomsky, *The Chomsky-Foucault Debate: On Human Nature*, USA: The New Press, 2015.

Noam Chomsky, *On Anarchism*, USA: The New Press, 2013.

Noam Chomsky, *Understanding Power; The Indispensible Chomsky*, USA: The New Press, 2002.

Noam Chomsky, *Who Rules the World?* USA: Picador, 2017.

Noam Chomsky, *The Responsibility of Intellectuals*; USA: The New Press, 2017.

Noam Chomsky, *Notes on Resistance*, USA: Haymarket Books, 2022.

AFTERWORD

Is Justice a Spectral Effect?

As it will be remembered, this book opened with the question "Does Justice Exist?" and will close with the question "Is Justice a Spectral Effect?". John D. Caputo drew our attention to the fact that justice does not have an essence, that it means different meanings and claims different demands in different contexts, and that justice cannot ever phenomenalize around a certain definition, law, rule or existence. As he points out, there were undoubtedly just institutions, just people, just laws; the injustice was the emphasis on the risk of fixing justice in these facts and closing its openness to the future.

This afterword, titled "Is Justice a Spectral Effect?" is also concerned with preserving the openness of justice to its future. Therefore, the fact that this book begins with a question and closes with a question is a manifestation of the nature of justice. In other words, if justice takes a strong stance against existence and fixation in terms of its openness to the future, then the end of such a book will not provide an answer or explanation as to what justice is; moreover, in order to maintain this questionability and openness, it will require closing with a new question or a closure without conclusion.

Derrida has introduced hauntology as a concept similar to ontology but at the same time significantly differentiated from it and placed it at the center of the deconstruction. Whenever Derrida starts talking about something, he uses the expression if there is such a thing, which in a sense points to spectrality. In this respect, spectres are at the center of deconstruction by challenging the existence. Deconstructing dualist logic, spectres challenge dichotomies such as presence and absence, body and soul, past and present, life and death. The spectre represents the mobilization of familiar Derridian concepts such as repetition and the postponement of existence. From a Derridian perspective, it is conceivable to argue that in moments of scattering and diffusion, when meaning cannot be firmly fixed and the security of conceptual boundaries is jeopardized, specters emerge and challenge existence by leaving a trace.

Accordingly, the spectre refers to beings that are neither completely dead nor completely alive, neither in the present nor in the past. It refers to beings on the threshold as the boundary of these two spheres. Just as the ghost stands out for deconstructing the sharp distinction between existence and non-existence, which is not reduced to a specific being; justice, likewise, harbors an important possibility with its aspect that neither comes into existence in the present nor is constantly postponed to the future. As is also known, Derrida

 | DOI:10.1163/9789004732902_015

deals with justice in the specters of Marx with the metaphor of a specter. Derrida's approach to justice with the metaphor of the spectre can be considered in relation to the fact that justice will never fully exist. As Caputo states, justice does not exist in any existing order. Justice calls for justice, justice comes, but justice never exists. In this sense, justice haunts us like a spectre, interrupting our sleep and following us like the specter of a buried corpse.

Justice that comes into existence in the form of all kinds of entities, laws, rules, criteria, etc. that point to justice is deficient in the sense that it points to an incomplete justice, not a complete justice. Since every situation in which justice is substituted carries the risk of causing injustice in the sense of closing justice to the future, every situation in which justice is substituted is important to be criticized, rethought and not opened to the future. Derrida's undeciable also comes into play in this context. Because decision structurally points to an end, but justice is not a presence to be reached in the sense of an eternity, it is always the 'to come'. The spectre of the undecidable always pursues the decision with a demand for justice. This specter ensures that justice cannot be fully realized in a law, so it is only through the undecidable that justice can always remain what is to come. While justice is always an urgent demand, it also haunts a decision made in the present. Lyotard has the same concern when he says that "*after every decision* we should *sit down and* think *if this is what is just*". Considering that the theories we produce about justice, the decisions we make, all kinds of situations that stabilize justice open a door to injustice, our assumptions about justice must always be on the alert. This reveals the elusive nature of justice, almost like a specter. Justice wanders around us like a specter and is by no means confined to a particular theory, but injustice exists and is present. In this respect, justice is like a specter that eludes us whenever we try to define it. Justice means different things in different contexts and makes different demands from different perspectives, but it has an aspect – spectrality – that can never be identified with the form in which it came into existence. The purpose of the last question in the interviews is to increase the spectrality of this phenomenon to some extent, but at the same time to lose this spectrality as soon as it appears. Justice is not something that can be defined, but rather something that eludes us in every attempt to define it. But injustice is not like that. Injustice can become concrete and can be shown with concrete examples. Justice, on the other hand, as soon as it takes a concrete form, is in infatuation with a future in the sense of always opening up to something better on the grounds that it would allow injustice.

Consider the importance Derrida attaches to the concept of 'to come'. The concepts of justice and democracy, which Derrida treats as names of the impossible, are woven with the hope of the coming of the one to come. In fact, deconstruction begins with hope and prayer for the arrival of something we cannot see the coming of. The fact that Derrida and the word prayer are mentioned together here may come as a surprise to the reader. Indeed, as a thinker who is assumed to be an atheist, to whom and for what will Derrida pray? But this surprise becomes comprehensible when Derrida's emphasis on the future is taken into account and considered together with the meaning he attributes to prayer. Prayer is a request for the future, for something that is not present at the moment but is desired to come. This is why Derrida emphasizes the importance of concepts such as justice and democracy, which he considers as making the impossible possible and says that we cannot stop seeking and demanding it even if it is never realized, and why he prays for their realization. It is a consequence of this concern that Derrida speaks not only of democracy but of democracy to come, not only of justice as law but of justice to come. Our dedication to the truth of democracy and justice is thought to be related to our promise to be committed to their promise-future, not just to the imperfect states of democracy and justice as they exist here and now. Here, the concepts Derrida puts on the agenda are always the promised and the to come. In other words, justice and democracy are what is promised, what calls us to the terms "justice and democracy". This is why Derrida says that the "democracy to come" is more important than democracy in the context of future democracy. Because we cannot say that the name of a future democracy will still be democracy. Justice is also like this. The faith in justice is linked to a passion and faith in what is to come. If faith is a passion for a coming that we do not know, then justice is something in which we can keep our faith. It is in this context that Derrida emphasizes that justice reduced to the existing (law-rule) is not justice and its deficiency by preserving his faith in the justice to come. In this context, although justice requires contingent laws, it cannot be reduced to a specific rule. The demand for justice always demonstrates that the given is open to being transformed into questioning. The point here is that contingent laws are needed when we are exposed to unforeseen events. Exposure to unpredictable events is both what gives conditional laws a practical rationality and what inspires one to either defend or oppose them.

While Derrida expresses that justice, which he calls the name of the impossible, is not in a moment reduced to the present, but is always coming, he also makes it the object of a belief that he actually desires their realization. Derrida, therefore, attempts to name them as a desire. This is a desire for the impossible. So we desire justice, we dream of the impossible and pray for its realization. It is not a simple logical contradiction to want the impossible to be possible, but something that is not existing at the moment, but something that we hope and pray for. Law is the only thing that can realize justice, even if it does not necessarily possess it in itself. Democracy in its current form is necessary to achieve the ideal of democracy, even if it is not the ideal of democracy itself now. All these concepts are the ones Derrida prayed for and expected to be realized, but their current form, however incomplete and imperfect, is important in that it brings us a little closer to the ideal of justice and democracy. The point here is not to present their current state as absolute and thus not to run the risk of closing the openness to the future.

Any idea of absolute immunity that could potentially close the future must also be deconstructed. For such an idea of absolute immunity is an obstacle to opening the thing to a future that allows it to live and at the same time destroys it. This is related to the nature of the future, which brings both threat and surprise. The absolute future is unpredictable, shattering our horizon of expectation. And yet, despite the unpredictability of the future, we should pray for a better future and try to achieve a better version of the status quo, which is what drives to act. In such a situation, there will be something that tempts us to act. This is a love of the future whose arrival we cannot see, but for which we keep hoping and praying. Being exposed to an unpredictable future opens one up to the possibility of both taking a risk and taking responsibility for what is to come. In this respect, the thing to come can be seen as a radical affirmation of the unpredictable. However, it should be reminded again that believing in such a future and praying for it implies an active state, in other words, an actual prayer, rather than a passive state of waiting. In this respect, the name of justice is also the name of hope. The future is always better. Not because it is so, but because we have hope for it. Such openness to the future does not mean that justice is a futile pursuit in the sense that it requires action, but rather that it carries the hope that justice will always be expected as "the thing to come" even if it never exists. We can never be sure whether the future will bring luck or threat or risk. This openness, on the other hand, is important in the sense that it encourages us to seek, interpret and be on the path that leads us to action, otherwise it will not be possible for an understanding that closes the future to lead us to act.

In "The Force of Law" Derrida says that justice does not really exist, justice is a call, and what exists is the law. Strengthening the remedy of justice is possible by making laws just. In this sense, justice is an unconditional call and has no sovereignty. Derida emphasizes the distinction between sovereignty and the unconditional. If concepts such as justice, hospitality, forgiveness and the gift of forgiveness, which he calls unconditional, are to be preserved and kept open to the future, it is necessary to distinguish between sovereignty and unconditional. Because these concepts exist as a weak call or demand due to their openness to the future, but they are calls without power or sovereignty, but their power lies in their unconditionality. This "unconditioned" without sovereignty is neither being nor nothingness, neither finite nor infinite, it does not exist but insists on its call.

Therefore, the desire to realize justice will come to the forefront in terms of motivating people to take action. In this respect, justice is a weak call, but its strength is in its weakness. The more one responds to the call of justice, the more this ghostly call of justice will come into being by becoming flesh and blood, which is closely related not to the aspect of justice that is reduced to abstract theories, but rather to the fact that it gives people the power to act and the motivation to do so. In other words, justice, if there is such a thing, is a call, justice demands from us as a spectral call, and the desire of justice to realize itself becomes flesh and blood through human beings. That is, the weakness of justice is countered by the power of human action. Caputo claims that the real death of God, whom he calls a holy ghost, happens when we do not respond to God's call. He argues that to the extent that we respond to God's call, this spectre is a spectre that will become flesh and blood and become embodied. Just like this, when we think of justice in terms of the metaphor of the ghost, the death of justice in the sense of its absence will occur when human beings do not respond to the call of justice. Justice calls, insists, but it is we humans who exist. Without a response, the call faces the danger of extinction because the only witness of the call is the response. Whether justice exists or not depends on whether we resist or help the call. This is the moment when justice corresponds to a weak call and human beings to the power to respond to it. It is only through our actions that we can make the world a more just place. We want justice to be restored, but it depends on us and our response to the call of justice, that is, our actions.

Caputo argues that it is through human beings that God does what he commands, that is, what needs to be done. In this sense, the desire for justice would be to respond to God's call to do justice, which offers an explanation of the function of religion in that it moves human beings to take action. If, as Derrida says, *religion is a response*, then those who respond to the call of justice can be called truly religious in the broad sense of the term. As a matter of fact, the fact that Derrida does not call God impossible should be considered in this context. The fact that the impossible is God and that God is conceived as a Being that makes everything possible does not solve the problems that we are responsible for and must solve. Because when we have such an identifiable being, when we know it, we make the impossible possible, which would mean closing the future by making the impossible possible. Therefore, the possibility of the impossible is not about a great being (God) coming to save us, but about the future and responsibility. What is our responsibility and why is it so much about specters, Derrida asks. Because the relation to the other cannot be separated from the problem of the ghost, the problem of the event and the problem of what must be done. The openness to what is coming, to the event that cannot be recognized beforehand, to the memory of hope, is where spectrality is located. If I am talking about specters, Derrida says, I am doing this in the name of justice.

In any case, specters come to haunt us and call us to take action. The questions and answers in this book are also matters to be heeded by those who want to hear the call of specters.

Index

anarchism 136, 137, 139, 140, 145–149, 155, 156, 158, 160, 164, 166, 170
anthropology 33, 115, 116
aporia 14, 44, 77, 86, 91, 98, 100–105, 107
autoimmunity 96, 97, 107

belief 14, 18, 22, 23, 25, 36, 42, 48, 49, 58, 65, 66, 74, 83–85, 88–90, 127, 147, 164, 168, 173
borders 17, 50, 51, 55, 103, 108, 113, 119, 123, 124

capitalism 28, 139, 143, 146, 147, 152, 161
citizenship 58, 94, 99, 113, 123, 125, 152
commitment 15, 25–27, 36, 37, 42, 54, 58, 59, 77, 84, 94, 113, 120, 127, 136, 139, 143, 162, 164
common law 61, 64, 65, 67
consensus 69, 111, 114
cosmopolitanism 92, 113, 114
critique 11, 19, 22, 28, 29, 33, 39, 43, 49, 53, 65, 73, 78, 105, 115, 120, 121, 129, 132, 146, 152, 160, 164
culture 12, 36, 39, 58, 86, 89, 90, 113, 117, 119, 123, 125, 126, 156, 161

decision 3, 13, 14, 18, 22, 23, 42, 59, 64–69, 77, 81, 82, 85, 86, 88, 91, 92, 101, 107, 121, 122, 128, 133, 158, 165, 172
deconstruction 8, 10, 12, 17, 18, 25–27, 31, 40, 43, 44, 50, 54, 59, 70, 73, 75, 95, 98, 100, 106, 107, 128, 129, 148, 156
democracy 14, 22, 53, 58, 60, 63, 88, 92, 94–97, 99–101, 103, 106, 107, 111, 113, 114, 118, 122, 127, 129, 130, 172, 173
difference 18, 19, 22, 36–41, 44, 45, 55, 58, 67, 75, 82, 83, 86–88, 94, 102–105, 114, 118, 122, 125, 128, 129, 140, 144, 157, 158, 160, 165
diversity 37, 58, 59, 94, 113, 143, 152, 162

Emmanuel Levinas 15, 18, 27–31, 33, 34, 36–39, 42, 43, 54, 55, 77, 78, 82, 83, 121, 129–131, 133, 139
enlightenment 22, 38, 42, 92, 115, 116, 147, 155, 156
epistemology 73, 78, 80–83, 128, 145, 152, 157, 158, 160
equality 58, 89, 113, 114, 120, 136, 138, 147, 153, 164, 165
ethical 21, 25–30, 33, 34, 36, 37, 40, 46, 47, 50, 54, 58, 59, 63, 67, 68, 70, 71, 73, 75–78, 82, 83, 86, 91, 94, 102, 113, 127, 128, 131, 136, 137
evil 9, 19, 23, 41, 42, 43, 45–47, 49, 51, 52, 77, 87, 129, 130, 132, 133, 169

Friedrich Nietzsche 20, 37, 49, 79, 80, 102, 120, 139, 152, 155, 156
friendship 63, 94, 95, 100–103, 107, 137
future 9, 13, 14, 17, 19, 22, 23, 52, 56, 61, 63, 98, 99, 103, 104, 107, 122, 129, 130, 149, 168, 171

Gilles Deleuze 80, 136–139, 143, 146, 150–152, 155, 157–162, 170
god 8, 9, 10–13, 15, 20, 21, 23, 26, 36–38, 40–43, 45, 48–50, 52, 53, 56, 75, 84, 92, 114, 130, 132, 157, 175

hermeneutics 8, 17, 18, 21–24, 36–39, 43, 44, 51, 52, 54–56, 127, 133
holocaust 34, 43, 45–48, 86, 87, 133
hope 13, 52–54, 82, 86, 91, 107, 110, 120, 129–131, 156, 168, 170, 172–174, 176
hospitality 11, 14, 18, 19, 32, 36–38, 40, 43, 44, 45, 50, 51, 52, 55, 68, 77, 86, 90–92, 103, 108, 109
human rights 113–115, 117, 123–125

identity 20, 25, 36, 52, 58, 94, 119, 146, 147, 152, 155
immigration 32, 50, 62, 68, 108, 109, 113, 131
injustice 19, 21, 23, 25, 34, 47, 55, 70–72, 78, 83, 85, 88, 90, 92, 111, 112, 125, 130, 132, 134, 145, 153, 154, 163, 168–170
interpretation 7, 8, 22, 41, 43, 44, 48, 52, 59, 61, 62, 66, 69, 73, 76, 79, 90, 99, 100, 113, 166

Jacques Derrida 8, 11, 15–17, 19, 21, 25, 27, 32, 36, 37, 41, 45, 49, 52, 59, 60 justification 5, 21, 33, 69, 84, 106, 114, 116, 117, 168, 169

law 8, 9, 14, 23, 30–32, 50, 55, 58–63, 65, 69, 70
legacy 94, 98, 104, 106, 107, 109, 116, 118
legal 58–60, 61, 63, 65, 69, 70, 76, 77, 86, 91, 108, 113, 114, 117, 122
liberalism 28, 88, 89, 114, 115, 118, 120, 121, 130, 152

metaphysics 20, 26, 27, 77, 78, 80, 82–84, 129, 130, 152, 160

otherness 36, 77, 78, 83, 102, 103, 121, 130

politics 28, 29, 32, 40, 52, 59, 63, 70, 71, 82, 89, 95, 100–103, 108, 110, 119

power 22, 29, 33, 36, 46, 49, 53, 54, 63, 71, 80, 84, 95, 98, 118, 121, 124, 127

recognition 7, 30, 47, 118, 119, 152, 153
relativism 41, 73, 88, 89, 113, 127
religion 7–10, 13, 14, 16, 22, 23, 33, 39, 48–50, 53, 54, 71, 97, 102
responsibility 9, 21, 25, 30, 31, 50, 51, 78, 94, 127, 130–133, 136, 137, 139, 149

unconditional 23, 32, 40, 50, 90, 99, 108, 109, 132
undecidability 13, 14, 48, 91, 111, 129
universal 15, 19, 20, 27, 28, 31, 33, 47, 55, 58, 59, 62, 63, 71, 77, 87, 92, 99, 113–115

violence 19–23, 27, 38, 63, 64, 68, 70, 82, 84, 87, 89, 116, 127

www.ingramcontent.com/pod-product-compliance
Lightning Source LLC
Chambersburg PA
CBHW051401240926
51852CB00002B/87
9789004727779